CALLAS: LA DIVINA

Maria Callas

CALLAS:
LA DIVINA

ART THAT CONCEALS ART

Stelios Galatopoulos

WITH FRONTISPIECE
AND 24 PAGES OF HALF-TONE PLATES

LONDON HOUSE & MAXWELL
Elmsford   New York

First published in United States 1970
by London House & Maxwell
by arrangement with J. M. Dent & Sons Ltd
Published by British Book Centre

A London House & Maxwell book

FOR
NICOLA ZACCARIA

CONTENTS

ILLUSTRATIONS

Maria Callas (*photo by Angus McBean*) Frontispiece

FOREWORD

I HAVE KNOWN Maria Callas for many years now, not only as a great artist but as an admirable woman and as a friend. For many years indeed, in fact since she came to Milan, to La Scala. This is a magnificent opera house as everyone knows, and the productions are almost invariably of an extremely high standard, but there are of course other fine opera houses elsewhere. Why is it then that La Scala holds a unique place among them? It is because this theatre has a positively magical quality, which, like everything which possesses this kind of magic, cannot be explained. I can only say that it is a theatre where opera has been a live and glorious thing, a social custom with a special meaning for its audiences, from the time of Mozart, through the great Romantic period, up until the present day.

When Madame Callas joined La Scala it was a very happy event for both. I am certain that it was the Scala magic which gave Maria her final, ethereal touch, and it was then that her singing took wings for its soaring flight all over the world. There she found the secret essence of the heroines of early Romanticism: Lucia, Norma . . .

Perhaps I should confess that my meeting with Maria Callas was not connected with her singing. Of course I have always been friendly with singers and musicians: Giacomo Puccini was to me a dear grandfather when I was a child; he invented my nickname, Biki, under which I have gained some fame in the field of fashion.

Fashion: this was the reason Maria first came to me, and by no means a trifling or irrelevant reason. The elegance of Callas, both on stage and in life, has been one of her many triumphs.

Maria Callas is an outstanding character: a life lived at the summit. She is comparable to such figures of our time as Picasso, Cocteau and Chaplin, for in her art she has the same revolutionary and exciting influence they had and have in theirs. And, like all of them, she never judges art and life by two different standards. In art—as in life—there is no distinction between lesser and greater things. *Everything* is important. Big achievements may be simple, like making a good cup of tea. Small details may be difficult, as in sending a satellite to the moon. Artists handle dangerous materials all the time as a matter of course, and great artists demand absolute standards, even in the most casual circumstances. Certainly Maria has no standards other than absolute. She cannot do other than try, very simply, very sincerely, to do her best.

But where did she acquire her extraordinary feeling for classicism? Where is the origin of her subtle sense of musical architecture, her vast tragic instinct? Where is the secret spring of this voice of hers, mysterious, evocative, full of wonderful light and shadow, of remote and penetrating echoes? The answer lies in a single name: Greece. Greece . . . with its bare, dazzling beauty, its deep Mediterranean soul, its winds sweeping the August seas, stirring the olive trees, descending the white gradients of the ancient theatres. Maybe the secret of Maria's art is there. In Greece she rediscovered the pristine power of acting, and brought it back, heroically, through her voice, to the opera stage. What an overwhelming and awe-inspiring task for a woman, alone with her art! But what a magnificent adventure!

This adventure is the reason for this book. Fortunately, with the advent of the gramophone, a new relationship has been established between singers and audiences: their voices can now be permanently captured on record and so reach a wider public. Recordings did not exist for Giuditta Pasta or *La* Malibran; but they do exist for Callas, and very fine ones too. Thus we may enjoy her voice even when she is not performing in our own locale, and we can meditate on the message of her art, a mysterious blend of the classical, romantic and modern spirits.

The book provides an insight into this fascinating enigma, showing how a unique art emerged from the everyday life of a woman, giving singing and acting a wholly new direction. It cannot but be a pleasure for everyone to become better acquainted with this woman, whom I already know so well: a kind, simple, dedicated and spirited woman of our time.

BIKI.

Milano.

I

INTRODUCTION

This is the reason that the artist lives and works and has his being: that from life's clay and his own nature, and from his father's common earth of toil and sweat and violence and error and bitter anguish, he may distil the beauty of an everlasting form, enslave and conquer man by his enchantment, cast his spell across the generation, beat death down upon his knees, kill death utterly, and fix eternity with the grappling-hooks of his own art.

THOMAS WOLFE

MY INTEREST in Maria Callas's work began through my passion for opera. It was as far back as 1947 that I first heard Maria Callas sing in a performance of Ponchielli's *La Gioconda* in the Arena of Verona. It was merely by chance that I heard her on that occasion, but ever since, during the last seventeen years, wherever and whenever it was at all possible, I have made a point of following up and attending her performances.

After my first experience of a Callas performance it was no longer either satisfying or adequate to hear operas sung by other singers. True, I had heard many fine singers in the world that had delighted me, but however good they were, there was always something missing. What was Callas's formula?

All I knew about Maria Callas before I first heard her sing was that she was Greek. I knew very much more after the performance, but still I was unable to explain that magic, the consummation that I had witnessed. Her voice remained in my ears and I felt I would never forget it nor mistake it for any other; a voice with so many phases and colorations that I could not describe it to anyone

1

who had not actually heard it. For I had never heard another voice like this. Other voices excel in either the lightness, the lyricism, the drama, but here all these qualities seemed to be present in one voice. Perhaps it would have been possible to describe it through painting, for it represented the kind of feeling which is expressed in the pictures of Leonardo da Vinci. But one would have to be a Leonardo da Vinci to do that adequately.

It was not until 8th November 1952 that I first heard Callas sing in Bellini's *Norma* at Covent Garden, London. Only then did I fully believe that it was possible for Italian opera to be what I thought it ideally should be; and what, in this case, Bellini intended it to be—what it had been in the days of Giuditta Pasta, Maria Malibran and all the other great singers of the past that one unfortunately can only read about. Here at last the miracle was performed again. On that night in London, for me, Callas sang with an inspiration that made all other voices I had actually heard before seem insignificant.

The desire to write a book about this artist was born after the London performance of *Norma*, and it has taken over ten years to materialize. During this time Maria Callas has made musical history, and this is the subject of my book. Although Callas the artist has been the prime purpose of this book, it could not be confined to this only, as Callas the artist and Callas the woman are quite inseparable. It is from life's clay and his own nature that the artist would find eternity.

Callas has not only been accepted by the world as a great unique artist, though not without controversy, but has also become a most controversial person herself.

Probably no contemporary artist has been discussed as much as Maria Callas: 'Maria Callas, the in-human being, tigress in her dealings with everybody, her colleagues and even her own mother. A woman yearning for love. Callas the female Shylock, the miser who extracts her every penny.'

And the opposite of this, with just as fanatical certitude: 'Callas, completely devoted to her art and caring for nothing else; a woman whose artistic ideals are of the highest. Callas the perfectionist. Callas, to whom money means nothing and will give help to other poor and deserving musicians.' And of course Callas the 'Monstre Sacré' as well as Callas 'La Divina'.

But we must forget all these controversial descriptions—that in some ways have wrongfully made of her nothing short of a monster, and in other ways an angel in disguise—if we are going to do justice to her at all.

Maria Callas is a very attractive woman, feminine, rather impulsive and always, like any true artist, wanting to be understood, liked and appreciated. In return she is devoted to her public and always tries her best not to disappoint them.

In her work she is a strict disciplinarian—a rare quality. She is a superb workman, very quick to learn, applying all her intelligence and education. She never jokes about her work and always performs as though her audience must be freshly conquered. Once conquered they must be tamed. So much for the 'tigress' in her. She is completely unaffected, and totally without mannerisms. Just as she lives her roles on the stage, in real life she is always naturally and simply 'Maria'. She is extremely modest about her artistic achievements, so much so that she is never satisfied and strives to improve and perfect. As she herself has said: 'I have set myself a standard that is almost impossible to keep, for in each performance I find I could and should have done much better; yet the public is always enthusiastic.' Nevertheless she speaks her mind and knows what she is talking about, with a fine sense of humour that often makes her already colourful personality electrifying.

Callas feels there is always something more to learn, and is always glad to discuss and analyse her work, about which she is by far her own sternest critic. This is the result of the sincere responsibility she always takes for everything she does.

It was in the ancient theatre of Epidaurus in Greece, after the dress rehearsal of *Medea*, that I told Maria Callas how wonderful I thought her performance was, and that, if it were possible, she had even improved since her previous appearance as Medea a couple of years before in London. Her answer was: 'With God's help that is what I must do. But tell me, which parts did you like best?' Then, as if she still had doubts about her great achievement, she said, 'Let's not praise me too much. The performance is not till two days' time. *Then* I must be good; it is my duty.'

She feels she owes the public her best every time, and when her aims are not fully achieved she is left with a feeling that she has let her public down.

She has never been known to reject any criticism as long as it is constructive. All the applause in the world cannot make up for her distress when she knows she has not given of her best. She sometimes gets angry with herself when she feels she is not performing well, and this has many times been unwittingly, and sometimes deliberately, misunderstood by her associates.

Her outbursts with opera managers have always been accorded the highest attention by the press, in fact never an opportunity has been missed for a so-called 'Callas Scandal'. These disagreements have always been, from her point of view, about artistic standards. Her friendships with opera managers like Covent Garden's Sir David Webster, Dallas's Lawrence Kelly and others are never mentioned by the press. The general public naturally forms an opinion based on what it reads in these matters.

Maria Callas has never accepted and never will accept the second rate. She may become touchy and difficult, moody and even obstinate, but only when her fundamental artistic beliefs are at stake. Strangely she has always thrived on opposition and, as she herself once said, 'When I am angry I can do no wrong'.

But whatever we think of Maria Callas the woman, there is one thing we must never forget to consider, if we are to be at all fair towards her; that Maria Callas the woman, not the sublime artist, is not an angel—alas! the only angels one knows of are in heaven —but a human being with her share of virtues and faults, and therefore one must make concessions. To use Leoncavallo's phrase from the Prologue in *Pagliacci*: 'A slice of life is what the writer has tried to describe. His only maxim is that the artist is human.'

The controversy about Maria Callas, as I have already said, also extends to her art, although it would seem that most people who do not accept her as the great and unique artist she is are those who have had very few, if any, opportunities of seeing her on the stage. Nevertheless there are those who, from personal experience, are not prepared to surrender unconditionally to her artistry. Some critics too have often complained of wobbly top notes and an unevenness in the voice, and there are people for whom an unsteady or even a strident note can ruin the whole performance, however great the performance may be. The only argument in such cases is that opera is as much a theatrical as a musical experience—a drama expressed in music—and Callas, more than anyone else in this generation, understands this, and even more important is able with the extraordinary gifts that nature has given her to express herself to the full. There have been many wonderful singers since the beginning of opera. Perhaps the greatest of them all were Maria Malibran and Giuditta Pasta, both singers having made their careers during the first part of the nineteenth century. Just as comparisons between them and others of their time were incongruous, they also are today with Maria Callas; her art is so distinct from any other living singer's. In fact we do have to go back to Malibran and Pasta when we discuss Callas, for it is with them that she has much in common; she does in fact compare more closely with Malibran than with Pasta. Callas has the same voice range, that is from low G to high E, as Malibran had, and, even more important, there seems to be a very great similarity in their approach to their interpretations. We have no direct evidence as to the tone of Malibran's or Pasta's voice, but we do know the way that Malibran employed her voice; in the variety and spontaneity she brought to her interpretations. In the same way today we can never foresee how Callas would render a part, for she seems to improve in her interpretations every day, with some touch of observation added, that never ceases to bring to the audience new light and interest. These are the qualities in an artist-interpreter that we can call 'genius', because it is always the case in an original creation, the product of inspiration and inventiveness of others' thoughts. There have been many singers, and still are today, with fine voices and lovely top notes, but with very little, if anything, else. As a result they have not succeeded yet to hold constant attention.

Not that Malibran or Pasta were always accepted by everybody without any reservations. We know that Eugène Delacroix would only accept Pasta, and that with the greatest admiration, but he did not appreciate Malibran, whereas Rossini considered Malibran one of his only three real geniuses, the other two being the bass Lablache and the tenor Rubini. It is to an amazing degree that Pasta's and Malibran's critiques read today; but for the name they could be about Maria Callas.

One cannot change people's tastes, whether they are favourable or unfavourable. One can, however, contribute towards helping people to understand and consequently appreciate the good things. To appreciate an artist one needs to appreciate the fact that an open mind is necessary, and that other things, usually completely irrelevant, should not be allowed to interfere. Callas is a big name, a great star many will say, and that is why people simply go crazy about her. This is all true but for the wrong reasons. Callas has become a big name, a great star, because of her art as a singer. It is precisely and primarily for this reason that Callas is even known to the world. The reply that Meneghini (Callas's husband from whom she is now legally separated) [1] gave to many who thought they would become New Callases can throw much light. 'Just bring me one who sings like Callas, who has a mind like Callas, a heart and temperament like Callas, an ambition and fierce dedication like Callas, and leave the rest to me.'

It is almost always forgotten that Callas did not rise to meteoric heights overnight, dazzling everybody. On the contrary nothing ever came easy, and she had to work exceptionally hard in order to be understood, appreciated and accepted. Even for success to come overnight it really takes years to do so.

Athens was truly excited when the young girl of seventeen sang *Tosca* at short notice. Many thought, no doubt, what a promising singer Maria was, but that was only a beginning; and besides her voice and style, good as they were even then, they were unfinished and imperfect. She went on ceaselessly striving after the highest ideals to become the leading soprano of the Athens Opera. But alas, this was not everything, for Athens is only but one city in the world. Years of hard work, disillusionment, heartbreak and sacrifice were to follow before triumph eventually came from all over the world. Yet the hard work continues, for Maria Callas has the even more difficult task of maintaining the name she has made. The world easily forgets people without merit but who by chance rise to stardom.

No wonder her fame is a lasting one, for it is based on sound foundations, whereas notoriety does not really survive the great test of time. Already she has set permanent standards in roles such as Norma, Medea, Anna Bolena, Violetta in *La Traviata*, Lucia di Lammermoor, Leonora in *Il Trovatore*, Tosca—to mention some of Callas's supreme operatic achievements—that all other present

[1] In April 1966 Callas, by taking up Greek nationality, found that her marriage, according to a Greek law passed in 1946, did not exist outside Italy.

and future artists who would attempt them will always be compared and measured up to her.

Callas today at forty-two has been singing for twenty-seven years. Quite recently she has been through a vocal crisis, by which it seems the top notes of her voice have suffered the most. Although it seems to have been a temporary one, there are a number of people—those naturally who had not heard her sing before—who think she has always been singing in this way. For them one can only wish that they might have the opportunity to hearing Callas again on top form.

In my discussions of her individual roles I have tried in each case to analyse a complete and particular performance. But in some instances I may not have fully succeeded in doing this, for over the years it is very easy to allow the memory of one performance of an opera to influence another of the same opera. As a result therefore I may well in some cases have included the virtues and shortcomings of different performances of the same opera.

Finally, although it is perhaps superfluous to mention it, I would like to say that, because of my personal admiration for the artist and her sincerely modest attitude towards her art, I have tried to treat everything about her with understanding and sympathy, and not superficially and rashly pass judgment upon her; it is so easy to condemn. Without this understanding of her on my part, I would never have attempted to write a book about this artist, nor indeed about anybody else. This is not to say that I would watch a performance by Maria Callas merely to enjoy a rewarding emotional experience. On the contrary, as far as artistic values are concerned I am always as critical as I am capable of being, which is how I know she would want me to be.

STELIOS GALATOPOULOS.

May 1966.

II

BIOGRAPHY OF THE ARTIST

I

Alas, that the longest hill
Must end in a vale, but still,
Who climbs with toil, wheresoe'er,
Shall find wings waiting there.

H. C. BEECHING

ON THE morning of the feast day of St Barbara, the noble patron of artillery, 4th December 1923, a third baby was born at the Fifth Avenue Hospital (then called Flower Hospital), New York, to Mr and Mrs Georges Kalogeropoulos, who had recently emigrated from Greece.[1] The baby had all the qualifications that normally would make any parents quite happy and content. It was healthy, beautiful and big, weighing just over twelve pounds. Nevertheless there was one drawback. This baby was a girl and to the Kalogeropoulos family, especially to the mother, who expected a son, a great disappointment. In Greece not long before the Kalogeropouloses lost their three-year-old son in a typhoid epidemic.

Georges Kalogeropoulos met Evangelia Dimitroadou while he was studying pharmacy at the University of Athens. They fell in love, and in August 1916, shortly after he graduated, were

[1] The actual date of birth is not certain. Maria Callas's passport gives the date as the 2nd, *Grove's Dictionary* the 3rd, but Callas's mother remembers it as the 4th. Callas herself considers the 4th as her birthday primarily in order to agree, naturally, with her mother and also because St Barbara is the patron of artillery for whom Callas says she has a special devotion.

8

married. Evangelia Dimitroadou was one of eleven children of an army officer who came from a Greek family of Istanbul.

Music was highly esteemed in the Dimitroadou family. The father especially had a fine voice.

Georges Kalogeropoulos and his wife settled at Meligala, a town in the Peloponnesus, where he opened his own chemist shop. In a year's time their first daughter, Iakinthy, was born and three years later they had a second child, a boy whom they called Vasily. Life seemed to be quite pleasant for the Kalogeropoulos family. Things went well in Meligala; the business was thriving and they felt quite content. Socially they established themselves among the leading citizens of Meligala. Even more important, their two children were growing more and more endearing. But happiness was not to last long. In 1923 a typhoid epidemic struck Meligala. Almost immediately Vasily, their beautiful boy, who was only three, died from typhoid fever. This was a terrible blow to the family, one that was never to be forgotten. All happiness disappeared from the Kalogeropoulos home and no meaning could be found in life. Day after day their grief for their loss knew no bounds. Georges and Evangelia were disconsolate. Time seemed to be unable to cure their grief: instead it increased it. There was one thing that seemed necessary to them. They should leave Meligala, which was full of sad associations. Not even anywhere else in Greece would it be easy for them to make a fresh start. Georges Kalogeropoulos soon had to make decisions. That same year he sold his house and business, and with his wife and daughter set out for distant lands. Like many Greeks, who have to seek their life away from Greece, Kalogeropoulos chose America, the land of wealth and hope. It seemed their only chance to start a new life and with time to forget.

In New York, whence they emigrated, Kalogeropoulos first got a job with a drug store in Astoria, a part of New York, and with the money he brought from Meligala managed to get a small apartment in the same district. Four months later their daughter Maria was born. They had hoped for another son to fill the emptiness the unforgettable Vasily left and thus regain some of their lost happiness.

Georges Kalogeropoulos, a hard-working man, within a year opened his own drug store in Manhattan where he also got an apartment for his family, at 139th Street, a neighbourhood which was very popular with many Greek emigrants. For practical reasons, like many with long foreign names, Kalogeropoulos changed his surname to Callas, this actually being a shortened version of Kalogeropoulos. Somehow a kind of new life started for the Callas family. And, if it did not come up to the happy and easier days at Meligala, before Vasily died, it was nevertheless an agreeable and promising start. And if their new baby was a girl, she soon began to endear herself to them. At the age of three she was christened at the Greek Orthodox Cathedral in New York as Cecilia Sophia Anna Maria Callas, later to be known to the world as Maria Callas.

It was at a very early age that little Maria and her elder sister, whom they now called Jackie, showed signs of musical appreciation and of possessing a singing voice. Their only source of music was the family radio from which they, especially little Maria, were picking out songs. This delighted Evangelia more than anybody else. She was herself, since the old days in Greece when she lived with her own family, fascinated by music. Her father's fine singing voice, of which the whole family felt very proud, had made a permanent impression on her. Now her ambition was readily fired with the possible prospect of seeking musical careers for her daughters. For further encouragement to the girls, a pianola was bought, and Evangelia, with her own savings, also acquired a gramophone and several records, most of them being vocal. Maria one day, when she was almost four, was discovered under the pianola, pressing its pedals with her hands in the hope of making music, and when the gramophone was played, and that was very often, she would listen together with Jackie for hours and then sing together with the performers.

Friends of the Callas family who called to see them found the two girls, especially little Maria, delightful with their amazing singing. Soon the neighbours knew too. Little Maria was becoming quite famous. Before long three additions in the singing members of the Callas household were made. Mother brought home three canaries; a canary for each of the girls and one for herself. Maria's canary was soon more than the usual pet. She would spend hours watching it, especially its throat, sing.

All this was pleasant and agreeable, but not active enough for

Evangelia, who arranged for a Signorina Santrina, an Italian teacher, to give piano lessons to the girls. Maria was almost eight. Georges Callas objected at first to his wife's musical ambitions, but soon agreed to her continual demands. But an irritability was beginning to creep into the household. Georges Callas was a hard-working man and tried his best to make his family as comfortable as he could. Financially they had to be careful, and being a proud man he never expected his wife to go out to work. Evangelia on the other hand, by often reminiscing of her much more comfortable life to which she had been accustomed with her parents, was often misunderstood as not being appreciative.

In 1929 the depression in America caught up with Georges Callas and he lost his business. It was a terrible blow, but he managed to get a job as a travelling salesman for a wholesale pharmaceutical firm. At least he could somehow support his family during the difficult times. The years that followed did not bring much happiness to the Callas family, who found themselves moving annually from cheaper to cheaper apartments. The girls' piano lessons could only be continued at great sacrifice, which Evangelia on her part was more than willing to make. This led to continual arguments with her husband, but in the end she had her way. Evangelia was not going to let the depression, or anything else for that matter, stop her from seeking musical careers for her daughters.

Maria was growing up rather a shy, quiet girl, well behaved and religious. She was always ready to attend church and never missed her Sunday school. But it was a lonely life for a child who could not have much opportunity to make many friends. She would hardly settle at school and begin to feel her way around when she was obliged to change school every time they moved to another apartment. She was a good pupil and did her school work conscientiously, but it was in music that she would seek some excitement and interest to an otherwise dull life. By the time she was ten she could already sing and accompany herself on the piano the 'Habanera' from *Carmen* and 'Je suis Titania' from *Mignon*, and of course her childhood favourite song 'La Paloma'. It is interesting to note that in the first aria she was unconsciously practising her lower mezzo-soprano notes, and in the second coloratura aria she was already developing her high notes.

It was not very long, in every new neighbourhood the Callas

family moved, before young Maria's singing would be heard. One bright spring morning when she was singing, accompanying herself on the piano, the sounds of her voice managed to attract the attention of the passers-by, and soon quite a crowd gathered to listen under an open window. It may have been the individuality of her voice, that was to create so many controversies years later, that attracted her first audience.

At school concerts too she was always popular with her soprano voice. But to her mother she was more than all this, she was an *enfant prodige*. Evangelia would lose no opportunity to show off her daughter's singing. The rather shy Maria must have been harassed on many occasions when her mother pushed her into several radio contests. Not a very happy experience, even though on one occasion she won first prize—a watch—on a recorded amateur radio programme.

But even her music soon became a chore to a great extent. Mother would always ambitiously urge her on, whilst father would, after arguments, agree reluctantly if at all. And then there were other problems that so many lonely children, unguided by the essential motherly advice during adolescence, suffer. There was the other older sister to whom, except for the singing, mother paid more attention. Looking into the mirror Maria could not see many attractions in herself. As a result of overeating—an outlet so many lonely people find—she became quite plump. Maria is also myopic, and the spectacles she wore from the age of five completed the picture. No doubt all these were in her mind exaggerated in the absence of someone who could offer even a few right words and thus help her self-confidence to develop. She naturally turned to find confidence in her singing. Since 1932, when she went to P.S. 189 School at Amsterdam Avenue in the Washington Heights district of Manhattan, they had not moved to another apartment. By staying at least during the last four years at the same school, there was a new stability and security to be enjoyed. It must have been during those last years at school that Maria discovered and believed that she was endowed with talent. When she sang people paid attention. This attention could easily be seen as a kind of love through the eyes of a child who hardly had its full share of love. Her singing voice was obviously her strong point and she was beginning to discover it herself. It was not impudence when one day she criticized the soprano who was singing 'Lucia di Lammermoor' on the radio. It was more of self-confidence, for when she detected weak points she felt that one day she could do better.

As 1936 was drawing to a close Maria's graduation was approaching and Evangelia Callas already made her plans. They may have gone through the worst time, but still, financially, the strain was considerable. Therefore hardly any bright prospects for musical careers for Maria and Jackie were visible, even in the remotest corners of the horizon. Between her and her husband there was discord which grew worse over the hard years. He was a hard-working and conservative man whose first duty was to support his family, whilst she was fired with ambition for musical careers for her daughters at any price. Their personalities were bound to clash. Under the circumstances Evangelia turned to the only place she could. Her family in Greece was still large and reasonably comfortably off. Once there she would seek the help of her family, and the musical education of the girls would be quite possible. Needless to say Georges Callas did not entertain any such ideas, but Evangelia was determined and she was convinced she was doing the right thing. She would go to Greece with her daughters, for a while at least.

At the beginning of December 1936 Jackie, now nineteen, sailed alone for Greece, where she would stay with her grandmother to await her mother and sister, who would be coming in a few months as Maria was not yet free from school. Her father would be remaining in New York.

On 28th January 1937 Maria was understandably excited. It was her graduation day. Her marks were very good and she was taking part, naturally, in the musical variety programme the school was putting on for the occasion of the graduation ceremony. The programme was composed of Gilbert and Sullivan melodies and Maria sang in excerpts from *H.M.S. Pinafore*. She sang well and the audience, which consisted of parents, applauded her warmly. When the thirteen and a half year old graduate left the stage she hardly knew that the next time she was to sing on the stage in the United States she would cause a sensation. But this was in many years to come, and it happened on the stage of the Lyric Theatre in Chicago.

A few months later, in March 1937, Maria and her mother, taking their canaries with them, sailed on board the *Saturnia* for the country of their ancestors, Greece. Georges Callas, when he said goodbye to his wife and daughter, was aware of the distance which was going to separate him from his family. He was not, nor were they for that matter, at all aware that the time would stretch to eight whole years with a world war between, before they would see one another again.

The *Saturnia* was not a luxury ship, but it was fairly comfortable and the trip pleasant. Maria was enjoying it, and very soon, together with her mother, made several acquaintances with their fellow passengers. It did not take very long either, with Evangelia around, for people to discover that the young Maria could sing. One evening after many requests she did sing, accompanying herself on the piano. She chose the 'Habanera' from *Carmen*. She had sung in public before many times, but now, maybe because she was no longer a schoolgirl, her approach was different. She not only sang, but gave a performance at the end of her song, characteristically throwing a red carnation to the captain of the ship who was amongst her audience.

The *Saturnia* anchored at the Greek port of Patras in the Northern Peloponnesus where at least two passengers, mother and daughter, together with their canaries, disembarked. This was Maria's first glimpse of Greece, and the beautiful town of Patras was a good introduction to the old country. Spring was just breaking through and the train trip that took them to Athens, though terribly slow as Greek trains go, was most pleasant. Eventually the train pulled into Athens railway station. Soon they were at grandmother's house where, together with Jackie, they were to stay, at least to begin with. They spent the first month seeing their old relatives and generally settling in. But Evangelia was anxious to arrange her affairs that had after all brought her to Greece. With the money her husband was sending them they could live fairly comfortably. American dollars could go a longer way in Greece. After trying two apartments they settled in a small but pleasant one at 61 Patission Street. Without much difficulty either a suitable piano teacher was found for Jackie. Maria presented a bit of a problem. Once they were settled Evangelia began to try everybody she thought might be helpful for Maria's singing career. She was herself quite sure that a great future lay ahead for her daughter. All the other relations and friends who heard young Maria sing liked her voice too, though nobody seemed to show any interest that could compare with what the mother expected. Anyway nobody offered any help, not even the wealthier members of the family.

In the end it seemed that the best they could do was for Maria to join the Odeon Athenon (Conservatory of Athens) which was considered to be the best conservatory of its kind in Greece. But it was not so easy as all that. Maria may have had the voice and talent required and was already a tall and serious girl, but she was only fourteen. The Odeon Athenon had its regulations about age. Although Maria had in addition an ambitious and determined (though hardly sympathetic) mother, she failed to gain admittance. Mother and daughter turned their eyes to the second best place to study singing in Athens. This was the Ethnicon Odeon (National Conservatory) where the Greek singer Maria Trivella, a good teacher if not a great singer, was teaching. There was going to be trouble here too when it came to Maria's age, but Evangelia this time acted quickly. Her daughter was after all born in America, and owing to her height and seriousness she could easily be taken for at least sixteen. So this time Evangelia stated her age to be sixteen and had no more trouble.

It was in September 1937 when Maria was admitted to the Ethnicon Odeon. At her audition for Maria Trivella Maria sang the 'Habanera' from *Carmen*. There was a significant expression in the singing of the young girl and Trivella was very impressed, so much so that she helped Maria to obtain a scholarship. Trivella showed an immediate interest in her promising student. Apart from the singing she gave her French lessons as well. Maria also, by her mother's arrangement, started to take Greek lessons in order to perfect the uncertain Greek she had learned in America.

Young Maria Kalogeropoulou, as she was naturally called in Greece, plunged into hard work, and under the capable guidance of her teacher her progress was beyond expectations. In 1939 the annual student production at the Conservatory was going to be Mascagni's *Cavalleria Rusticana*. Maria was chosen to sing Santuzza, the title role. The performance was to take place in April, and Maria, who was according to the Conservatory seventeen

but in reality she was only fifteen, made her first appearance on the
stage. Her efforts were rewarded with the first prize in opera at the
Conservatory.

Maria continued her studies with Maria Trivella until the
December of 1939, when at her mother's wish she went to the
Odeon Athenon. She was sixteen years old now, and at the Odeon
Athenon Elvira de Hidalgo had recently joined the teaching staff.
The Spanish Elvira de Hidalgo had until then been a famous
coloratura soprano of great reputation in the opera houses
of the world, where she had sung with the most famous
artists, including Caruso. Taking advantage of her presence in
Greece the National Opera in Athens also made her their artistic
adviser.

When Maria presented herself at the Odeon Athenon for her
audition, no longer merely plump but fat, with pimples on her
face and nervously biting her finger-nails, de Hidalgo, as she later
recalled, found the whole idea quite incredible. But when Maria
began to sing 'Ocean! Thou mighty monster' from Weber's
Oberon it was a different story; a story that was the beginning of a
five-year period of hard work, achievement and eventually
triumph. De Hidalgo seems to have begun her teaching immediately, for, losing no opportunity at the audition, after she
expressed her pleasure, said to her new pupil: 'Now that you have
sung "Ocean" so well you must put this music away. In twenty
years' time you can look at it again. This is no music for a young
girl.' De Hidalgo no doubt was so impressed with the voice, if not
with the appearance, of her new student, that she arranged her
admission to the Conservatory to be free of tuition fees. Maria was
thrilled, and with even greater enthusiasm threw herself into hard
work. No interest other than that of becoming a truly great singer
was going to find room in her heart. Social life of any kind did not
interest the young singer, and she had practically no friends of any
consequence. With one exception, however. Her teacher, Elvira
de Hidalgo, very quickly became also her best and only friend.
Maria would spend all her available time with her even when she
was not studying, which was not very often.

With de Hidalgo Maria was to discover, and make her own, the
secrets of *bel canto*. Already her fast growing repertoire included,
apart from opera, much other vocal music so necessary for the

serious music student.[1] In 1940 Maria sang Angelica, in a student production again, in Puccini's *Suor Angelica*. Also Amelia and Aida in Verdi's *Un Ballo in Maschera* and *Aida*. She made a bigger impression than her Santuzza, but nevertheless these were still student performances. Jackie, who apart from her piano was also taking singing lessons, was chosen to sing in the chorus of *Suor Angelica*. Under de Hidalgo's wonderful teaching Maria was constantly improving her voice and vocal technique. More important still under the expert guidance of her teacher, her natural instinct for dramatic expression was beginning to develop, and once again music was in no way a chore as it once had been in America. Shortly afterwards, with the help of de Hidalgo, Maria made her first professional appearance. This was Beatrice in Suppé's operetta *Boccaccio* at the Athens Opera. Maria had also to share the performances with another singer. It was not much of a part, but still it was the first time she performed on the stage with professional people, and Maria certainly did her part most professionally.

Meanwhile war was raging in most of Europe, but it was not till 28th October 1940 that Mussolini declared war on Greece. The Greek army, small but brave, proved more than a match for the large invading one. Soon the Italians were repelled, forced into Albania, west of Yugoslavia, all through the winter. Then Hitler's army came. On 6th April 1941 Salonika was badly bombed, and after sixteen days of bloodshed the heroic Greek army was obliterated.

On 27th April 1941 the Germans occupied Athens, and later in the same year Italian troops arrived as well.

With the occupation of Athens Maria's career, like everything else, came to a standstill. Any communication with her father in New York was now impossible. Greece was in a chaotic state, and starvation was soon killing the old and weak. Like many others Maria on many occasions had to walk miles to far-away farms in the hope of getting some vegetables. These war years, like the depression in America, were to leave their strong impressions on Maria.

A few months later, when life somehow eased a little and the

---

[1] The soprano parts in Handel's *Messiah*, Pizzetti's *I tre canti Greci*, Bach's *St Matthew Passion*, Mozart's *Requiem*, Haydn's *Requiem* and Lieder by Schubert and Brahms.

Germans allowed schools, theatres and public places to reopen, de Hidalgo was able to arrange for Maria to become a permanent member of the Athens Opera, which somehow managed to function during those chaotic years of the occupation.

The Callas family even made acquaintance with several Italian officers, who very often brought them food. Maria would delight them by singing operatic arias from Italian opera. Also Maria, who was always advised by de Hidalgo that it was essential to learn Italian, now found her opportunity. She began to study it and, being able to practise conversation in Italian, mastered the language in a matter of a few months.

One day in July 1942 the soprano of the Athens Opera, who was to sing *Tosca*, was suddenly taken ill. Probably through de Hidalgo's advice the Opera House management rushed Maria to the theatre to replace the indisposed soprano. There were just about twenty-four hours to go and a dress had to be made for her. This difficult task, for Maria was quite big, was assigned to a young stage designer Nikos Zografos, who promptly altered a black velvet dress he found in the wardrobe of the Greek National Theatre (the opera and theatre companies were sharing the same theatre in Athens in those days). A tall hat and sceptre to match the waistless dress gave the young singer the best appearance possible. On 4th July Maria sang a most impressive Tosca and created quite a sensation both with the public and the critics; she was only seventeen and a half years old.

It has been said that the indisposed soprano who was to have sung Tosca sent her husband to stop Maria taking her part, and that Maria scratched his face and apparently got a black eye herself. There were several people present on that evening. Strangely none of them remember such an incident. Nikos Zografos, who made her dress for the performance, her first stage dress, does not recall anything of the kind. Neither does the stage director nor Maria herself. They all remember, however, her success. Even years later in 1956 in America this alleged incident was recalled and made headlines.

Maria Kalogeropoulou now became one of the Athens Opera leading sopranos at 3,000 drachmas per month. This was about forty-five shillings. It was very little but it did mean something in those days. Money, after food, was after all the most scarce thing.

Maria Callas

RIGHT. Maria Callas with her husband, Gianbatista Meneghini. Milan, 1958.

RIGHT. 'I knew immediately that in Maria Callas there was a future great singer' said Maestro Tullio Serafin. Here, in 1960, they are discussing *Norma*.

Some of the finer points of *La Vestale* at rehearsal, La Scala, Milan, 1954, are discussed by Callas, Antonino Votto, Victor de Sabata with Arturo Toscanini.

ABOVE. Maria Callas and Luchino Visconti after the first performance of Gluck's *Iphigenia en Tauride* at La Scala, Milan, during the 1957 season. BELOW. With Iphigenia's grace and dignity, Maria Callas takes her curtain calls (Visconti's production of *Iphigenia en Tauride* at La Scala, Milan).

Bellini: *Il Pirata*

Perhaps never before has there been a singer whose means of expression
were better suited to impersonate this heroine. This is really Bellini's and
Callas' Imogene.

Spontini: *La Vestale*

As Giulia in Spontini's rarely performed opera which Callas
resurrected.

LEFT. Rossini: *Il Barbiere di Siviglia.* Callas as a very individual and controversial Rosina. RIGHT. Puccini: *Turandot.* Early in her career Callas invested the character of the cruel and cold Princess with just the right blend of imperiousness and coldness.

Verdi: *Il Trovatore*

Callas' assumption of the role of Leonora was basically that of an
aristocratic lady and a major contribution to Italian opera.

The commander of the Italian army of occupation, a particular Italian opera lover, was quite impressed by the efforts of the Athens Opera artists, no less of Maria herself, so much so that he arranged for them to visit Salonika during the summer. Half a dozen singers, including Maria and a piano accompanist, were to give potted concert versions of Italian operas.

Maria, accompanied by her mother, arrived with her colleagues to Salonika where they would stay for almost a month. One thing they did not have to worry about: this was food, which the Italian commander saw was good and plentiful. To quite an appreciative audience, which consisted mainly of Italian soldiers, the Greek artists sang as well as they could and not for money either. At their own request at the end of their performances they were all paid in food supplies which they happily took to Athens. Food was after all better than ready money.

This was the first time that Maria sang professionally away from Athens and was glad of the new experience. A few months later, early in 1943, Maria was given the role of Santuzza in *Cavalleria Rusticana*—the very first role she had sung as a student at the Conservatory.

Manolis Kalomiris, one of Greece's most illustrious composers, was producing his new opera *Ho Protomastoras*, based on the book of that other illustrious Greek writer Nikos Kazantzakis. The leading role of Smaragda of this new modern Greek opera was entrusted to the young prima donna of the Athens Opera. Maria sang the difficult music in March 1943 and earned an ovation. (This was the only modern opera Maria had sung to date.) In just over a month the versatile Maria was entrusted with yet another role, that of Marta in the Greek *première* of D'Albert's opera *Tiefland*. With her in the cast was the baritone Evangelios Mangliveras, one of Greece's most famous singers. Mangliveras, with a successful career behind him, had sung with success abroad as well as in Greece. Although he was now vocally past his prime, his amazing acting abilities and great experience still commanded the utmost attention. When they met at rehearsals their friendship was immediate, and Mangliveras taught his young singer friend various important points of stagecraft.

Tiefland was a success, and this time, as well as her singing, Maria's acting abilities were noticed, thanks to a great extent to

B

Mangliveras. With the *Tiefland* performances over Mangliveras's interest did not diminish. In fact it developed to great affection, and eventually he asked Maria to marry him. Maria admired and respected the great artist, but for the moment could find no room in her heart for anybody. There was room only for music.

Meantime Maria arranged a private return visit to Salonika. Accompanied by her mother, she arrived in Salonika to prepare for her two scheduled recitals. She was this time going to sing rather for the people of Salonika than Italian soldiers. Italian arias and a set of German *Lieder*, by Schubert and Brahms, all accompanied with piano, was her programme. When Maria appeared on the stage of the White Tower Theatre some people let a slight chuckle of laughter escape them. It seems that Maria, who was quite plump, fitted the image of a prima donna that many people expect. Yet for this reason this expected image often produces smiles and sometimes laughter. But this was all for a very short moment until Maria began to sing. The people of Salonika immediately appreciated that here was a voice worth paying attention to, worth listening to.

With Italy's surrender to the allied forces in September 1943 the Greek resistance movement was greatly strengthened, and soon they drove the Germans out of the Greek countryside. Within a year only Athens and the greater Greek cities were left occupied.

In the late summer of 1944 Maria was invited to sing the leading role in Beethoven's opera *Fidelio*. The soprano who was originally chosen for the part could not learn it in time. Maria could and sang the role of Leonore so imaginatively that her characterization made a great impact. Leonore turned out to be her greatest success so far. And in the finale of the opera, when Leonore frees her husband from prison, Maria jubilantly sang 'Oh, namenlose Freude' ('Oh, nameless joy') in the vast theatre of Herodes Atticus on the Acropolis before an oppressed people and their oppressors, the army of occupation, she seemed to be assuring them that the hour of liberation was imminent. And as it happened it was only a few weeks later, on 12th October 1944, that Athens was liberated by the Greek resistance troops. The liberation was unfortunately the beginning of something even worse than the German occupation. Hardly was the rejoicing over when on 3rd December civil war broke out. The issue of the civil war was

Communist domination. Street fights, with more people dying than ever, followed, and life came to a chaotic stillness which was more terrifying than the time of the occupation. Food was for a time impossible to find, and the winter that followed was the severest for years. Like most other families Maria with her family remained shut up in their home for days. Street fighting continued and sometimes came so close to Maria's house that it was terrifying. One night, whilst Maria and her mother were in the room where they kept their canaries, their flat was machine-gunned. Their shadows must have been seen on the blinds. They switched out the light immediately and fell on the floor. After some time when it was quiet they ventured to get up. They were thankful neither of them was hurt, but soon found out that their canaries, those other singers of their household, were lying dead on the floor of their cage.

It was mainly owing to the intervention of the English troops that the civil war ended after forty bloody and brutal days. Maria Kalogeropoulou, the brightest star of the Athens Opera, however, was beginning her own battle. It seems that Maria's success was the kind that would incite jealousy. Possibly her exciting personality, which seems to penetrate everything she does and is conveyed to her audiences, separates her from the crowd of other artists and she appears to monopolize success. Jealous colleagues, especially those who had not stayed with the Opera during the German occupation and who always resented her success, found their opportunity and began to put pressure on the Opera House new administration to discontinue the young prima donna's membership of the Athens Opera. The superintendent of the Opera, to keep the peace, decided not to renew Maria's contract. These factors would not have intimidated the young but determined singer, but now the American Embassy in Athens were strongly advising her to return to the United States to enable her to retain her American citizenship. Furthermore Athens could hardly offer much more for such an ambitious artist. With the ending of the war Maria heard from her father, who sent her some money too. But she needed more money if she was to travel to America. She managed to obtain a loan from the American Embassy to cover at least her fare, and she also gave a recital at the Rex Theatre in Athens.

Almost immediately, after a final appearance with the Athens Opera in Millocker's operetta *Bettelstudent*, Maria left Greece to join her father and seek a new career in New York where greater opportunities existed. After all in Greece she had been the National Opera's brightest star. Surely there would be a place for her in the New World, with better prospects of reaching the top. To all these hopes there was one dissenting voice. Her great teacher Elvira de Hidalgo, although she agreed with Maria leaving Greece, insisted that Maria's future lay most definitely in Italy and not in America or anywhere else. Once she became established in Italy the whole world would come to her. De Hidalgo's words were to be proved right, but Maria's mind was made up, perhaps chiefly because she had a father in America to go to. Full of ambition and hope Maria sailed on the S.S. *Stockholm* for the New World where she would try to further her career, the only thing that really mattered, the only thing for which any sacrifice would be worth making.

Her father was there to receive his daughter when she landed in New York. Only she was no longer a little girl but a grown-up young lady of twenty-one. It seemed a long time since the depression, war and hardship, and father and daughter were moved to tears of joy. Georges Callas had by now managed to have his own pharmacy again and a fairly comfortable apartment on West 157th Street. Maria went to live with him, and for a time she occupied herself by just keeping home for her father and seeing old acquaintances. Life was for the moment pleasant, and Maria felt a new kind of security near her father. America, the land of plenty, appeared for someone who had come from a country that had been occupied a new world. In a few months her mother joined them too. Jackie decided to stay in Athens for the moment. But soon the novelty of all these newly found joys of life wore off. Maria knew what her vocation was and certainly turned anywhere she might find suitable work.

America proved to be a great disappointment, for nobody seemed interested in a young girl of twenty-one, even though she had been a star in the Athens Opera with several roles to her credit. With some help from the Greek singer Nicola Moscona, who was a permanent member of the Metropolitan Opera, but more through Maria's persistence, she auditioned for Edward Johnson, then the head of the Metropolitan Opera. The result was a contract to sing Leonore in *Fidelio* and the title role in *Madama Butterfly* in the Metropolitan's forthcoming season. Both operas were to be sung in English. Strong-willed and determined to get ahead, but only in the way she considered right, Maria, in spite of great hardship, turned the contract down. She would not sing a German opera in English, and at that time weighing 190 lb. would certainly not appear as the fragile Butterfly. Maria suggested she should sing *Aida* or *Tosca* instead, but Johnson would not hear of it. He had made his offer and that was that. Maria too had given her answer. It was a brave decision to take, and it seems Maria knew what she wanted. Another audition followed, this time with the San Francisco Opera, but nothing came of it. They found her quite good, but as she was unknown they advised her to go to Italy and make a name for herself first. 'When I make a name for myself in Italy I shall not want you,' was her reply. Nothing came either of a project for establishing an opera company in Chicago by E. Richard Bagarozy, a New York impresario, in which a new soprano Marie Calas, as she was to be called, was to sing the title role in Puccini's *Turandot*. The opera company went bankrupt before it began its season and that was the end of that. Maria had met the Bagarozys about a year before. Bagarozy's wife, Louise Caselotti, herself a singer, coached Maria, who for over a year visited the Bagarozys daily.

Bagarozy was originally a lawyer in New York. His main interest in life, however, was opera. He married an opera singer. Soon he gave up his profession and became an impresario. His ambition was not only to manage the affairs of other singers, but he also hoped one day he would manage his own opera company. He came very close to succeeding in this. For this venture Bagarozy went into partnership with an Italian impresario Ottavio Scotto. Chicago—with its memories of great operatic performances in the past still fresh, but having no opera at the time—was the chosen city. As many European opera houses as a result of the war were not functioning in 1946, Baragozy and Scotto engaged easily quite a number of young European singers. Marie Calas was going to be the star. But the promised financial support failed to appear, and as the American Guild of Musical Artists demanded a considerable deposit that would safeguard the salaries of the members of the chorus, there was consequently no Turandot with Marie Calas or anything else.

One of the many other artists who would have appeared with the Chicago company was a young bass, Nicola Rossi-Lemeni. He was a frequent visitor at the Bagarozy flat and Maria became quite friendly with him. Just about this time the famous tenor, Giovanni Zenatello, the Sovritendente of the opera performances at the Arena of Verona in Italy, was looking for a soprano to sing the role of Gioconda in Ponchielli's opera. Rossi-Lemeni, who was already signed on to sing at the Arena of Verona in the forthcoming season, suggested to Maria that she audition to Zenatello. Maria liked the idea and did audition for Zenatello at his house in New York. Zenatello liked what he heard, and without any fuss offered her a contract for five performances of *La Gioconda* at twenty pounds each. Maria accepted the offer at once. Certainly not for the money, which was very little, but she wanted to sing the opera if only for the good prospects such an engagement offered.

Maria Callas sailed again for Europe on 17th July 1947. On the day of her departure she signed a contract appointing Bagarozy her agent for a period of ten years, agreeing to pay him 10 per cent of all her gross fees earned from her singing. Bagarozy in return undertook to use his best efforts to further and promote her career. Maria was in financial difficulties again for the trip to Europe. Her father gave her some money and her godfather, Dr Leonidas Lantzounis, made her a loan which paid for her passage from New York to Naples and then on to Verona. Maria arrived in Naples on board the S.S. *Rossia* on 27th June 1947. From Naples she made her way by train to Verona.

Verona was to prove the turning-point in her career, for it was here that Maria Callas met Maestro Tullio Serafin and Signor Gianbatista Meneghini, two gentlemen who, each in his own way, were to play a great part in her future and her career and life.

Maria could not help thinking of her teacher and friend Elvira de Hidalgo back in Greece. Would she be proved once again right when she had said that Maria's future lay in Italy? Well, she was now in Italy, even if she came via America, and she was to sing Gioconda. Elvira maintained that once her fame was established in Italy it would spread all over the world.

Maria waited and worked hard, constantly preparing as 3rd August, the day of the first *Gioconda*, approached. At the final rehearsal Maria had an unfortunate accident. She fell and sprained her ankle. In spite of the pain this caused her she did not let things like this get in her way.

When the little candles that customarily burn in thousands during the overture of an opera performance at the Arena were extinguished nobody guessed how triumphantly de Hidalgo's words were to be justified. Not even the maestro, Tullio Serafin, or Maria herself, knew this was the beginning of a triumphant career that was destined to change the operatic world and bring a renaissance of Italian Opera.

II

Io son l'umile ancella del Genio creator:
ei m'offre la favella, io la diffondo ai cor . . . [1]
Cilea—ADRIANA LECOUVREUR.

Maria Callas's Italian début took place on 3rd August 1947, under the eminent conductor Tullio Serafin. She had a considerable success and, to judge by the enthusiasm of the 25,000-strong audience that crowded into the huge arena, they must have thought her a most exciting Gioconda in Ponchielli's opera. The music critics were pleased with her too, though without any great enthusiasm, but most important of all Maestro Tullio Serafin was the first among Italian musicians to appreciate the young singer's genius. 'I knew immediately that in Maria Callas there was a future great singer,' Serafin was to reminisce years later. In fact a great friendship was begun, and Maria was to follow the great maestro's valuable advice and guidance in the years of triumph that were ahead.

It was also during this time in Verona that Maria met Giovanni Battista Meneghini, a Veronese industrialist many years her

[1] I am only the humble handmaid of the creative genius: it gives me words, which I diffuse in men's hearts . . .

senior. Maria, who had been rather a lonely person with hardly
any friends—her time had always really been devoted to her voice
—found in Meneghini an unusually close friend, for he was just as
devotedly interested in her voice and in encouraging her in the
promising career she was embarking on as she herself was. Their
friendship was immediate and they became inseparable.

With the Verona *Gioconda* performances over, Maria was quite
free to seek other engagements. Understandably her attention
was turned towards the great Italian theatre, La Scala of Milan. It
is any singer's ambition to sing in this old theatre and Maria was
no exception. But the gates of La Scala do not open easily, however aspiring singers may be. Anyway Maria managed to obtain
an audition. When she eventually sang in this audition Mario
Labroca, who was then the Artistic Director of La Scala, quite
liked what he heard, but rather coldly just talked about certain
vocal defects he had noticed. Anyway he could not offer her anything for the moment. Yet before Maria departed he promised her
that she would be considered as a possible singer for the role of
Amelia in Verdi's *Un Ballo in Maschera*, which La Scala was
planning for the forthcoming season. On this note Maria left to
wait hopefully. She may not have been engaged immediately, as
any young singer who had already known success might have
hoped to be, but she had at least good reason to wait hopefully,
as Labroca's final words to her were quite promising. She waited
and waited, her hopes diminishing as the months went by without
anything happening. La Scala was silent as far as she was concerned. Meantime, in November, another singer was engaged for
La Scala's *Un Ballo in Maschera* and this ended Maria's waiting.
But another message arrived for the disappointed singer. Her
friend Tullio Serafin had not forgotten her. He was now inviting
her to sing Isolde in Wagner's *Tristan und Isolde* and in *Turandot*,
both productions under his baton at the Teatro La Fenice in
Venice. Maria accepted the offer at once and without any hesita-
tion, until suddenly she realized that she did not know the role of
Isolde. 'You have a month to learn it,' Serafin said. 'I know you
can do it.' In fact she prepared the role of Isolde completely under
Serafin's guidance and musical teaching and she did learn it in
just a month's time, in time to sing it on the opening night on
22nd December 1947. As Isolde Callas achieved an undisputed

triumph.[1] At last the great role was not only sung, but was magnificently interpreted. Early in January she sang her second and final role, that of Turandot. It was no less successful than her recent Isolde. But her success in Venice was noticed in Italy much more than her Gioconda in Verona had been six months before. Almost immediately several other engagements followed in rapid succession. But first Tullio Serafin had to be consulted. Did he think it would be the right opera and the right place? In fact nothing without the sanction and advice of Serafin was undertaken. She sang *Aida* in Rovigo in the early part of 1948, and Leonora in Verdi's *La Forza del Destino* in Trieste; *Turandot* again in Verona, *Aida* at the Terme di Caracalla, Rome's open-air opera, and again Isolde, this time in Genoa.

During the summer of 1948 Maria began to prepare, with Serafin, Bellini's great role, Norma, a role that was destined to be so much her own and, like so many others, to be labelled 'a Callas role'. But this was a little ahead yet as other surprises lay in store both for the singer and the opera public.

The 1948–9 season of Venice's La Fenice presented the exceptional Isolde of the previous season in a new Wagnerian role, that of Brünnhilde in *Die Walküre*. The second opera that was scheduled for production at La Fenice was Bellini's *I Puritani* with Margarita Carosio in the leading role of Elvira. Because of the great lack of suitable singers, *I Puritani* is a rarely performed opera even in Italy. In particular, the demands of the leading role are far greater than that with which the ordinary coloratura soprano can cope. Carosio, though not quite the perfect interpreter of the role, was, however, competent and anyway possibly the best available soprano. But Carosio, a few days before the performance, suddenly fell ill and had to withdraw. A substitute for this role, and particularly at such short notice, was impossible to find, Serafin again produced the right idea. Apparently Serafin's daughter, who was staying at the same hotel as Callas, had heard her sing an aria from *I Puritani* in her room. She was so moved that she told her father about it. With what must have been some trepidation the management of La Fenice, again following Serafin's advice, invited Maria Callas, after an impromptu

---

[1] The opera, like the other two Wagnerian operas, *Parsifal* and *Die Walküre*, that Callas had sung, was sung in Italian.

audition, when Maria sang an aria from *I Puritani*, to undertake the coloratura role of Elvira. Maria, who only knew just about one aria from the role, thanks to her teacher de Hidalgo in Greece who introduced her to the music of Bellini and Donizetti, accepted the offer, which was really more of a challenge. She had six days to learn it and at the same time there was Brünnhilde on her hands. No two roles could be less similar, but as Callas was to prove time and time again on so many occasions during her career, she achieved the incredible. She did learn the role in time and, a few days after her dramatic Brünnhilde, scored a stupendous success as Elvira. Musical Italy enthused about the event, and Maria Callas was heralded as nothing less than phenomenal. In fact comparisons went back to the fabulous versatility of Lilli Lehmann.

Altogether 1949 was a very eventful year for Maria Callas. Apart from appearing in *Walküre* in Palermo, in *Turandot* at the San Carlo in Naples, and dazzling Rome by singing *I Puritani* and very shortly afterwards Kundry in Wagner's *Parsifal*, she married Giovanni Battista Meneghini in Verona on 21st April. Ever since Maria had met Meneghini he had been her constant companion, always ready to give her his spiritual support when things were not going quite smoothly. For practically two years, ever since they had become friends, Meneghini had not wavered in his devotion to her. He already managed her affairs. But there were many things to consider. The great difference in their ages and their families' virtual disapproval certainly did not speed things up. Meneghini's family stubbornly would not approve. But the day came when their minds were finally made up. Two days before Maria was leaving to fulfil an important South American engagement they were married.

Maria Meneghini-Callas now crossed the Atlantic again; this time heading for South America. Meneghini could not accompany his wife. He was so much tied up in some important business commitments that it was necessary for him to be in Italy. Maria's engagement was important too. She was making her début at an important theatre and would also be singing in three different operas. So hardly had the Meneghinis been united in matrimony when they had to be separated because of business commitments.

At the Teatro Colon in Buenos Aires, again under her beloved maestro Tullio Serafin, Maria made her South American début in

Turandot. The new soprano made quite an impression both in *Turandot* and *Aida* that followed with the Argentinian public and critics. She did not, however, gain their unreserved enthusiasm. Not until she had sung her third and last role. In *Norma*, the role she had meticulously studied the previous year with Serafin and was now singing for the first time, she won a personal triumph. With the South American engagements over, Signora Meneghini was most anxious to return to Italy and the husband she left behind. Clearly she felt quite lonely in South America. It was almost four months that she had to stay away and it seemed a lifetime. Maria's homecoming must have been a very happy occasion for her. During her absence Meneghini had acquired a comfortable and pleasant flat in Verona, with a view of the Arena, just in time for his wife's arrival. Whatever life had in store there is no denying the next few months that followed must have been some of the happiest in Maria Callas's life. All the things that she had lacked in the past seemed to have been acquired at the same time. It was a wonderful new experience for Maria to live in her own flat and to have the security of a husband, particularly one who was so interested in her career. The days that followed after Maria's return from South America were like a belated honeymoon. But time passed, as it usually does under such circumstances, much too quickly and it was already December. Maria had now to concentrate on further engagements which were constantly increasing in number. Such is the life of an aspiring artist, and Meneghini was most understanding.

In December 1949 Meneghini-Callas found herself opening the season at the San Carlo in Naples in the role of Abigail in Verdi's *Nabucco*. Then in Rome again, where her Norma was acclaimed by the Romans. 'Her Norma is divine,' was one of the many rapturous comments on this performance. Both these operas have always been very difficult to cast, and especially the leading soprano roles. Maria's performances made a great impression and her name was now well established. Soon all the Italian theatres were after her services. Or rather nearly all, for La Scala, Milan, the greatest temple of melodrama, was still inaccessible. Ever since her audition there in 1947 she had heard nothing from the theatre. Deep in her heart Maria must have been longing for the day when she would sing on the famous stage of La Scala where all the great singers of the past had sung. An invitation did finally come in April 1950 for a gala performance of *Aida* during the Milan Fair. This was not quite the kind of invitation that the artist would have wished for. She was to replace the indisposed Renata Tebaldi. Nevertheless the invitation was gladly accepted. When once she was actually heard at La Scala this could lead to greater things. Her début at La Scala turned out to be a brilliant affair, both socially and artistically, but in spite of this La Scala still offered no contract to their successful guest artist. Maria sang a second *Aida* as scheduled, and the Meneghinis departed from Milan, satisfied with Maria's performances but without a contract from La Scala. Antonio Ghiringhelli, the superintendent of La Scala, was quite silent.

At about this time another contract of a somewhat different nature was offered by 'Cetra', the Italian recording company, and with this an extraordinary recording career began; one that was to take Callas's art to all the corners of the world.

There was a new début to be made. Maria was crossing the Atlantic again during the early part of May 1950, this time heading for Mexico. Meneghini, owing to important business commitments again, could not accompany his wife, but as she was only to be away for about a fortnight they made arrangements to meet in Madrid on Maria's return. Maria was not travelling alone either this time. Her friend Giulietta Simionato, the mezzo-soprano, who was also singing in Mexico, was accompanying her. On their way to Mexico they had to make a stop in New York where Maria arranged to see her parents. Both her mother and father were in New York, and it had been three years since she had seen them—when she sailed away to sing Gioconda. Many things had happened since. She was now quite a famous singer, and of course she was Signora Meneghini, happily married and financially secure.

In New York Georges Callas met the two singers at the airport. Evangelia Callas unexpectedly had to go to hospital with an eye infection. The stop in New York was only going to be for a few hours, so Maria almost immediately went to see her mother. It was a happy meeting in spite of the circumstances. Maria could only spend a short time with her mother. There was so much to talk about, especially about Maria's successful performances in Italy.

Although Evangelia had heard most of it before in letters, she was delighted to hear it all over again. It was even more delightful for Evangelia when Maria, just before she left, invited her mother, who was hoping to be up in a few days, to come to Mexico so that she could hear her daughter sing. It had been a long time since her mother had seen her on the Athenian opera stage. She could now hear her re-create the great heroines of Italian opera, and, besides, the change would help her to recuperate better.

In Mexico Maria made a most successful début singing *Aida* and *Tosca*, and a new role for her, Leonora in Verdi's *Il Trovatore*, was added to her fast-growing and amazing repertoire. Her mother, who soon joined her, was there to witness it all. Evangelia was now able to admire her daughter. The difficult years of the depression and the long German occupation in Athens seemed as if they had not happened. Maria was a prima donna and that is all that mattered. Perhaps Evangelia also enjoyed herself, being in the limelight of her daughter. Almost any mother would. Soon the fortnight was over and Maria was on her way to Madrid where her husband was awaiting her. Feeling very happy with her performances she bade the Mexican capital goodbye, promising to return the following year. Her mother saw her off at the airport, both of them feeling very happy for having met after such a long time. As Maria waved her last goodbye from her seat in the plane she little knew that it would be her last goodbye to her mother for many years to come. Mother and daughter were unfortunately not to see each other for almost twelve years.

The Meneghinis were soon back in Verona where they could spend a few weeks alone without any engagements for Maria, at least not until 19th October.

During the autumn of 1950 a short festival of rarely performed operas was organized in Rome by a very enterprising intellectual group, 'the Amfiparnasso'. The performances were to take place at the Teatro Eliseo, and Maria Meneghini-Callas was invited to sing, for the first time in her career, the comic role of Donna Fiorilla in Rossini's rarely performed opera *Il Turco in Italia*. 'The Amfiparnasso' naturally turned to Maria, who so far had sung every role offered her in Italy with success. In fact she got the reputation that she could sing any role. Her versatility was so amazing that even then she was accepted as the woman with many

voices. Callas showed an unusual flair for Rossini's vivacious and
sparkling musical comedy and reaffirmed her reputation as a
singer who could sing practically any role. She seemed to have
found the right style, and with a delicate subtlety she proved that
she had deeply grained comic qualities in her. The opera was
produced by Luchino Visconti, the genius of the Italian stage and
cinema. During the Rossini opera Maria struck up a close friendship with him, one that is still in existence today. The two of them
found they had many things in common, for they both approached
opera from a dramatic angle. They both found great interest in
their discussions and enjoyed each other's company greatly. It
was a few years after that Visconti was lured by Callas into the
world of opera, a collaboration that led to some of her greatest
triumphs.

The Verdi Celebrations were held in 1951 and Callas offered her
own substantial contributions. First there was *La Traviata* for
Florence. This was her first appearance in this role but it was not
necessary, as usual, for her to have to learn it in an impossibly
short space of time. She had meticulously studied the role with
Tullio Serafin some time before. The role of Violetta had particularly captured her imagination and, as she was discovering, the
music of this opera was just what suited her voice. In fact she was
beginning to realize what the right kind of music for her voice
was. Now there was a chance to show how the role of Violetta,
'the Lady of the Camelias', should be sung and portrayed. On
15th January her most sensitive and moving portrayal confirmed
all hopes.

Twelve days later Maria was singing Leonora in *Il Trovatore* at
the San Carlo in Naples. Although she sang extremely well, and
made Leonora very individualistic and aristocratic, the Naples
music critics did not seem to appreciate this, and in fact treated it
with polite indifference. After Naples Maria sang *Aida* at Reggio
in Calabria and repeated her Violetta at Cagliari.

The year 1951 was also the year of the hundred and fiftieth
anniversary of the birth of Vincenzo Bellini, the Sicilian composer.
Bellini's operas had, since the days of the great singers for whom
most of them had been composed, been neglected, as singers with
the right style and technique were rare. Now, with the arrival of
Callas on the operatic scene, Bellini's operas were again revived,

as people were rapidly discovering that, with the right singers, this music could still cast a spell. Maria was soon established as the world's leading exponent of Bellini's music. *Norma* was her first contribution to the Bellini Celebrations in Palermo, Sicily.

About this time Maria had to go to Milan. It was not for any normal performance but for a rather special audition. Arturo Toscanini was in Milan looking for a suitable soprano for the role of Lady Macbeth in Verdi's opera *Macbeth*. He was planning to present the opera in New York. Maria auditioned for him in Milan; the introductions were made by Toscanini's daughter, Contessa Wally Castelbarco-Toscanini. The famous conductor liked what he heard, and at the time it seemed that there were no major obstacles in the way. But the performances never materialized. The maestro's health was deteriorating rapidly and the world was not to witness what would have been an outstanding event, for in Callas Toscanini would have found what Verdi ideally demanded.

Since the previous year, when Maria had sung at La Scala, the famous theatre had maintained a complete silence and had shown no interest in the up and coming prima donna. In Maria's heart there was always naturally the hope that one day she would take her rightful place at La Scala. However, for the moment she was so busy singing in most of the Italian theatres, in Mexico and South America to think much about it.

Now suddenly, out of the blue, La Scala was asking for her. Ghiringhelli, the superintendent, remembered the guest artist who helped them out during the previous year's emergency when the soprano Renata Tebaldi could not appear in *Aida* due to sickness. What was more incredible, the invitation was exactly the same this time. Would Callas help La Scala and again replace the indisposed Tebaldi in *Aida*? Maria did not need much time to decide. This time she promptly refused: if La Scala wanted her she would be delighted to sing but only on the terms of a top rank artist and not as an understudy. This was the way she was forced to answer the invitation that in normal circumstances she would have wished to accept more than anything else.

Meanwhile her mind had to turn towards her next important assignment. Florence holds its famous 'Maggio Musicale Fiorentino' in May and June. Being Verdi's year the festival was

appropriately opening with a rarely performed opera of the
'middle Verdi' period, *I Vespri Siciliani*. It is by no means the best
of Verdi, but with the right interpreters the opera, in spite of a
certain unevenness, can be most exciting with the wonderful
situations and rousing tunes it contains. Exactly such an interpreter Florence found in Maria Meneghini-Callas, who sang the
leading role of Elena, thrilling her audience. This performance,
which was full of revelations, gave the festival an electrifying
start. Hardly had the applause died down when Ghiringhelli, with
open arms and contract on hand, presented himself to her. La
Scala was yielding to the successful prima donna. The invitation
this time was a royal one with all the honours. Maria was offered
three leading roles. La Scala would stage for her Bellini's *Norma*,
and she would also sing Constanze in Mozart's *Die Entführung aus
dem Serail* at La Scala's first ever production of the opera. And on
top of these Maria would have the great honour of opening the
forthcoming season at La Scala in the very same role of Elena in
I Vespri Siciliani. It was a contract that any artist would go a long
way to obtain, and Maria was happy beyond description. All those
years of hard work and hardship were not in vain. The golden gates
for her to reach her goal were now open and Maria cried for joy.

The season at La Scala was opening in six months' time, and in
between this time Maria had a very busy schedule. She was to sing
in an even more rarely performed opera than *I Vespri Siciliani*.
Haydn's *Orfeo ed Euridice* was written in 1791, and it was left to
Florence and Callas to give it its first stage performance. Maria
created the role of Euridice and proved how well she mastered the
classic florid style in singing.

With her final contribution at the 'Maggio Musicale' over
Maria had only a few days to prepare for her trip to Mexico. This
time she was not going alone, however. Her husband was now
able to accompany her. Meneghini, who was a wealthy industrialist, together with his brother, ran the family business in
building materials. Since his marriage, however, Meneghini had
been constantly giving up much of his share of business affairs to
his brother, so that Meneghini would be able to devote much
more time in managing his wife's affairs that her career presented.
This was their first long trip together and they were to stay away
all through the summer. Mexico City was the first stop, and then

São Paulo and Rio de Janeiro in Brazil. Maria also invited her father to join them in Mexico.

Georges Callas was at this time living alone in New York. His wife had decided to return to Athens again. It was obvious that they were gradually reaching the point of not being able to live together. Maria thought the change would do a lot of good to her father. It would also provide a chance for him to meet his son-in-law whom he had not seen. Deep in Maria's heart there was more than this. Her father, a very conservative man, had always held different ideas about the stage and never really believed that his daughter would one day be a famous prima donna. If he did he had never shown it, and he had certainly never given any encouragement. Now for the first time he could see his daughter perform on the stage, and perhaps the experience would make him change his views.

In Mexico City Maria sang *Aida* and Violetta in *La Traviata* with enormous success, especially as Violetta, a role she was singing for the first time in the Mexican capital. The public went wild over their applause, and the critics were running out of words of praise about the beauty of her voice and her overwhelming dramatic power. Maria was very happy with her success, especially because she had her husband and father with her to share it. Georges Callas was so much taken by the experience of seeing his daughter perform that he forgot all his doubts and reservations about the stage. His daughter had now proved to him differently, and he even developed an interest in opera, an interest he certainly did not have before. He was so proud of Maria that he even forgot for the moment his other domestic problems. His all too short holiday in Mexico ended and he returned to New York a happy man.

The Meneghinis went on to São Paulo where Maria was to make her Brazilian début in *Aida* and then also sing in *La Traviata*. Brazil was not, however, to be the happy place Mexico had been. From the beginning things were far from being smooth. Maria fell ill and did not sing in *Aida*. She recovered in time to sing in the *Traviata* performances which she shared alternately with the Italian soprano Renata Tebaldi. Both sopranos sang with success and they were glad to meet again. It had been over two years since they had first met and become friends when they were both singing during the 1949 season at La Fenice in Venice. This friendship was not, however, to last much longer. The events that followed in Rio de Janeiro, where both sopranos were appearing after São Paulo, brought it to an end and transformed it into a kind of a feud.

In Rio de Janeiro Tebaldi was the first to make her début. She sang in *Traviata* and completely won the Brazilian public over. She became the talk of Rio until one week later when Callas made her début in *Norma*. The public gave Callas a standing ovation, and the critics saw in her a great singer with extraordinary dramatic powers. Tebaldi, unlike in São Paulo, seemed to be over-sensitive. Although both sopranos had sung with great success, a kind of rivalry was created in the eyes of the public. An event that followed brought about a complete rift between the two singers.

At a benefit concert where several artists were taking part it was agreed that each artist would sing one item only. Tebaldi, however, unexpectedly broke the rule and gave two encores. This would have been of no serious consequence in itself. But there was another. When Callas next sang in *Tosca*, immediately after the performance she was called by Barreto Pinto, the director of the opera house, who announced to her that he had decided to cancel the remainder of her performances. Vaguely he explained that the reason for taking such a step was a supposed hostility the audience were showing towards Callas. Callas, who naturally found this most humiliating, was very annoyed and insisted that the opera house's contractual obligations towards her should be carried out. She did not sing in the second and last *Tosca*, but sang her two scheduled *Traviatas* with enormous success. Contrary to Pinto's argument, people turned out in thousands to cheer her. The biggest surprise and the final straw came when Renata Tebaldi sang in Maria's second *Tosca*. It all seemed that a conspiracy had taken place in order to stop Callas from giving performances for the Brazilian public.

It had been a most unpleasant time, and with the *Traviata* performances over the Meneghinis were most anxious to leave Brazil. Besides, Maria had a forthcoming engagement to fulfil in Sicily. On 3rd November 1951, the actual day of the hundred and fiftieth anniversary of Bellini's birth, Maria sang *Norma* to open the new season at the Teatro Bellini in Catania, Sicily, the composer's birthplace. A few days later she also sang in Bellini's *I Puritani* and then rushed back to Milan to prepare for her forthcoming appearances at La Scala.

It had been a most successful and busy year and, apart from the unpleasantness in Brazil, quite a happy one as far as her career was concerned. But in other respects the picture was not so pleasant. Maria's parents, although officially still married, in effect no longer lived together. Her mother had decided to return to America again in order to sue her husband for maintenance. As far as Maria's marriage was concerned she was very happy with her husband, but his family had never accepted the fact of losing Meneghini to a foreigner and an artist. But despite all these distressing events Callas's career continued. All she could think about for the moment was her forthcoming début at La Scala. She threw herself into hard work with complete dedication.

It is the custom in Milan that La Scala opens its gates for the new season on 7th December, the feast day of St Ambrose, who is the patron saint of Milan. It is a great and important day both socially and artistically for Milan, and a great honour for the artists who are chosen to sing on such a night.

The 1951–2 season was opening with a spectacular production of Verdi's *I Vespri Siciliani*. Maria Meneghini-Callas sang the leading role of Elena and took the Milanese audience by storm. The critics received the new soprano at La Scala enthusiastically. The *Corriere della Sera*, one of Milan's most important newspapers, described Maria's throat as miraculous and her technical agility as unique. This was a beginning, an auspicious one, in a theatre where, in the years that followed, she was to achieve some of her greatest triumphs; but the best was yet to be.

In just over a month there followed *Norma*, and Maria gave La Scala its most noteworthy performance of this opera in over thirty years. The third opera, Mozart's *Die Entführung aus dem Serail*, that Maria was scheduled to sing was quite a rarity for Milan. Mozart's operas have never been very popular with Italians, and in fact the opera was having its first ever production at La Scala. Maria mastered the difficult role of Constanze and sang with a brilliant *bravura* that delighted the highly critical Milanese audience.[1] In

[1] The opera was not sung in the original German but in Italian.

spite of the success which Callas found in her first Mozart opera she has never shown any interest in singing Mozart's music on the stage again.

Callas finished her first season at La Scala most successfully and had every reason to be happy. But absolute happiness is as rare as perfection is in life. Her fame was rising rapidly and she was becoming a very much sought after singer. Furthermore her marriage was proving to be a success. Nevertheless dark shadows from other directions were being cast on her happiness. Her mother, who had sued her husband and got her maintenance, decided to live in Greece with Jackie, her other daughter. Now she began to demand financial support from Maria and, quite openly, began to rebuke her daughter. Meneghini, the rich son-in-law, was also included in this. Furthermore it was demanded of Maria to sponsor completely Jackie's new career in Italy. Jackie, in all probability at her mother's decision, was changing from a pianist to a singer. Maria refused to help, as she did not consider Jackie's career her own responsibility. Bitter exchanges followed between both mother and sister in Greece and Maria until communications ceased entirely.

Hardly had she finished her appearances at La Scala when Maria had to go to Florence. The 'Maggio Musicale' was that year presenting only works by Rossini. Maria was to sing in *Armida*. This opera, which is technically extremely difficult, especially its numerous florid passages, had not been performed for 116 years. With the advent of Callas it seemed possible to revive this opera. The idea came from no less a person than Tullio Serafin, who also conducted the opera. Callas came up to expectations and was acclaimed in this extraordinary difficult *bravura* role.

Maria had already been a success in a considerable number of different operas, and consequently she had established herself as one of the leading prima donnas in Italy. In Mexico and in South America, apart from the unpleasantness with Pinto, she was quite a favourite both with the critics and her large public, who always filled the theatre to capacity whenever she performed.

Elvira de Hidalgo's words back in Greece—that Maria ought to go to Italy where, once her fame was established, all the other countries would follow—proved to be absolutely true. Now that Maria was an established prima donna in Italy her fame—it seemed like a matter of course—was spreading in other European countries.

The first invitation came from the Royal Opera House, Covent Garden, in London, for Maria to sing in *Norma* in the forthcoming June. This was going to be the first production of *Norma* in the English capital since 1929 when Rosa Ponselle, the last of the great Normas, had sung it. But Maria was unable to accept the invitation due to a previous engagement which was taking her again to Mexico. Eventually it was arranged for her to appear at Covent Garden in the forthcoming November.

In Mexico Callas for the first time sang Gilda in Verdi's *Rigoletto* and Lucia in Donizetti's *Lucia di Lammermoor*. Of the two Lucia was a stupendous success. The Mexican public were the first to find out that at last in the operatic history of the twentieth century here was a dramatic soprano who was capable of executing Lucia's florid music with the utmost ease. Maria's characterization of Lucia was a major achievement and a role which she subsequently perfected with refinements of expression. Maria was to be acclaimed in *Lucia di Lammermoor* in many theatres in the years that followed.

After Mexico Maria's life continued to be one great rush. In fact it became even busier.

The 1952 season at the Arena of Verona was opening with *La Gioconda*, and Maria returned there to the scene of her Italian début back in 1947 to sing again the very same role. It had been exactly five years since she had opened the season at the Arena, thus really starting her spectacular career. They had been five hard-working years, difficult in many ways, but all this could be forgotten in comparison with what Maria had achieved. She had become a famous prima donna and by no means in the ordinary way. She had brought new ideas and new excitement to the operatic stage, and people were beginning to understand and accept her art.

As Maria walked on the vast stage of the Arena to face the thousands of people, for a moment time stood still and her heart burst with joy.

At about this time Callas accepted a new long-term recording contract with the British recording firm E.M.I. She had already recorded for 'Cetra', but this new contract promised much more artistically, for the recordings were to be made in La Scala itself, using its outstanding conductors, orchestra and singers.

It was soon time for her to depart for London for her forth-coming début. Since Maria left Greece she had not seen her sister Jackie, who was living in Athens. In the meantime many things had of course happened. Unlike her elder sister she was now married, and as a prima donna, if not quite world famous yet, she had won considerable fame wherever she had been heard. It was now Jackie's turn to be invited, and Maria was very happy to have her sister with her in London. After all her mother and father had both in turn admired their daughter in Mexico and Chicago. Any sister would be happy and proud to see Maria on the stage, and particularly in one of her greatest roles.

On 8th November 1952 Maria Meneghini-Callas made her London début in Bellini's *Norma*. It proved to be the highly charged event that was expected. She created a sensation in the English capital, her first European capital outside Italy. Ebe Stignani, the great Italian mezzo-soprano, was in the cast. The two ladies together gave London its most noteworthy post-war operatic performance. It was a memorable evening, and the standing ovation that the English public gave Callas was unprece-dented within living memory.[1] The English critics too im-mediately saw in her a greatness as a singer that seemed to make other contemporary voices almost insignificant. Not that the voice was considered flawless. Yet the way Callas used her voice to express the inner emotions of the character of Norma was a stroke of genius. Still, there was a critic who would not surrender unconditionally. The late Ernest Newman, in the Covent Garden foyer after the performance, found himself surrounded by a crowd of people who wanted to hear his opinion. After all he was the eldest music critic in London, and the only one who had heard some of the great Normas of the past. Newman said very little: 'She is wonderful, truly wonderful.' And then, raising his umbrella and almost in a high-pitched voice: 'But she is not a Ponselle.'

Callas sang another four performances, always having en-thusiastic receptions, and then departed for Milan. Her London

---

[1] Even many years later people, those who saw these *Norma* performances, would always remember Callas's London début and nostalgically refer to it as the greatest thing they had ever heard on the operatic stage.

début could not have been more successful and Maria was very happy. Covent Garden was after all the most important theatre outside Italy in which she had appeared. A love, that exists to date, between Maria and London was born.

Back in Milan it was almost St Ambrose's Day, and Maria began practically straight away rehearsals for Verdi's *Macbeth*, with which opera La Scala was opening its new season. On 7th December 1952 Callas sang the role of the wicked Lady Macbeth according to the meticulous instructions which Verdi had given. Her performance reached great heights, and she electrified the audience in the sleep-walking scene—the climax of her art. Even Verdi would have approved. The Milanese certainly did, for they were all too eager to appreciate Maria's efforts. It was now possible for La Scala to revive operas hitherto neglected because of the lack of right interpreters. La Scala needed Maria just as much as Maria needed La Scala.

In January 1953 a concert was scheduled at the Festival Hall, London. There was going to be a performance of Verdi's *Requiem*. Callas, in the company of the great tenor of the generation, Beniamino Gigli and Ebe Stignani, were going to be the soloists. This announcement generated great excitement amongst the music lovers of England. But it was not to be. Due to an epidemic in Milan Callas had to cancel her appearance and thus deprived the world of hearing her in this work, for she has never sung in it since. Shortly afterwards Maria gave Florence her first Italian Lucia di Lammermoor, a role that she was to repeat in many theatres, and an experience which introduced a new golden age of opera. She also sang Lucia to open the spring opera season both at the Teatro Carlo Felice in Genoa and Teatro Bellini in Catania in Sicily.

Back at La Scala she sang *Il Trovatore* and *Gioconda*, for her old successes had now to be given to La Scala audiences as well before another successful season came to its close. She also shared a brilliant concert for R.A.I., the Italian radio, with Beniamino Gigli, and Maria sang excerpts from Rossini's *Armida*, Charpentier's *Louise*, Mozart's *Die Entführung aus dem Serail* and Meyerbeer's *Dinorah*.

In April Callas returned to Rome and sang in *Norma*. It was three years since she had been acclaimed by the Romans in this very same role. She scored a great success, but in her second opera, *La Traviata*, opinions were sharply divided. In some of the local press Callas's interpretation of Violetta that defied and in some cases modified many of the customary conventions drew a storm of disapproval. The public, which was also divided, turned out in masses fighting for tickets to see her, and quarrelling amongst themselves during the intervals. The year 1953 was the hundredth anniversary of *La Traviata*, and La Fenice, the theatre for which Verdi composed the opera, invited Callas to open their new season in this very same opera.

We are never surprised when we frequently hear that great success is accompanied by a good deal of bitterness; the greater the artist, the greater the controversy, and Maria Callas was no exception to this rule. The more successful she was, the more resentful her rivals became. The public too, always ready to enjoy such rivalries, helps much in creating them. Reports of Callas's and Tebaldi's affairs in Rio de Janeiro during the previous season reached Milan in various versions. As both prima donnas were now appearing extensively during the season at La Scala, the public took it for granted that they were bitter rivals. Sections of the public would on many occasions show their preference for one or the other singer. However, Maria was used to fighting for everything, and to become queen of La Scala she was prepared to fight even harder. 'When nobody antagonizes me then I shall know I am no good,' was reported to have been one of her remarks on the situation.

Meanwhile the 'Maggio Musicale Fiorentino' again found a rarely performed operatic masterpiece for Maria to sing. Cherubini's *Medea* had long been forgotten and was having no performances of any consequence, even in Italy. This was mainly due to the lack of suitable interpreters of the title role. Callas found in *Medea* a role that is suited to her *par excellence*, and gave it a characterization that is unique in this century. The role demands much and only an artist of her calibre could do justice to it, but the rewards it offers are great both for artist and audience. It did not take long for it to be labelled a 'Callas role'.[1]

---

[1] The performance, like all performances of *Medea* that Callas was to sing in later years, was given in Italian with Franz Lachner's recitatives which replaced the original French dialogue.

In the early summer of 1953 London was celebrating the coronation of Queen Elizabeth II. Although Covent Garden had commissioned Benjamin Britten to write *Gloriana*, a new opera for the occasion, they also planned a gala season of Italian Opera in which Maria Meneghini-Callas, the unforgettable Norma of the previous season, would be the star. On 4th June, two days after the coronation, Callas sang her first Aida in London. It was a memorable occasion, but to the ears of English critics she was a controversial Aida. True she had brought with her dramatic powers a strange and moving realism to the role as had never been heard before in the English capital, but some critics found that Callas sometimes sacrificed a smooth line too much for the sake of dramatic expression. A fortnight later she repeated her Norma and then gave Londoners a new role. Verdi's *Il Trovatore* has always been a favourite and often performed opera in London. With Callas it seemed now that the opera was given a new meaning. The way Callas filled Verdi's trills and arpeggios with all the dramatic expression that the composer intended, made even the oldest opera-goers feel they were hearing this familiar music for the first time.

Summer was well on its way when the Meneghinis, after a month in London, returned to Italy. They went straight to Verona, their home town, where Maria about two weeks later opened the season at the Arena of Verona. She sang Aida.

The year 1953 had been a very successful and busy one. Maria's life seemed to be a continuous song from stage to stage with little else as there was never any time. Not that she did not enjoy it. It was exactly what she wanted, but there were times she could well do with a rest. This was, however, a luxury she could not afford for the moment. There was always an engagement waiting. Now there were recordings to be made, and in November she would be singing *Norma* at Trieste. September and part of October seemed to be the only time for a rest, and the Meneghinis enjoyed every minute of it. Soon Maria would be embarking on an even more strenuous year.

The 1953-4 La Scala season opened without Callas. Alfredo Catalani's opera *La Wally* was performed to commemorate the sixtieth anniversary of his death, and the title role of Wally was sung by Renata Tebaldi. *La Wally* was quite successful, and

Tebaldi's singing, if not quite exciting, was nevertheless beautiful. Three nights later La Scala presented the Florentine production of *Medea* with Callas. All the excitement that had been lacking the previous evening came back to the theatre. It may have been partly because of the opera, but undoubtedly Callas's personality that penetrated so deeply in her master-characterization of Medea was the main reason. By comparison many people were now finding Tebaldi's singing, though beautiful, rather monotonous. During the season at La Scala, Tebaldi sang in three more operas, *Otello*, *Eugene Onegin* and *Tosca*, with considerable success. Despite this it was Callas who was the reigning queen of the season; as Medea, Lucia di Lammermoor, Elisabetta di Valois in Verdi's *Don Carlo* and Alceste in Gluck's opera, she thrilled and electrified the Milanese audience. The ovations she received in *Lucia di Lammermoor* were delirious; floral tributes were scattered across the stage and many considered her Lucia the greatest they had ever heard. The tension she created on the audience in the famous 'mad scene' of the opera was so moving that the audience, as an emotional release, interrupted her scene with a prolonged standing ovation. Callas's Lucia was a personal triumph that no living singer can easily equal, for the standard she had set is extremely high.

Maria Meneghini-Callas was now the queen of La Scala and she was there to reign. But another kind of battle in Maria's life was coming to a victorious conclusion; in sixteen months she had managed to reduce her weight from 204 lb. to 140 lb. The tall heavy girl became the elegant young woman. For the first time in her life she became clothes conscious, sufficiently so as to make her eventually one of the best dressed women in the world. The transformation was complete; she had become a swan. Her appearance would now enhance her stage characterizations even more. Having lost her excessive weight she seemed to have lost with it the inferiority complex she had had about her appearance. What was most important of all was not the actual loss of weight, but the fact that her appearance became an added feature of her art. Yet another of Callas's expressive gifts was finding fulfilment, and with it she was acquiring a feeling of security and satisfaction.

Maria's transformation naturally was noticed, and for a time it was very much talked about. People began to give their own incredible versions as to how Maria had slimmed. These versions stretched from starvation to tape-worms. But Maria paid little attention to all these. She had found an emotional outlet in over-eating during her youth. Now her success and security no longer demanded overeating. To the many inquiring reporters Maria had only this to say: 'If I had a reducing system, don't you think I could become the richest woman in the world?'

In July she created her first role since her loss of weight. This was in Boïto's *Mefistofele* at the Arena of Verona. She made Margarita a touching woman full of humanity.

Maria Meneghini-Callas made her American début not at the Metropolitan Opera, New York, but at the Lyric Theatre of Chicago, the city in which she very nearly sang *Turandot* as Marie Calas for Bagarozy's Opera Company that went bankrupt in 1957.

Chicago was finally establishing an opera company after a period of over twenty years, and all efforts were made for it to be worthy of the city's memorable operatic past. This great task was undertaken by two young and able impresarios, Lawrence Kelly and Carol Fox. Unlike Bagarozy, they managed to acquire the necessary funds. Callas was their trump card.

Maria, with her husband, arrived in Chicago to find that they were eagerly expected. As she would be singing so near New York she invited her father to Chicago. She had not seen him since the time they had spent together in Mexico. Maria was in effect the only tie Georges Callas had with his family. The same could also be said for Maria, and father and daughter were happy for the reunion. Georges Callas, who even developed a great interest in opera, was always happy and proud of his famous daughter.

On 1st November 1954 Callas sang *Norma* and more than materialized Chicago's expectations. She surpassed them and Chicago acclaimed her 'queen of opera'. There followed *Lucia di Lammermoor* and *La Traviata*, both operas, like *Norma*, being considered Callas specialities, and the Chicago public, and the critics no less, appreciated them to the full.

It had been seventeen years since Maria first left the United States for Greece after her graduation from P.S. 189 School in New York. The plump thirteen-year-old girl who thought herself the ugly duckling, but who sang well in excerpts from Gilbert and Sullivan's *H.M.S. Pinafore* and got a warm round of applause at the graduation ceremony, was now transformed into a swan and a great prima donna.

The admiration for Callas was not restricted to her stage appearances alone. Contrary to rumours that Callas was a tempestuous and difficult person, the reporters who gathered into Chicago found her a charming and patient woman. Everything was going smoothly and the good feelings between Maria and the Chicago public were mutual when suddenly and unexpectedly, amidst this excitement, the man who seven years before failed to give Chicago an opera company showed signs of existence. Richard Bagarozy, with whom Maria had signed a contract appointing him as her agent for ten years back in 1947 in New York, now on 4th November filed a suit against her. His claim was for $300,000. Callas promptly denied the claim on the grounds that the contract was signed under duress, and also that Bagarozy, by doing nothing at all to promote her career, had failed to carry out his contractual obligations.

In spite of this unexpected episode the mutual love between Maria and Chicago public did not waver. Maria's appearances continued to be the focus of Chicago's attention. The New Opera Company was successful enough to ensure its next season. The time came for Maria and Meneghini to say goodbye to Chicago. There were just three weeks before the opening of La Scala's 1954–5 season when Maria would be singing a new role.

Spontini's rarely performed opera *La Vestale* was chosen for Callas to revive. To help her in this task she had her old friend from Rome's *Il Turco in Italia*, Luchino Visconti, as producer. This was the beginning of a wonderful partnership which produced the most thrilling results. *La Vestale* had long been absent from the Italian stage, and in this revival La Scala was sparing no effort in making it a success. Ebe Stignani, Nicola Rossi-Lemeni and Franco Corelli completed the fine cast, whereas Visconti was given the unprecedented sum of £50,000 to spend on the production. Furthermore the presence of Arturo Toscanini during the rehearsals and at the first performance increased interest and anticipation.

Toscanini's personal relationship with Victor de Sabata, La Scala's musical director, having been restored he was again, after twenty years, showing interest in La Scala's activities. At rehearsals he would discuss with the conductor Antonino Votto and Callas some of the finer points of the opera.

La Vestale was a great success as a spectacular production and also provided a vehicle for Callas to show the range of her vocal gifts. Despite these, the opera could not emerge from obscurity to enter the standard repertoire. Perhaps its libretto is too outdated.

Maria's second opera in this season was Giordano's *Andrea Chenier*. Despite the hostility shown during the performance by a claque, Maria gave her role, Maddalena de Coigny, a superb all-round characterization.

A claque is a group of people who are paid to applaud an artist. They are a kind of professional applauders. The claque has been in existence since opera started, and even today it exists in many countries. Though it is admitted that some applause at certain times is most encouraging for any artist, and many artists do in fact pay a claque, Maria never believed in this and has herself always refused to pay for her applause, as it then in her opinion ceases to be applause. Consequently it was very easy for anybody to direct the hostility of the claque against her. It seems that some rival singer hired the claque as a means of ruining this performance. Once again Callas won in the end, for there were enough people in the theatre to show their genuine appreciation for her art.

Then came Bellini's *La Sonnambula*, again under Visconti's direction. Callas worked wonders with the role of Amina. Her svelte new figure and appearance were all she needed to complete her superb interpretation of this charming character. The Callas-Visconti combination was beginning to show results, and their third effort, *La Traviata*, was sensational. With this Violetta one could really fall in love. Callas had been successful in her previous appearances in this role, but it was only now that she achieved perfection in her interpretation of the frail woman. However, before the *Traviata* performances Maria gave La Scala her early Roman triumph, the comic characterization of Donna Fiorilla in *Il Turco in Italia*. In this, her most taxing season at La Scala, she sang five different roles. Also between *Andrea Chenier* and *La Sonnambula* Callas appeared as Medea in Rome. Part of the Roman audience—those who admired Tebaldi—thought it right to show their loyalty by being hostile to Callas. This hostility was shown

by making noises in the theatre, thus diverting the attention from
the stage. Furthermore Callas's insistence in having many rehearsals in order to achieve perfection in movement and singing
with the other artists of *Medea* caused the resentment of some of
her fellow artists. All these, together with the hard work she put
into her performances, were causing her a great strain. Her Medea
was, however, a greater triumph than ever before. She sang and
played the role with rare conviction. Now that she had the figure
she made full use of all her resources.

In Milan too that she was the 'queen of La Scala' was a fact, but
her crown weighed heavily on her at times: Callas always had and
always will have her antagonists. Even some of her colleagues
were becoming rather perturbed, for it was Callas who mono-
polized everything, particularly success. Beside her other artists
suffered partial or total eclipse, however good they might be.
Nothing causes more resentment.

It was only to be expected, from time to time, that other and
usually inferior artists would find themselves fighting with Callas.
Maybe they cannot meet with her exalted standards and the hard
work she puts in and demands from others in everything she
undertakes in her effort to achieve perfection. The press are not
exactly saints, and often use anything like this as an excuse for a
full-scale scandal. It is usually the unpleasant things that make the
best headlines, and it is certainly the unflattering rather than the
favourable things that people seem to remember most easily. Her
feud with Renata Tebaldi—if feud in the real sense of the word
there ever was—was always under fire by the press. True there
was a clash between the two singers in the early days of their
career in Rio de Janeiro. Probably neither of them was to blame.
In any case when they first met they were very friendly. Anyway
the important thing is that if the press did not build up the whole
thing, never losing an opportunity, there could hardly have been a
feud. Callas may have passed remarks that were really answers to
provocative questions. It is the easiest thing in the world to repeat
these remarks, using exactly the same words, but at the same time
distorting their meaning. When asked whether she thought of
Tebaldi as a great rival, Callas's answer was that they were not
rivals. 'Our repertory is different,' she stated. 'Should there come
a time when Tebaldi sings *Sonnambula*, *Lucia*, *Gioconda* and then

goes on to *Medea*, *Norma* and *Macbeth*, then there will be scope for possible comparison. Well, it's like comparing champagne with cognac or Coca-Cola.' The perversions of this remark were too fantastic for words. There were no distortions or hardly any mention, however, of Callas's remark that she thought Tebaldi a fine musician.

Callas's success and fame throughout the world were bound to disturb many people—there is nothing like success to incite jealousy. True, in comparison with ordinary people, she may be temperamental, sometimes even tempestuous and hypersensitive. This is after all inevitable in a woman who believes fervently in her art and needs all the ambition, drive and will-power she can possibly muster. If she is to achieve perfection how else than by insisting on the highest possible standards in others; she herself has always given all. Callas's love and devotion to music that started as early in her life as she could remember was an act of dedication and not a marriage of convenience that would have happened from petty motives. Therefore as a result she would devote all the resources of her love, ability and enthusiasm without respite.

Because of this integrity she often feels compelled to make decisions without considering the effect they will have on her associates. The result is controversy. For the sake of the spirit of musical truth in her art all ordinary obligations must go by the board.

It must not be thought that Callas is at odds with every other artist. It has been of course hinted in the press at the slightest provocation whenever there was an argument about Callas that she is unpopular with her colleagues. This is not true. Artists of great standing like Elisabeth Schwarzkopf, Giulietta Simionato, Franco Corelli, Tito Gobbi, Nicola Zaccaria, Jon Vickers, the conductor Nicola Rescigno and others, have the greatest respect for Maria Callas and say they are always inspired by working with her. When Elisabeth Schwarzkopf, the distinguished German soprano, heard Callas sing Violetta in *La Traviata*, a role that she herself had sung on many occasions, such was the admiration that she felt for Callas that she said she would never sing this role again. Jon Vickers, the famous Canadian tenor, when in 1963 he was asked about his experience as a singer, paid great tribute to

Callas by saying: 'I have sung with Callas—surely this is the greatest experience of all.' No less does she cherish the respect and admiration of famous conductors like Tullio Serafin, Herbert von Karajan, Victor de Sabata and great producers like Luchino Visconti, Franco Zefirelli and so many others.

Life naturally was much easier for Maria having her husband by her side, ready to help her and to give her the necessary reassurance and encouragement when she needed them most. It was five years since Maria married, and although she had a pleasant and comfortable flat in Verona she could hardly consider it much of a home, for she could only spend very little time there. As a famous singer, it was demanded of her to travel often, and having to work so hard very little time was left for normal home life. Since her engagement at La Scala the Meneghinis had obtained an apartment in Milan's Grand Hotel. Now in the summer of 1955 they bought their first real house in Milan. No. 40 Via Buonarotti Michaelangelo was to become Maria's castle, which she took great pride in decorating sumptuously. She would spend all her available time on shopping trips through Milan's fashionable stores. Maria could now play the role of housewife, a role that every woman dreams about at some time in her life. Meneghini too now freed himself completely from his business interests in Verona. He sold his share in the family business to his brothers and took up full-time duties in managing his wife's affairs, which were increasing in an amazing way.

One of their first visitors was Elvira de Hidalgo, who came to Milan to see her brother. Maria felt like a little girl, happy to see her friend and former teacher. There was so much to talk about, both about old times and the present. And how wonderful— Maria could receive her old friend in her own home.

The summer months passed all too quickly and the Meneghinis, during the end of September, were travelling to Berlin where Maria was to make her début as Lucia. La Scala was taking its production of *Lucia di Lammermoor* for two performances during the Berlin Festival, when Callas would repeat her great success as Lucia under the baton of Herbert von Karajan. The Berliners treated these appearances with great enthusiasm and anticipation. Twenty-six years before Arturo Toscanini had given Berlin the same opera with Toti dal Monte as Lucia and conquered the hearts of all Berlin. Callas sang on top form, and with her dramatic powers that she masterfully combined with her extraordinary technique conquered Berlin. It was an unconditional surrender. From then on the Berliners would have a new standard for comparison.

With the Berlin triumphs behind them, the Meneghinis were able to spend a few days at home in Milan. The next destination was a return visit to Chicago.

On 31st October 1955 the Lyric Theatre of Chicago embarked on an even more enterprising season than its first one. Callas sang in Bellini's *I Puritani*, a completely unknown opera in Chicago, and she received the unanimous praise of the critics and the enthusiasm of the public. There followed Verdi's *Il Trovatore* and the performance proved to be a masterpiece. Ebe Stignani and Jussi Björling were in the cast that could not be bettered anywhere. This role was probably Maria's greatest triumph in Chicago and the critics were competing with each other in finding fervent effusions in their eulogies. Björling, the greatest tenor for this opera at the time, declared: 'I know now that there is perfection in the world. This is Callas's Leonora in *Il Trovatore*.' Callas's last offering in the Chicago season was her first appearance in a role that she had once been forced to refuse because of her excessive weight. There was no obstacle now, and she created a youthful and fragile Cio-Cio San in Puccini's *Madama Butterfly* who might have come straight from the Kabuki Theatre, Japan's national theatre, itself. Chicago was delirious and Callas was very moved with the reception that was so lovingly given her. On 17th November, when she sang her final performance of *Madama Butterfly*, after her final curtain calls, which even for Chicago broke all previous records, Maria walked into her dressing-room where a different kind of reception awaited her. She was served with a summons making her liable for court action, brought by Bagarozy. As bodily contact with the defendant is legally required the server pushed the summons into Maria's kimono. The sum of money claimed was again $300,000. Maria was at first dumbfounded. The whole thing seemed like a trap. The management of the theatre, having assured her of their protection by maintaining careful vigil, were now letting her down in such an appalling way. Her dumbfoundness soon gave way to outrage. Feeling

C

betrayed she exploded: 'Chicago will be sorry for this. I will never sing here again.' The press immediately made quite a scandal out of this, a very sad ending to a most wonderful friendship between Callas and the whole of Chicago. The Meneghinis, upset and disappointed, left Chicago for Milan, while solicitors were employed to represent Maria if necessary.

St Ambrose's Day approached again, Callas's fifth. This time it was to be *Norma* in a special gala performance. In spite of slight vocal strain, that was unfortunately noticeable, Callas again gave a great portrayal of the tragic Druid priestess, a portrayal which over the years reached great dimensions. But it was again in a revival of the controversial Callas-Visconti *Traviata* that she most excited the audiences which flocked to see all twenty performances of this opera.

Callas had captured the imagination of the Milanese. With her unique characterizations of the great heroines of Italian opera she lured to La Scala a new audience, which was finding in opera a new interest. Any announcement of something new that Callas would do at La Scala would immediately become one of the main topics of conversation among the Milanese. In fact it was taken for granted in the Scala seasons that Maria would take on new roles as well as appearing in some of her past successes. So after the great number of *Traviatas* Callas gave Milan two completely different characters: the *coloratura* role of Rosina, in Rossini's *Il Barbiere di Siviglia*, and the dramatic soprano title role of Giordano's *Fedora*. Opinions about her Rosina were divided, both amongst the critics and the audience. Although she sang exquisitely, many thought that Maria's all too powerful personality was not sufficiently subdued for once, so that Rosina was not quite the convincing *ingénue* she ought to be. On the other hand, she gave such a highly memorable Fedora that even Sardou, the dramatist—not to mention Giordano—would have been left spellbound.

With the *Fedora* performances over Maria Meneghini-Callas arrived in Vienna to give two performances of *Lucia di Lammermoor*. La Scala was taking its production of this opera to Vienna for two performances in the rebuilt Staatsoper Theatre, which was celebrating its first season. Here too, twenty-six years before, Arturo Toscanini with Toti dal Monte had appeared in *Lucia di*

Lammermoor; a memory that the Viennese treasured. Herbert von Karajan, then a young man, had walked miles to reach Vienna to hear this performance, an experience which he had never forgotten. It was estimated that twelve thousand people and the better part of the Viennese police force fought over the four thousand seats. Callas sang Lucia under Herbert von Karajan on 12th June 1956 for the highly critical Viennese, and even surpassed all expectations. Vienna, like Berlin, had now a new standard to go by.

After the Vienna interlude Maria and her husband took a well-earned rest, for Maria was preparing for her return to the New World. Finally, all arrangements were completed, and she was due to make her début at the Metropolitan Opera, New York, in *Norma* on 29th October 1956. For some time the Metropolitan Opera had been negotiating with Callas without success. Callas had her artistic standards, in which she firmly believed. The Metropolitan had other ideas, and then there was the question of fees. The highest fee that the Metropolitan paid its artists was far below the fee that Callas was getting for her performances in other opera houses. Callas's personality would clash with that of Rudolf Bing, the director of the Metropolitan. One of the most apt remarks that Maria was reported to have made when told that the salary she expected was higher than that of the President of the United States was, 'Let *him* sing then.'

Still, the day came when all differences between Maria and the Metropolitan were ironed out.

She arrived in New York, the city of her birth, fully aware of the atmosphere of enormous anticipation. Her publicity was controversial, but there was nothing unusual about that. She was, however, very tense and was extremely disturbed to discover, at the first rehearsals, how dated the Metropolitan *Norma* settings were, and how seriously they clashed with her own specially designed costumes. Allotted rehearsal time at the Metropolitan was far below the standards she considered necessary for perfection. On the other hand, never before had the Metropolitan Opera box office receipts been so high: $75,000 from all tickets sold. The press had discovered her mother who seemed glad to give interviews in Athens, with various versions of the last letter that Maria had written—the one that finally broke their relations. The

letter was alleged to have had words in it to the effect that Maria
was not interested in what became of her mother. It is bad
enough when situations like these are exposed, but when the
people involved think they can find comfort in the press it is fatal
for all concerned. The press made the most of this and other things,
such as Maria's past clashes with colleagues, giving the impression
that the *diva* was always to blame. As a result she naturally felt the
strain. Further, Callas's arrival in New York did not go unnoticed
by Bagarozy, who served her with another summons. Maria agreed
to receive the summons, and on 21st December, the day she was
leaving New York, appeared to testify in the Supreme Court.

Callas had a rather cool reception on her first entrance on the
Metropolitan stage and began singing rather unevenly, certainly
not in her best voice. But as the evening wore on things began to
change; the Callas magic was fast returning. The evening which
had begun rather coolly was now ablaze, and Maria knew that she
had won yet another battle. A fiery *Tosca* was to follow and then
she sang *Lucia di Lammermoor*. The New York critics praised
Maria for her extraordinary dramatic talent, but their opinions
were divided about her actual singing which, however fine, was
not completely devoid of vocal imperfections.

Back in Milan the season began without Callas, with Antonietta
Stella singing *Aida*. Meanwhile Maria returned to London after
an absence of four years, this time of course slim and elegant,
almost beyond recognition, but very well remembered for more
important reasons. Only two performances of *Norma* were
scheduled, and London fought over the tickets as never before.
There were many who went to the performance on 2nd February
1957 to find out whether she could still sing Norma with the
wonderful Norma-like figure she had acquired; Callas did not let
her London audience down. She was as good as ever, indeed
better. She was to the London public, who now forgot any
reservations it had held before, Callas *La Divina*, and with the
duet 'Mira O Norma' from the second act of *Norma* she, together
with Ebe Stignani, gave Covent Garden its first encore in a
quarter of a century. With the two *Norma* performances over the
Meneghinis stayed on in London, when Maria recorded for
E.M.I. a completely different role, that of Rosina in *Il Barbiere di
Siviglia*, and to see old friends.

The 1957–8 season at La Scala was well on its way when Maria returned in March to sing Amina in a revival of the Visconti *La Sonnambula*. Any possible reservations about her performance now vanished; she seemed to have found a new naturalness and made Amina another of her own roles. Taking advantage of her presence, La Scala staged a spectacular production of Donizetti's *Anna Bolena* during the Milan Fair. This was unfamiliar even to Italian audiences until Callas sang in it.[1] She found in it everything a singer and actress of her calibre could wish for, and she succeeded in completely identifying herself with the role. This was a characterization that undisputedly went down in the history of La Scala's major achievements. Visconti was again the director, as he was in the third and final production of the season—Gluck's *Iphigenia en Tauride*. Vocally this role lay very comfortably in Callas's middle register, and she sang Gluck's music with impeccable style and taste. This was her sixth season at La Scala, and in June 1957 President Gronchi of the Italian Republic bestowed on her the honorary title of *Commendatore*, a title very few women have ever received, for her services to Italian opera. This was a great honour for Maria, a foreigner in Italy. The gesture of the Italian Government was a proof that Maria's efforts and achievements for Italian opera were greatly understood and appreciated.

Thus the season at La Scala—happily—ended for Maria on a high note. Immediately after its season La Scala planned a visit to the very modern Cologne Opera House in Germany, where in July Maria, with other La Scala artists, gave a performance of *La Sonnambula*. It was a happy occasion and the press was very complimentary. As for the public, they were so impressed with the performance that they went home that night feeling they had been present at one of the theatrical experiences of their time.

A brief stay in Milan and Maria was travelling again. This time, August 1957, she was homeward bound. Twelve difficult, glorious and rewarding years had passed since she left Greece. She was returning now to give two concerts during the Athens Festival in the ancient theatre of Herodes Atticus, where once she had triumphed in Beethoven's *Fidelio*.

Maria was very happy to be in Athens, and deep in her heart

[1] Previous revivals of the opera in Italy were in Leghorn in August 1881 and at Bergamo, Donizetti's birthplace, in October 1956.

she was rather anxious to succeed and show her countrymen that the great fame she had acquired was real. But Maria soon discovered that her path was not altogether smooth. Most of the local press was hostile. A good deal of the hostility centred on Maria's relationship with her mother, who left for New York before Maria's arrival in Athens. In any case Maria had nothing to say about this, good or bad. This was a personal matter that could not be discussed publicly by her.

The Greek parliamentary opposition party also found it convenient to use Maria's high fee as a political weapon against the Greek Government. On top of all this Maria's indisposition, due to the hot and dry summer climate in Athens, led to a cancellation of her first concert practically at the last minute, for, unwisely, the festival authorities expected Maria to make a superhuman effort. A few evenings later, on 5th August, Maria faced a very antagonistic audience which crowded into the huge theatre of Herodes. But all doubt and resentment were quickly dispelled and forgotten when Maria began to sing. It was clear that she was appreciated and accepted by her own people, and this is surely the greatest reward any artist can wish for.

When Maria returned to Milan she fell ill. For some time now overwork and emotional strain had caused her to suffer from nervous exhaustion, and it was against her doctor's orders that she left with the La Scala company to appear in four performances of *La Sonnambula* at the Edinburgh Festival. La Scala was taking four productions to the Edinburgh Festival, where the festival authorities signed the contract with the understanding that it would be possible for Callas to be in the company. So Maria pulled herself together and made the trip rather than put La Scala in a difficult situation.

The opening performance at the King's Theatre, Edinburgh, found Maria in rather poor voice, and the stage lighting was so bad that it nearly wrecked the production. The second performance found the *diva* on much better form, but on her third evening she was feeling so ill that the performance was only saved from disaster by her dramatic ability. Meanwhile an extra fifth performance was announced, but Maria, despite her doctor's advice to withdraw immediately, decided to give her agreed fourth performance only. This she did and, sufficiently recovered, gave her best performance. Callas was able to sing the role of Amina in the way she wanted, so being able to carry out her intentions through the medium of her voice. The fifth performance was sung by the young soprano Renata Scotto, who had originally been engaged for this performance. Callas, amidst great publicity, left Edinburgh to rest for a week in Venice where Elsa Maxwell was giving a party in her honour. This proved to be unfortunate. Maria also informed the San Francisco Opera, where she was expected to appear in just over a month's time, that she would be unable, for reasons of health, to carry out her contract. Elsa Maxwell's superficial remark that never before had a star given up a performance for the sake of keeping her word to her (that is, coming to the party) did not help public opinion in favour of Callas.

Back in Milan Maria demanded that La Scala should make a public statement about her Edinburgh performance, as the world press had already blown the whole thing up into a large-scale scandal. The superintendent of La Scala, Antonio Ghiringhelli, the only person who could have put things right, surprisingly decided to remain silent. This was the beginning of the end.

Callas, after a long rest, gave a concert to inaugurate the newly formed Dallas Opera on 17th November 1957.

Lawrence Kelly, who with Carol Fox directed the Chicago Lyric Theatre, had by now broken their partnership, and Kelly became the director of the Dallas Civic Opera. Callas and Kelly had already known each other and become friends in the days when Maria sang in Chicago. Kelly, who particularly appreciated and admired Callas's artistic gifts, was determined to lure her to his new opera house. Everything to show goodwill was attempted most ambitiously. Callas was even asked if she would care to sing all the three roles in the *Tales of Hoffman*. 'My dear, would you pay me three fees?' was the well-meant, bright answer. After several discussions, mainly on artistic matters that all came to most agreeable conclusions, were exhausted Callas was very happy to sing in Dallas.

She was back in good form again and Dallas gave her a reception fit for a queen. The phrase on everyone's lips was: 'Dallas for Callas.'

Another happy event took place during this time, actually four days before the concert. Her long lawsuit with Bagarozy came to an end. A settlement out of court was made, and that was the end of the whole unpleasant affair that dragged for nearly three years. Maria was also tired of being a courtroom character, as she has said. Bagarozy died suddenly in New York just a year later.

The American trip had been quite successful, and Maria returned to Milan feeling much better. No one of course had even the remotest suspicion of what the next few weeks had in store for her. She soon discovered, however, that relations were strained between her and La Scala. It would seem that although Maria unjustly got the worst of the Edinburgh Festival episode, La Scala in addition was now aloof. However, Maria still opened the 1957–8 season as Amelia in a new production of Verdi's *Un Ballo in Maschera*. A few days later, on 27th December 1957, she went to Rome to open the season there on 2nd January 1958 in a gala performance of *Norma* before President Gronchi of the Italian Republic. During the ordinary rehearsals Maria had some trouble with her throat—not an uncommon thing amongst singers. But taking care of herself by resting she felt perfectly all right on 31st December at the dress rehearsal. On the same day in the evening she also made a television appearance singing 'Casta Diva', the aria from *Norma*. The following day, however, which was the day before the actual performance, Maria woke up to discover that she had lost her voice. With the help of medical treatment her condition improved by the following day, and at the same time she informed the theatre of the situation. During the first act of the opera Callas sounded tired and unsteady, especially in her high notes. Soon her low notes began to give in as well. She was fighting a losing battle. Her voice was going rapidly and there was nothing she could do about it. She managed to finish the first act before she lost her singing voice completely. There was no second or third act that evening, for Callas was unable to continue. This caused a large-scale scandal, for the theatre failed to put on an understudy and this unfortunate performance of *Norma* ended with Act I. What followed instead were overexcited arguments and anger all aimed at Maria Callas, who locked herself in her dressing-room. Neither the management of the theatre nor any representative of Callas appeared to offer the least kind of explanation to the audience. Through an underground passage that connects the theatre and the Hotel Quirinale, where the Meneghinis were staying, Maria took refuge in her hotel suite. The Roman public, which gathered around the hotel, demonstrated wildly, cursing Callas while she remained silent. Having provided medical reports to prove her physical illness, and having sent her apologies to President Gronchi, she thought it unnecessary for any further comment on her part. Not surprisingly the Italian press blew up the situation to a large national scandal. Soon the Roman scandal was making big headlines in the international press. Maria immediately got the reputation that she is a most unreliable artist who would walk out of a performance at the slightest whim. This is of course untrue, for Maria Callas has seldom cancelled any of her performances. In fact if one takes the trouble to look at facts one finds, to give an example, that out of 157 performances (up to May 1958) at La Scala, she had cancelled only one performance because of a bad cold, and on another occasion there was a general cancellation due to an epidemic. Not bad by any standards.

Two days later the Rome Opera House, which originally claimed that it could not provide an understudy, presented another gala performance of *Norma* with the Italian soprano Anita Cerquetti. When a week later Callas recovered her voice she was not allowed to give the remaining two of the scheduled performances. This left no alternative for Maria but to place a legal action against the Rome Opera House. She claimed payment of her fee for the agreed subsequent performances that she was not allowed to give. Meanwhile the Rome Opera House placed a counter-suit for £8,500 on the grounds that Callas's walk-out was unjustified. The case was to take over seven years to be settled. In April 1965 the Rome civil court gave its verdict in complete favour of Callas by awarding her £1,030 and rejecting the Rome Opera House's counter-suit. The opera house was also ordered to pay costs.

Back in Rome in 1958, however, Maria, after having been refused to sing, could find no reason whatever to remain in Rome. If anything the Meneghinis were now anxious to return to their home in Milan.

In Milan Maria found that her relations with La Scala were even more strained than when she had left them. She had no

*C

appearances to make in Milan for the moment, but in a few days
she would be appearing in America. Maria and her husband took
advantage of the short time they had in hand and rested in the
peace and privacy of their home. The recent events had been very
trying for Maria and a rest was essential; and when presently she
began to receive hundreds of letters from friends and admirers,
who expressed their sympathy for her on account of her Roman
misfortune, she felt much better. This was very important for
Maria and helped her to regain her faith in her work. All these
friends and admirers proved to her that she was necessary to them,
and that her long devotion to her work was not in vain. A few
days later Maria, with renewed strength and enthusiasm, accompanied by Meneghini, left for America.

First she gave a very successful concert in Chicago. The
unfortunate events of her final appearance in *Madama Butterfly*
back in 1955, when she swore she would never sing in Chicago
again, were all forgotten. Chicago opened its arms affectionately
to embrace their willing *diva*. Appearances followed at the
Metropolitan Opera, New York. Three operas, *Traviata*, *Lucia di
Lammermoor* and *Tosca*, were the chosen works. In spite of the
difficulty that she found in getting herself acquainted with the
production of *Traviata* (practically no stage rehearsal apart from
the dress one was allotted), Callas gave New York a Violetta that
was incomparable. The New York public gave her in return an
ovation that was equally incomparable. *Lucia di Lammermoor* and
Tosca followed with great success. The latter was conducted by
compatriot Dimitri Mitropoulos.

The American trip proved quite successful in every way.
Artistically Maria gave her best. Socially she was just as much the
most sought-after person. This was in a way something new for
Maria, who was always far too busy with her work to devote much
time to social affairs. Now it so happened that she found herself
among the social group that is known as the 'international set'.
This was no doubt because of Elsa Maxwell, who had all her life
been interested in famous personalities. Maxwell found a special
interest in Callas, who was not only perhaps the greatest artist but
also a woman of great and attractive personality. Maria enjoyed
her very brief excursion in this kind of life. Also, now that she
was in New York, she also saw a lot of her father, who frequently

admired his daughter on the Metropolitan's stage. Afterwards Maria sang two *Traviatas* in Lisbon and a concert in Madrid before it was time to go back home in Milan.

Returning to Milan Maria found the atmosphere still very chilly. It would seem that time did not heal any of the wounds. On the contrary with time things seemed to be getting worse. When eventually Maria met Antonio Ghiringhelli in public he chose to ignore her presence. After this they were naturally no longer on speaking terms. This, however, did not affect the operas scheduled for her. When she sang in *Anna Bolena* it was more of a trial than a gala performance. Remembering what had happened in Rome, and this was Callas's first appearance in Italy since, it was decided to have two hundred policemen in the theatre just in case. She was certainly a persecuted queen. But the wronged Queen Maria won the trial, for she played her role with a rare conviction. No one in Milan mentioned the Roman incident, but the La Scala management still retained their hostility towards her. This was a terrible and unfortunate situation. Under such conditions of strain no artist could fulfil his vocation and Callas was no exception. While she was preparing for a new role, that of Imogene in Bellini's *Il Pirata*, it was clear that the *diva's* long, and until then happy, association with La Scala was about to come to an end. Even so she was a resounding success in *Il Pirata*.

The end came with her last performance of *Il Pirata* on 31st May 1958, and, as Imogene at the end grieves the fate of her lover, now captured, Callas sang the words 'Vedete il palco funesto' ('Behold the fated scaffold') with a bitter smile at the corner of her mouth, her arms raised, pointing towards the proscenium box, where the superintendent of La Scala was sitting, for all to see the cause of her leaving. The word *palco* in Italian also means 'box', and this was the way Maria Meneghini-Callas made her exit from the leading opera house of the world, the theatre where she had known her greatest triumphs, the theatre she had always loved. Ghiringhelli soon found his opportunity to retaliate. While Maria was taking her curtain calls the safety curtain of the stage suddenly came down by his order, making it clear to artist and audience that the performance was quite finished. The audience of La Scala, however, gave her an unforgettable ovation, which continued outside the theatre late into the night. Piazza La Scala was filled with people, many of whom had brought their floral offerings. When eventually Maria came out of the theatre, escorted by a couple of friends, flowers were thrown along the path she walked. Nobody could quite comprehend why things got to such a state at La Scala that Maria was being forced to leave. Maria was just as unhappy. At certain moments it even seemed that the whole affair was temporary, an affair that would be put in order given a few days. But this was not at all so, and Callas was not to re-enter La Scala for the next eighteen months.

In the days that followed Milan must have seemed a different place to the ex-queen of La Scala. It was an unfortunate conclusion to a partnership that had achieved so many triumphs both for Callas and La Scala. The trouble had really begun in Edinburgh the previous year, and the events that followed only helped to make matters worse. Although there had never been any direct insoluble differences between Maria and La Scala, the atmosphere that was created in the theatre left no alternative to her but to end her association. Fortunately for Maria she did not have to stay in Milan for long immediately after the break with La Scala. Shortly thereafter she returned to London, the scene of former triumphs, for a series of appearances.

On 10th June 1958, in the presence of Queen Elizabeth II, Prince Philip and many members of the royal family, and practically the whole of the British Cabinet, Covent Garden celebrated its centenary in a glittering gala evening. Callas participated in this concert, singing the 'mad scene' from Bellini's *I Puritani*. A few days later she delighted the British public by making a television appearance in which she sang arias from *Tosca* and *Il Barbiere di Siviglia*. Ten days later she began a run of five performances as Violetta in *La Traviata* at Covent Garden, and although not in her best voice on the opening night, she recovered in the performances that followed and, with her compelling dramatic force, gave London its best Violetta for many years.

After London the Meneghinis, with forthcoming engagements at the Metropolitan and Dallas civic operas, began a well-deserved three-month rest. It was summer already and their peaceful villa at Sirmione on Lake Garda seemed to them to be the nicest spot in the world.

The Metropolitan season, however, did not materialize. Maria was to have opened the Metropolitan season in a new production of Verdi's *Macbeth*, but Rudolf Bing, the director of the Metropolitan, insisted that Maria should appear first in *Macbeth*, then in *Traviata* and then again in *Macbeth*. Although Maria agreed with the choice of operas, she would not, however, sing them in this order owing to the completely different voices required for each. These negotiations unfortunately did not lead to any agreement. The Metropolitan insisted on their programme, which Maria did not consider right for her to undertake. The result was that the Metropolitan cancelled her contract. Contrary to the Metropolitan's belief that artists would give their right arm to return to the Metropolitan, Maria simply did nothing about it. Rudolf Bing promptly stated, 'The Metropolitan is grateful that the association is ended.' 'Prussian tactics,' was Maria's short answer.

The demands of the Metropolitan, which caused the rift between her and Bing, were unreasonable, and as far as she was concerned there was no argument. 'My voice is not an elevator,' she appropriately summed up the situation.

While all these negotiations were going on Maria gave a concert tour in the United States and also appeared in *Traviata* and *Medea* at the Dallas Civic Opera.

After the Metropolitan appearances were cancelled Maria was showered with offers from various American companies. The only one she accepted was an invitation to sing at Carnegie Hall and Washington, D.C., for the New York American Opera Society, in concert performances of Bellini's *Il Pirata*. If the New York audience could not hear her at the Metropolitan, then they could do so at Carnegie Hall. People turned out in their thousands to cheer her and a practically unknown Bellini opera. A citation by the Mayor of New York was presented to Maria Meneghini-Callas. Having been honoured by her native city she took her leave to return to her home in Milan. Soon she was to embark on a spectacular concert tour in Germany, but before that she gave a special performance in a—to her—new European capital. It was a gala concert on 19th December 1958 at the Paris Opéra before René Coty, President of the French Republic. It was a benefit concert for the Legion of Honour, and it was hailed as the greatest event of the season. Callas donated her $10,000 fee to the cause. For the Parisians Maria sang a few excerpts from Verdi and Rossini, and then appeared in the complete second act of Puccini's *Tosca*. Feelings were mutual. Paris was completely captivated, and Maria was captivated too.

In an exchange scheme between Covent Garden and the Dallas Civic Opera, Covent Garden was to put on the Dallas production of Cherubini's *Medea* in return for their own production of *Lucia di Lammermoor*, and in this way it was possible for London to see Callas's *Medea*. On 17th June 1959 Callas gave London its first *Medea* in over ninety years. It was a powerful performance, and so complete that it left nothing more to be desired. The way Callas combined vocal and dramatic resources in her characterization of the grandiose Medea left the audience greatly impressed and moved. The five performances of *Medea* undoubtedly constituted the most exciting musical event of the London season.

Aristotelis Onassis, the Greek ship-owner, gave one of his most sumptuous parties in honour of the great *diva* at the Dorchester Hotel, London. It was a splendid affair and everybody of importance was there. The Meneghinis, who received a wonderful reception on their entrance to the party, stayed until 3 a.m.

The performances of *Medea* continued with tremendous success. When they were over the Meneghinis bade London goodbye, promising that they would return the following year. Neither husband nor wife had at the moment any reasonable doubt as to their promise. But life can be unpredictable for anyone. The events in Maria's life that followed were to change her way of life greatly. In fact this London visit was to be the last time that Meneghini would accompany his wife as her husband and manager. Before this, however, fate gave the Meneghinis a little more time.

On their way home Maria gave a concert in Amsterdam. This was her first visit in Holland, and the concert became the highlight of the Holland Festival. Soon the Meneghinis were relaxing at their villa at Sirmione on Lake Garda in Italy. Ten days later, however, they accepted an invitation from the Onassis for a Mediterranean cruise. On 22nd July they embarked on Onassis's fabulous yacht *Christina* at Monte Carlo. Sir Winston and Lady

Churchill with one of their daughters, long time friends of the Onassis, were on board. Several other guests completed the party. The *Christina* took her distinguished guests through the Italian and Greek seas as far as Istanbul, anchoring at various places in Italy and Greece where they all went on sightseeing tours. In Istanbul the Onassis and the Meneghinis were also received by the Patriarch of Constantinople. Three pleasant and in many ways exhilarating weeks went by as the *Christina* sailed through the calm waters. On 16th August the cruise was over and then the storm came after the calm. The summer that followed was the stormiest of Maria's life. After eleven years her marriage to Meneghini broke down and they were separated. The break was so sudden and unexpected that even the closest friends of the Meneghinis had not remotely anticipated it. Maria Callas may have been quite outspoken at times, but at the same time, deeply, she is a shy person. This may sound contradictory, but it seems the one thing brings the other. She does not readily trust nor make friendships, yet she is an impulsive woman. Maybe the long years of struggle, with rivalries and jealousies around her, to reach the top have left her sensitive to hostility and suspicion. For eleven years she was a devoted wife, and nobody knew how Maria really felt. Her marriage broke up suddenly and Maria said hardly anything. Maria's name now became romantically linked with Onassis's. Meneghini, because of this and mainly because he could no longer have complete control over his wife's business affairs, made the first move in separating. Yet he could hardly bear his loss. If only he could have maintained his absolute control. Maria on the other hand did not blame anybody. For a woman whose parents were not happy together, and eventually separated, the question of marriage must loom all the more seriously. Maria had only this to say: 'It is not important who is to blame. The breaking of my marriage is my greatest admission of failure.'

Maria's separation from Meneghini left her more or less without a family. She was not on good terms with her mother and sister, and her father was living alone in New York. Georges Callas had after years of separation eventually obtained a divorce from his wife in 1957. It was at one time suggested that Callas would have her own company and give regular seasons at the

Monte Carlo Opera House in which Onassis is the biggest share-holder. Although nothing materialized out of this idea, the friendship between Callas and Onassis is still alive.

Parting with Meneghini, Maria became her own manager, and under great strain endeavoured to fulfil her already confirmed engagements. It was during these difficult times, however, that she was reconciled with La Scala. Antonio Ghiringhelli was there to receive her when she arrived at La Scala for a recording engagement, when she recorded Ponchielli's *La Gioconda*.

Immediately after Maria finished her recording at La Scala she embarked on the *Christina* again—this time without Meneghini. Onassis's sister, Mrs Garoufallides, was on board. There was another important person absent—Mrs Tina Onassis. A few days later Maria left the yacht to fulfil a concert engagement at Bilbao in Spain. She was in very poor form and got a very cool reception during the first half of the concert. The second half was, however, another story. She pulled herself together and saved her reputation and gave the audience what they originally expected. As soon as the concert was over Maria joined the *Christina* again until 22nd September. On the 23rd she gave her first London concert at the Festival Hall. In spite of the great strain she must have been feeling during those times she was in great voice. In the sleep-walking scene from Verdi's *Macbeth* she surpassed herself. This was the first taste she was giving London of her electrifying characterization of Lady Macbeth. Everybody's heart was filled with anticipation, as it was expected that Callas would be appearing in *Macbeth* in a new production of the opera at Covent Garden during the forthcoming season. Another concert followed in Berlin and an appearance on British television seemed to complete her engagements in Europe. On 27th October, in the midst of great publicity, mainly about her private life, Maria crossed the Atlantic to fulfil a concert engagement in Kansas City and appearances at the Dallas Civic Opera.

It was during this time too that Maria was reconciled with the Metropolitan. While Maria was in New York, on her way to Dallas, it took one telephone call for peace to be restored between her and Metropolitan's Rudolf Bing.

Immediately this was known people started speculating whether Callas would be returning to the Metropolitan in the forthcoming season. But Maria was not making any new plans, even if the Metropolitan would meet her on her own terms. All she was determined to do for the moment was to carry out her already accepted obligations, and this was more than enough.

In Dallas she sang Lucia and rushed back to Italy. Meneghini had filed a suit for legal separation, and the hearing was scheduled for 14th November in Brescia. He considered it pointless for them to live together as Maria would no longer let him have complete control over her business affairs. The hearing lasted for only six hours, and a separation was granted by mutual consent on the grounds of discord and conflicting business interests. As soon as the hearing was over Maria was again on her way back to Dallas. She arrived on the day of the dress rehearsal of *Medea*. All the strain and fatigue she must have felt did not seem to matter much, for her performance as Medea received superlative comments.

Meanwhile Mr and Mrs Onassis were putting an end to their marriage, and Maria Callas's name continued to be romantically linked with Onassis's. Much to the disappointment of the press, who are always much too eager to settle in their own way other people's matrimonial problems, Tina Onassis named another woman as co-respondent and got her divorce.

London's Covent Garden was preparing a new production of *Macbeth* for April 1960. It was hoped that Maria Callas would sing Lady Macbeth; the English musical world was delighted and waited with excitement. But it was not to be, for Maria found herself unable to fulfil any major commitments. The strain of recent events seemed to have been too much for her. She must have been very close to nervous exhaustion during those difficult and unhappy times. Maria Callas was retiring from the operatic stage—temporarily anyway. She would not accept any engagements and the world wondered and speculated about the *diva*'s retirement.

The Golden Voice was silent.

III

Art is a human activity having for its purpose the transmission to
others of the best and highest feelings to which men have risen.

COUNT LYOF NIKOLAYEVITCH TOLSTOI

It had been almost a year since Maria Callas had stopped singing.
After thirteen years of so many triumphs on the operatic stages
of the world, since her Italian début at Verona, her personal
affairs were now taking priority over her art. During all these
months she continued to live alone at her house in Milan, but
often she would find the relaxing atmosphere of Monte Carlo
more attractive. Since the end of her marriage in 1959 Maria had
undertaken relatively few engagements. In fact she had only fulfilled her previously confirmed engagements which consisted of
two or three concerts and a few opera performances in America.
A few weeks after the separation order from Meneghini was
issued at Brescia Maria was seen with him in public. Immediately
rumours were circulated that there might be a possible reconciliation between them. But the rumours were groundless. Meneghini
did call at Maria's house on the occasion of her birthday on 4th
December, and also there were several formalities to be sorted out
regarding the division of their property. Their separation was
irrevocable. Meanwhile the friendship of Onassis and Callas
continued. Contrary to reports in the press of a possible marriage,
no such step was taken. Callas, who had been born in New York,
retained her American citizenship in spite of her Italian marriage,
and therefore could have obtained a divorce from Meneghini if
she had wanted it. Months went by but Maria did not even ask for
a divorce. The press waited patiently, watching her every move,
and although Maria began to spend considerable time on the
Christina, no announcement of any kind regarding her private life
was made, much to the disappointment of the press.

Nine months had gone by since her last stage appearance as
Medea in Dallas. During this time Maria Callas seemed to have

found a different life among Onassis's circle of friends. Perhaps for the first time in her life she found that it was possible to enjoy life and leisure for its own sake, without having to give anything in return. But such a life alone is not possible for a woman who has her vocation. Her mission in life is such that before long it will call her.

The summer of 1960 came and news spread around the world that Maria Callas was making her comeback to the operatic stage. Greece was the place. But prior to this Maria had agreed to give a concert at Ostend in Belgium. Perhaps a concert could have served as a warming-up, particularly as Maria had not sung in public for nine months. But it was not to be, for the concert had to be cancelled owing to Callas's unfortunate and sudden attack of laryngitis. This was a bad start for a comeback, but Maria did not lose her courage. Instead she looked after herself in order to be on her best form for her forthcoming opera performances in Greece. In August, under the auspices of the Athens Festival, Maria Callas was returning to Greece to sing Norma in three performances at the vast ancient theatre at Epidaurus. This was the first time that opera (previously only ancient Greek drama performances had taken place here) was being staged in this open-air theatre with its amazing acoustics. This was the first time that Maria Callas had sung in opera in Greece since the days when she was Maria Kalogeropoulou, the leading soprano of the Athens Opera. Now Maria Callas could give Greece one of her greatest characterizations. For this she had with her a very old friend and great musician—Tullio Serafin. During the end of July Callas arrived in Greece to prepare for *Norma*. In some ways it was a new Maria. There was none of the irritability and strain that was so often evident during the latter years of her marriage. She was now a very calm and patient woman; it could be possible that she had at last achieved an emotional balance. An apartment was built for her next to the Museum of Aesculapius, which is opposite the theatre, as Epidaurus is almost five hours by road from Athens. It was three years since the concert at the Herodes Theatre in Athens had taken place. This time there were no crises, artistic or political; Greece received her with open arms and the public had never fought like this for tickets in Greece before. Georges Callas, who had arranged to spend his summer holidays in Greece, was the only member of Maria's family present. Everything was arranged and planned for this performance, the first of its kind in Greece, to make it a memorable one. Except for one thing; the usually predictable Greek weather suddenly became most capricious. The gala first performance had to be cancelled at practically the last minute, as unexpectedly, and surprisingly for the month of August, rain began to pour down a short time before the performance was due to start and continued all through the evening. Thousands of disappointed people began the long journey back to Athens. Shortly after the festival authorities announced that the first performance would take place instead of the second which was cancelled. There was no mishap of any kind on the night of the new gala performance, and people returned in their thousands to fill the vast theatre to capacity. It was estimated that eighteen thousand people saw the performance, which they could hear perfectly. There was no trouble of any kind, not even in making a dress for Maria, like the time when she substituted, at twenty-four hours' notice, for Tosca. No jealous soprano sent her husband to stop Maria from singing either. On the contrary the singers of the Athens Opera who were not taking part in the performance were in the audience to admire their famous compatriot. On her first entrance Callas, as the Druid Priestess, looked regal. The audience, which gasped at first, released their tension by giving her an ovation; Maria had not yet even sung a note. She was nearly in tears. The feelings her countrymen were evoking in her were even greater than the strength of her art. She began to sing, unevenly at first, but with a strange mysticism that seemed to blend with this place, sacred to the Greeks, and in fact to any visitor. She went on to give a most wonderful performance that brought tears to all. When in the third act of the opera Callas, together with Morfoniou, another Greek singer, sang the celebrated duet 'Mira, O Norma' ('You see, O Norma') which marks the reconciliation of the two women in the opera, the enthusiasm of the audience knew no bounds. One might say this was identified as the complete reconciliation of Maria Callas and her fellow countrymen. At the end of the performance there were no flowers. Instead a wreath of laurel of the Greek earth was offered to Greece's famous daughter. Maria now knew that she was not only appreciated but also loved by her countrymen. Surely this could make anyone happy, and Maria was no exception. Unfortunately there was yet another mishap in store for her. By the next and final performance she had fallen ill. In spite of her doctor's orders not to sing because she had a high temperature, she insisted on giving Greece the promised performance. These were Callas's first opera performances in Greece since the early days. Her fee, which was about $10,000—a great departure from her 300 drachmas per month during the war—she donated to a scholarship fund (the Callas Scholarships) for poor but able young singers.

The Greek Government thought this to be the right moment to express its appreciation for Maria Callas's art by decorating her with their Medal for Merit.

It had been a successful comeback and a very happy one for Maria. Summer was practically over when Maria sailed on the *Christina* for Monte Carlo, but not before she promised to return to Greece in the following summer. Maria could relax in Monte Carlo for only a comparatively short time as other engagements were awaiting her. Soon she returned to Milan where she made a new recording of *Norma*, and then began work on a new role for an old theatre. Maria Callas, after an absence of two and a half years—she had recorded *La Gioconda* at La Scala fifteen months before—was making a comeback in her beloved theatre La Scala. The role that was chosen for Maria's comeback at La Scala was that of Paolina in Donizetti's *Poliuto*.

On St Ambrose's Day 1960 La Scala reopened its gates for a new season. Prince Rainier and Princess Grace of Monaco, friends of Onassis and Callas, and also many other distinguished guests, were amongst the audience at La Scala. It was a more glittering opening night than La Scala had ever seen before. The ex-queen of La Scala had returned to her throne. Once again Callas succeeded in bringing to life a forgotten operatic role. In her hands Paolina became a credible and interesting character. The Milanese audience greatly appreciated her return. The subscribers to La Scala decided to celebrate Maria's return by arranging a small ceremony in the theatre foyer, and an historic gold medal was offered her. Maria was deeply moved by the devotion the Milanese audience were showing her; a devotion that she considered to be a great honour. This was a gesture that had never before been made to any artist in all the history of La Scala. The *Poliuto* performances continued to bring excitement in Milan, but when they were over Maria did not, however, undertake anything else. She was indeed back on the stage but, unlike in the past years when she used to sing so much, her performances were to be few and far between, and although she still kept her house in Milan, Maria spent the whole of the winter in Monte Carlo with only the occasional visit to Milan. It was not until the spring of 1961 that Maria made her next appearance when she took part in a benefit concert at St James's Palace in London in aid of the Edwina Mountbatten Trust.

Summer was beginning and Maria joined the *Christina* for a Mediterranean cruise. Soon it would be time to return to Greece to sing once again at the Epidaurus Theatre. This was a different life, for Maria found the way to relax and enjoy leisure. Social life, which had been absent in her youth, could hardly be said to have filled her life during her marriage to Meneghini. There was never enough time for anything except her work. Now she found out how to live for herself. Nevertheless she was still the dedicated and hard-working artist, but the occasions on which this was demanded of her were very few. When she arrived in Greece she was still Callas the dedicated artist.

In the appropriate surroundings of the Epidaurus Theatre she was going to personify Medea in Cherubini's opera. The action of the opera, like the classical Greek play on which it is based, takes place in Corinth, which is in the Epidaurus district. No other theatre could be more appropriate for the re-enactment of the tragedy of *Medea*. Maria, who took great pride in personifying Medea in the ancient theatre, prepared her role with meticulous care. As in the previous year, when *Norma* was presented, thousands of people made the long journey from Athens to Epidaurus. The *Medea* performances were scheduled earlier in July that year in order to avoid any similar mishap because of the weather, as when the gala performance of *Norma* had to be postponed. It was all the more amazing when again, two and a half hours before the performance, rain quite suddenly began to pour down. But this lasted for only a few minutes and then the sun shone brilliantly again. The opening performance found Maria on top of her form. She sang and played Medea with a conviction that completely captivated the twenty thousand strong audience. The performance in its totality was nothing short of a theatrical miracle, and Maria Callas was treated with the reverence befitting a Greek goddess. The city of Athens bestowed on her their Gold Medal, giving her the freedom of the city.

Georges Callas again made the trip to Greece to be near his daughter. This time it was more of a family reunion than it had ever been for Maria. Her father was not alone. Her sister Jackie was also at the performance. It was possibly the first time she had seen her famous sister perform since the early days in Athens. It was a happy meeting and it was the first time that Maria had her father and sister with her on such an occasion. A week later, at the second and final performance of *Medea*, Evangelia, her mother, was in the audience. After the performance Evangelia stood before her daughter in the privacy of her dressing-room. For a while they were speechless. All that had happened in the past seemed unimportant, and peace was restored between mother and daughter.

Again Maria donated her fee from her performances to the scholarship fund she had founded the previous year.

Meanwhile Maria had other engagements to fulfil; she was to return to La Scala, where she would sing in a new production of *Medea*. On St Ambrose's Day, 7th December 1961, La Scala as usual began its season. Early Verdi, *La Battaglia di Legnano*, was the chosen work in which Franco Corelli and Antonietta Stella were the leading singers. It was an interesting rather than an exciting evening. The following evening Maria Callas appeared in *Medea* and brought to it all the excitement that is traditionally associated with the opening of La Scala, and which had been lacking the previous evening. Maria was very successful and the audience responded favourably to her, and appreciated all the new refinements which she brought to this great role of hers. It was reported that even Ghiringhelli of La Scala commented on Maria's singing, saying that every moment of it had been a work of art.

For some time now several film companies had on various occasions tried to persuade Callas to make a film. Callas always refused because she never considered herself a prospective film star. Now, however, a somewhat different proposition was made. Cherubini's *Medea* was to be filmed on the stage of La Scala with

Maria Callas in the title role; a film that would at least be valuable
for posterity. Although Callas showed some interest in the project
at first, it unfortunately never materialized.

Meanwhile La Scala was planning a grand revival of Meyerbeer's star-studded opera *Les Huguenots*. This was to be in the
spring, during the Milan Fair. Although no definite plans were
made, it was expected that Callas would appear in this production
with the Australian soprano Joan Sutherland—the Clotilde to
Callas's Norma of her London début—as one of the other stars.
With the *Medea* performances over Maria ran away from Milan to
Monte Carlo, continuing her semi-retirement from the operatic
stage. Since the London *Medea* in 1959 Maria had made very few
appearances, but many people believed that before long she would
emerge again completely. But this was not to happen—not for
some time anyway. What did happen during the next few months
was only a recording engagement in London and a short concert
tour in Europe.

On 27th February 1962 Maria Callas appeared on the concert
platform at the Festival Hall, London, to face a cheering crowd.
It had been a long time since her last public appearance in the
English capital, on this same stage. But she was not forgotten.
On her first entrance at this concert she was given a very warm
reception. The concert was a success, though not without some
unfavourable comment from some critics, who thought Maria's
voice had deteriorated somewhat. Other critics, however, found
that although there was a certain deterioration, especially in the
high notes, in other ways her voice was even better than before,
with a newly acquired suppleness and greater refinement of
expression. Nevertheless the resultant impression that remained
with the public was that the voice of Maria Callas, in spite of some
outstanding virtues which it had exhibited, was showing signs of
deterioration. A large part of her programme consisted of music
usually considered suitable for mezzo-soprano, such as 'O don
fatale' from Verdi's *Don Carlo*, and an aria sung in French from
Massenet's *Le Cid*. A recording of French arias sung by Maria
Callas in French had appeared a few months before, and, with the
wonderful rendering she gave Massenet's air, it was evident that
a new repertoire was open to her. In the rondo for Cenerentola,
Rossini's *coloratura-mezzo-soprano d'agilità* heroine, and in the

final scene from Donizetti's *Anna Bolena*, Callas confirmed to her London audience that in *coloratura* singing she was still unrivalled. For the first time in her career Maria Callas also sang publicly in English 'Ocean! Thou mighty monster' in its original English form from Weber's *Oberon*.

After her London appearance Maria stayed on in London for a few days to record a Donizetti-Rossini recital. She then left for Germany for a concert tour. Four cities were chosen—Munich, Hamburg, Essen and Bonn. An accident in Bonn nearly marred what turned out to be a triumph. A painful eye irritation (due to contact lenses) forced her to enter hospital for treatment. It was only a short time before the concert that she was able to leave the hospital and give the concert, which turned out to be the most successful of her German tour. It was already spring, and back in Milan La Scala was ready for their production of Meyerbeer's *Les Huguenots*. Everything went according to plan, except for one thing. Callas did not appear in it after all. She did, however, repeat her *Medea* performance at La Scala a little later—in fact practically at the end of the season. Not since 1960, when Maria had sung in *Poliuto*, had she appeared in something new; and understandably the public were rather disappointed when the *Medea* performance was announced. Nevertheless the public rushed to obtain tickets which were sold out in no time—and in spite of being the end of the season when the Milanese begin to disappear from Milan for the summer.

But alas, it would have been better if this unfortunate performance of *Medea* had not taken place, for it came as close to disaster as any Callas performance could ever come. Maria was vocally at worse form than ever before; worse than anyone could imagine it would be possible for her. She tried again to play Medea in her usual convincing way, and as far as any question of style and good taste was concerned Callas scored again as always. In fact she more or less scored in everything except in one, the most important point, that of voice. But this time her other virtues were not enough, for it was quite obvious that her voice had deteriorated to an extent which was alarming. It was not long after that the press began to write that Callas was losing her voice, and for a while the main news about her revolved around her social life. It was true that Maria, perhaps for the first time in her life, was enjoying the social whirl she had found herself part of. Ever since her friendship had begun with Onassis, Maria's mode of life had changed completely. The dull, hard-working days were over, or seemed to be over. Maria was undertaking very few performances. In fact only a few concerts were going to be her only appearances in the next two years. She would only carry out already promised performances. The reason for this self-chosen semi-retirement was not, however, what it seemed. Maria was facing a major crisis over her voice. Contrary to foregone conclusions, there was nothing wrong with her vocal chords. The trouble was something different. She was struck with serious sinus trouble that affected her right jaw and stopped her resonance chambers from working. Consequently for some time she was unconsciously forcing her voice, pushing on high notes, as she could not control her hearing adequately.

With *Medea* at La Scala over, Maria was quite free from any engagements and spent the summer resting in Monte Carlo and on Mediterranean cruises to Greece with Onassis's yacht *Christina*. There were no performances at Epidaurus in the summer of 1962. After two summers of extremely successful appearances at Epidaurus, Callas decided not to appear during the third summer, but possibly to return in the summer of 1963.

The press continued to take note of her every social appearance and would occasionally mention possible stage appearances. But these were only rumours that did not materialize. However, an unexpected appearance in London took place on 4th November 1962 when Maria made a surprise appearance on British television's programme 'Golden Hour' from Covent Garden. She sang an excerpt from Verdi's *Don Carlo* and then the 'Habanera' and 'Seguidilla' from Bizet's *Carmen*, and thus gave London its first indication as to what a formidable Carmen she might make. Callas had never sung in *Carmen* on the stage before, and immediately after her television appearance Covent Garden as well as opera houses elsewhere tried to persuade her to appear in this role that was already promising so much. Callas, however, did not consider it right—not for the moment anyway. On this occasion, the first since the disastrous *Medea* at La Scala, she was in good form vocally, and although the public liked what it had seen and heard, it was not altogether convinced of Callas's vocal recovery.

To sing three arias on television is one thing, but to sing a complete performance at the opera is quite another. The public was right, anyway, for Maria was far from well, and quite contrary to reports that she cared more about her social life than her work, she was working very hard, for Maria again became a full-time pupil, studying to overcome the new extraordinary technical obstacles her voice was presenting, while the musical public, that can be as ruthless as it can be loving, were digging the grave for Maria Callas the singer. In addition to this Maria developed a hernia near her appendix. Fortunately this, like her sinus, was curable and an operation was successfully performed. But time was needed for a complete convalescence, as too much of her strength was expended and the muscles of the abdomen were damaged with unavoidable effects on her singing apparatus.

The years that followed found Maria studying hard. It was more like the old days in Greece when Maria Kalogeropoulou lived for her voice under Elvira de Hidalgo's guidance. The most famous singer in the world became a student again. It must have needed a lot of courage on her part, but Maria has always proved that she could carry out her convictions—especially those about her voice. Meanwhile any announcement for a possible appearance of Maria Callas would immediately generate excitement and anticipation, even among those who were apparently convinced that she was quite finished.

The year 1963 already promised some exciting appearances by Maria Callas. Apart from La Scala, she would sing in a new Visconti production of *Il Trovatore* on 28th February at Covent Garden. When Georg Solti, Covent Garden's new artistic director, announced this as early as July 1962 England's musical world received the news excitedly. The *diva* had not appeared in opera in the English capital since 1959, when she had amazed everybody with her Medea. Also arrangements were finally made for her to appear in Paris. For a long time there had been talk about her appearing in *Medea*, then *Norma* was scheduled. But with the changing of the Paris Opéra management it was decided that in the spring of 1963 Callas would sing Violetta in *Traviata*.

La Scala meantime was planning a visit to Russia. It was understood that the Russians expected Maria Callas to appear with La

Scala, and this immediately started the speculation as to whether the *diva* would go.

A wholly inactive winter followed. When the *cartellone* of La Scala were posted, the name of Maria Callas, much to the consternation of the Milanese, who were eager to see their opera queen a permanent member of La Scala, was absent. It was rumoured that La Scala did offer her a role in Monteverdi's *L'Incoronazione di Poppea* and that of the Countess in Mozart's *Le Noce di Figaro*, but whether this was true or not the fact remained that another season at La Scala would go by without its *prima donna assoluta*.

The London *Trovatore* was also postponed for a later season. Maria spent most of her time in Monte Carlo and Paris, with occasional visits to her home in Milan. By May she was feeling fit enough to embark on a European concert tour.

Six concerts were scheduled: Berlin, Düsseldorf, Stuttgart, London, Paris and Copenhagen were the chosen places. With the exception of the Paris concert, the programmes (which included some French arias) were the same. Everywhere she was enthusiastically received. Everybody was delighted to see her back, even if for the moment only on the concert platform. Vocally, however, Callas was not on top form. Trouble with high notes in some items of her concerts was sometimes too noticeable to be ignored.

Yet in other items she had no trouble and brought back all the excitement of old times. Still no opera performances were announced. Maybe Callas, after twenty-five years of endless hard work, self-sacrifice, and certainly doing her duty towards her art, would now want to live and enjoy a more normal life, free from the incessant burden of responsibility that her career demands.

All these seemed to be logical conclusions for a time. But one forgets that Callas, both the artist and woman, is dedicated to art, for what is certain is that Maria Callas in 1964 started to 'sing' again. Possibly she can only overcome the emotional uncertainties of life through the medium of her art. On 21st January 1964 she returned to London to sing *Tosca* at Covent Garden. It was as far back as May 1959, when she gave Londoners her incomparable Medea, that she had sung in opera in the English capital. Crowds fought like never before for tickets, which were sold out for all the six performances in no time. Callas at Covent

Garden was again the greatest musical event; and again Londoners were not let down. To start with the voice was in much better form than at the previous year's concert. This was the greatest Tosca within living memory, and for the first time in the history of English criticism all the critics agreed. Due to Callas's subtlety the drama of *Tosca* had never seemed more vivid and compelling. Both the critics and the public found several revelations in this opera, yet on close examination of Puccini's score these had been there all the time. Callas merely carried out, through her creative powers, the composer's intentions, which she understood to the full. A few days after the performances had ended Callas, with Tito Gobbi and Renato Cioni, the artists with whom she had sung at Covent Garden, appeared on television in the complete second act of *Tosca*. This was one of the most exciting performances that had ever been viewed on television.

With the London triumphs over, Maria returned to Monte Carlo and Paris, where by now she had established a permanent residence in the smart Avenue Foch. Her visits to Milan, where she still had her house, were becoming with the years less frequent, until in March 1964 she decided to sell it. Maria said goodbye to the only house she had owned, the only one in which she had known any real happiness up to that time. This was the house that had been her castle in the most triumphant years of her career. Now another strong bond with the city of Milan was broken.

La Scala's visit to Russia was at last definitely arranged for the autumn of 1964. Callas was asked to sing in *Anna Bolena*. It would seem that no arrangements were made again for her to appear in the 1964–5 season at La Scala, and consequently she decided not to go to Russia either. As a result La Scala decided not to take their production of *Anna Bolena*, as no other living soprano can do justice to this exacting opera. Meanwhile Callas was preparing for her forthcoming appearances in Paris. *Norma* was eventually the opera decided on, and eight performances were scheduled for her in May and June. First she made some recordings, singing Verdi, Beethoven, Weber and Mozart; the last three composers for the first time on records.

Although Callas was now living in Paris the Parisian public knew very little about her art. True Callas as an opera singer had won world fame and was certainly widely known from reports and recordings, but she had only sung in Paris on two isolated occasions before, and both these times it had been in concerts. Therefore it was only very few of the Parisian audience that had any first-hand knowledge of the great prima donna. This was the first time that Callas was to sing in a complete opera in Paris, and the excitement the announcement generated was unprecedented in this generation as far as the French capital was concerned. The French press considered the occasion an historic one for the Opéra. As 24th May, the day of the first performance, was getting closer the excitement and great anticipation reached greater heights. Callas had not sung in *Norma* since the summer of 1960 at Epidaurus in Greece, and apart from her recent *Tosca* at Covent Garden, London, she had not sung in opera for some time. Music lovers arrived from many other countries in order to hear Callas in one of her greatest roles. Feelings were rather divided. Some people were looking forward, confident that Callas could still cast a spell with her singing; others feared that she would not.

The gala opening performance was a most glittering event for the Parisians who crowded the theatre. In fact, socially, the Parisian high society considered it an absolute must. Although everything in the auditorium was perfect, it was by no means the same on the other side of the footlights. Vocally Callas was far from top form. It was her exceptional dramatic powers and the way she coloured every vocal phrase that proved her superiority in this, possibly the most difficult role in all opera. Those who went to hear primarily a voice were disappointed, and quite rightly so, for she sang the role of Norma with the minimum amount of voice possible. But those who went to witness an incomparable characterization left fully satisfied. Difficulty in some high notes and a lowering in volume were most evident on this night, which was a combination of torment and triumph for her. It was evident that Callas had not yet found her real form vocally. All the promise she showed after her highly successful *Tosca* in London, only a few months before, had hardly materialized. But of course one must not too readily compare the two operas that had brought Callas back to the stage. Puccini's music in *Tosca* is by far the easier to sing, being much less demanding as it vocally requires primarily various degrees of intensity, whereas the exacting melodies of Bellini's *Norma*, with their abundant flowing phrases, require the singer to provide so much different vocal colour in addition.

It is true, however, that from time to time now Callas can on occasion rise above her vocal difficulties. The third performance of *Norma* found her on top form. She dared everything—the high notes and the cadenzas. Everything seemed to come easily. Consequently Callas's performance was fully realized. The Callas magic was again complete. The next performance proved this. Vocally it was saved from disaster by Callas's dramatic mastery. The high notes were not attempted. But she found her form again in the performances that followed.

This ended the Paris performances of *Norma* which, in spite of everything, were great. For even if Callas was considerably less vocally wonderful than once she used to be in this great role of hers, she proved with her unique dramatic gifts and impeccable musicianship that she is still the reigning Norma of our generation, but only less so.

But even more important—important though the *Norma* performances may have been—was that Callas, despite her at times very flawed technique, indicated to experienced listeners that she was promisingly well on the way to complete recovery. Her serious sinus trouble had definitely passed its crisis and she was looking stronger. This great hope showed further evidence in materializing fully when Maria, not long after her final performance in *Norma*, recorded in Paris a complete version of Bizet's *Carmen*. Although the role of Carmen lies vocally in the lower register with few high notes, it was evident that Callas's voice quality was far better than it had been for a long time. In fact it displayed definite signs of the quality her voice had had at its best. Again Callas began to employ the same technique that she had before her sinus trouble and her other physical handicaps had forced her to become a student again in order to overcome, with a new technique, the extraordinary technical obstacles her voice had then presented. When a few months later, in December, the records of *Carmen* were released, Callas's highly individual performance of this heroine, which is so difficult to cast successfully, was enthusiastically received by the music critics. It would seem that only she could do justice to the role of Carmen today.

More than ever before opera houses, and no less the musical
public, hoped that this was the first step towards witnessing
Callas embodying Carmen on the stage. Callas, however, had no
such plans, not in the near future anyway. With the Paris engagements over Maria was quite free.

A few days after the recording was completed Maria left for
Monte Carlo. Summer was well on its way, and it was time for a
Mediterranean cruise. This summer, as a guest of Onassis, she
was again going to Greece. Onassis had bought a small unin-
habited island, Skorpios, which is very near the island of Lefkas
in the Ionian Sea. His idea was to build a splendid country house
and turn the island into his private estate. Already construction
had started when the *Christina* anchored at the natural harbour of
the island. The days were peaceful and Maria began to relax and
enjoy being away from the crowded cities. During their stay there
they often visited, on board the *Christina*, the nearby island of
Lefkas, where at that time of the year a festival of folk-dancing
and singing takes place. It was here that one day Maria quite
spontaneously took part in the festival. In the central square of
Lefkas, where the festival of folk-dancing and singing was being
held, she sang several traditional Greek songs. It was a very
happy occasion for everybody. The inhabitants of Lefkas were
excited and honoured beyond description to have with them the
Greek Maria Callas, the greatest singer in the world. Maria too
was delighted to sing the songs of her country to her fellow
countrymen, and she was moved when the ten thousand inhabitants of Lefkas enthusiastically saw her off as she sailed away on
the *Christina*.

It was a very happy holiday, and Maria returned to Paris
invigorated and feeling all the better for it. In November all
formalities were finalized and Maria, who had been living in a
flat in Avenue Foch, bought an even more beautiful and bigger
flat a few doors away. She hoped to move into it in the following
spring, and this confirmed once again that Maria was making
Paris her permanent home.

The year 1964 was drawing to a close. It had been quite an
eventful year for Maria Callas and, if not completely successful
outwardly, inwardly it had been quite satisfying, with great
promise and hope for the future. Maria had started to sing in

Donizetti: *Anna Bolena*

Maria Callas at her most queenly as 'The Tragic
Queen of England'.

Donizetti: *Lucia di Lammermoor*

Delirium at La Scala. . . . Callas sings Lucia.

Verdi: *Macbeth*

As Lady Macbeth, Callas electrified all those who were lucky enough to
hear her at La Scala, Milan, in 1952.

Bellini: *Norma*

Callas as the Druid Priestess made operatic history. Undoubtedly the great *Norma* of our times.

Bellini: *Norma*

'Feriam . . .' One of *Norma*'s most moving scenes when she is about to kill her children and one in which Callas surpasses herself.

LEFT. *Norma*. Maria Callas as Norma, the demi-goddess to the Druids. RIGHT. Verdi: *La Traviata*. Callas achieved perfection in her deeply felt interpretation of Verdi's loveliest creation of 'La Dame aux Camélias'.

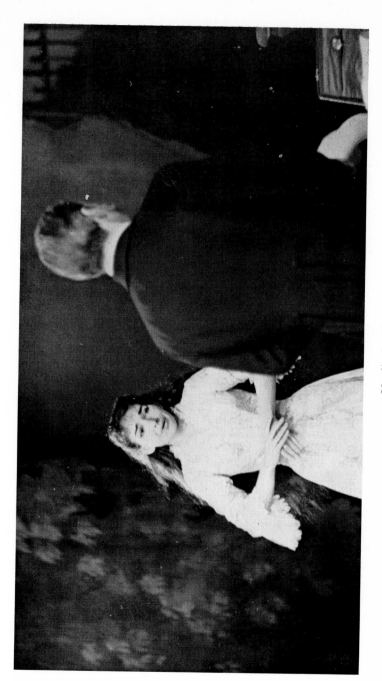

Verdi: *La Traviata*

Ditte alla giovine. . . . The hands cry too.

Verdi: *La Traviata*

A superb creation full of compelling force.

opera again and, above all, she had overcome the major troubles of her vocal crisis. However, time would tell.

With Callas becoming a Parisian it seemed that the Opéra of the French capital could count on her more frequent appearances there. When the Paris Opéra programme was announced in late autumn for the forthcoming season Callas's name, much to the delight of the Parisian music public, was included. She would sing in *Tosca* in February 1965, and again in *Norma* in the following May. In an exchange scheme between Covent Garden and the Paris Opéra, the London production of *Tosca*, in which Callas had appeared early in 1964, was to be taken to Paris, while the Paris production of *Norma* would be seen in London. It was hoped that Callas would also sing in both productions in London. The plan was for her to repeat *Tosca* in London in March and possibly sing in *Norma* later in the season as well, but no definite arrangements were made about her London appearances.

Meanwhile another important announcement was made regarding Callas's appearances. It had been six years since she had sung at the Metropolitan Opera, New York. That was the time when Rudolf Bing had cancelled her contract when he failed to understand Maria's explanation that she could not sing in *Macbeth* and in *Traviata* in the impossible order which he demanded. Although their quarrel was short-lived, it was only now that arrangements were made and Maria would return in the winter of the forthcoming season to sing in *Tosca*, her recent London triumph. This was considered a big event in the musical circles of New York. There had been several rumours in the past of a possible return of Maria Callas to the Metropolitan Opera, but nothing had materialized. Now it seemed that the Metropolitan Opera management were at last prepared to meet Callas on her own terms as far as artistic values are concerned, these having in the past been the major obstacles in Callas's relationship with the Metropolitan. This resulted in the appreciative American public being deprived of the witnessing of many of Callas's famous characterizations. Rudolf Bing offered Callas the role of Violetta in *La Traviata*, but Maria thought the role, for the moment, vocally not the most suitable for her return to the Metropolitan. Eventually *Tosca* was chosen, and only two performances were arranged to take place in March 1965. She would

D

also be singing in this opera in Paris before her Metropolitan appearances.

The year 1965 also promised some very interesting recordings by Maria Callas. A complete recording of Verdi's *Macbeth* had long been overdue. Also Verdi's *La Traviata* would be recorded. Although a recording already existed with Callas as Violetta, it was rather an old one, and besides, Callas's interpretation of this frail and unique heroine had deepened greatly since the early days of her career when she had made the recording.

But there will always be doubts and questions. Already the Covent Garden production of *Il Trovatore* intended for Callas was produced without her. Such is the life of an artist, and Maria Callas's life is by no means an exception. When all is said the artist cannot really be separated from the human being.

Anyway 1965 began most promisingly. On 19th February Callas began a series of eight performances of *Tosca* at the Paris Opéra. All the splendour and excitement that had become an integral part of Callas's performances was back at the magnificent Palais Garnier.

Everything started off most successfully. The *diva*, apart from a small lowering of volume in her voice, was vocally in very good form, better than she had been for some time. The voice was steadier and the high notes were mellower, and physically Maria appeared to be stronger. She went on to give the Parisians, and the many visitors who again made the journey from many parts of the world to Paris to hear her, a most rewarding interpretation. She showed many refinements and modifications, even since her previous appearances in this role in London just a year before. Clarendon, possibly France's most eminent music critic, described the performance an unforgettable theatrical experience. 'I have seen Puccini's *Tosca* many times—hundreds, but last night I was convinced it was really the first time,' he wrote.

So great was the demand for tickets that an extra performance was announced and sold out in a very short time. Hardly had the applause died down at the last performance in Paris when Maria had to leave for New York, her home town, to prepare for her two appearances at the Metropolitan. It was exactly seven years since she had last sung at the Metropolitan, on which occasion she had also sung in *Tosca*. New York had always before been rather a controversial city for Maria. In such a place where publicity and the press seem to be more superficial and rushed than in other places, it was bound to create fervent friendships and hostility at the same time. As far as the Metropolitan was concerned, Maria found that hardly anything had changed. She could not help being sharply, though justly, critical about the shabbiness of the Metropolitan's production of *Tosca*, and just like the time when she had rehearsed *Traviata* on a terrace, again, quite incredibly, she was not given a stage rehearsal. Fortunately she had sung in *Tosca* many times with the same baritone, Tito Gobbi, who was happily again singing with her; a very important point, especially in this opera. As usual Maria overcame these obstacles in the way she can so well with her experience in such matters. Meantime the great intrigue started for tickets. Crowds, hoping for standing-room tickets, formed outside the theatre days before the sale of the tickets began, and touchingly the crowd hung a banner on the front of the Opera House reading 'Welcome Home, Callas'. Indeed it was a welcome home. When Maria appeared on the stage on 19th March she was greeted with an applause that roared for four whole minutes, an experience unparalleled even for her. From then onwards the performance became a personal triumph, for Maria quite clearly reclaimed the throne at the Metropolitan. Not that her voice was not found to have diminished in size in the years since she had last been heard at the Metropolitan. But the artistry with which she used her voice was a stunning revelation of what the human voice can do to serve as a dramatic vehicle. The next morning the two most important New York newspapers, the *New York Times* and the *Herald Tribune*, put their reviews, full of encomiums for Callas's performance, on their front pages—a thing that in New York normally happens only on the morning after the opera's seasonal opening. There was now nothing of the hostility shown towards her in previous years. It seemed that even those who formerly, without any comprehensible reason, did not like Callas, had now succumbed to her magic. The whole event was too much of a triumph for Maria, with all the modesty she has as a true artist, not to realize it herself. And it made her happy to be back in her home town and to be friends with the world—for at moments of such complete acknowledgment and acceptance it seems to be the 'whole world'.

Six days later Callas gave the second and final performance and then left for her home, Paris, where she was anxiously awaited. There was just one month before she would sing in *Norma* at the Paris Opéra. It was also intended that she would make the new recording of *La Traviata* during this time. But there was hardly enough time to prepare for *Norma*, and the recording was wisely postponed for a year.

As spring was happily breaking in the beautiful French capital, Maria worked happily preparing for this great role of hers: Norma, the Druid Priestess, who gives everything for love. With just as much enthusiasm the musical world looked forward and with all the more reason for it. The *diva* had recently been in very good form, singing much better than for some time, and possibly in no other role could she be heard to greater advantage. Everything looked most promising. But life seldom follows a smooth or premeditated path. But what unexpected events were in store for Maria were a little ahead yet. Meantime she recorded for the French television a half-hour programme in which, apart from the interview, mainly about her views on singing in opera, she sang three excerpts from Massenet's *Manon*, *La Sonnambula* and *Gianni Schicchi*. The concert was to be televised on 18th May, during the period when Maria would be giving her *Norma* performances. Everything was progressing well until three days before the first performance of *Norma*, which was scheduled for 14th May. Maria was not at all well. There was a sudden lowering of her blood pressure and pharyngitis began to worry her throat. There was a heat wave in Paris, and extreme dryness in the atmosphere had always affected her in this way. As for the low blood pressure, it seemed to be, at least to a certain extent, psychological. Meneghini had recently been in some way stirring trouble. He had, since their separation in 1959, always been watching Maria. Now Meneghini decided to apply for a new court hearing, hoping that the court would give a decision that only Maria was to blame for the breaking of their marriage. Such a decision, if favourable for Meneghini, apart from the moral point of view, would also have benefited him financially, as he would then as a matter of course, according to Italian law, be entitled to a bigger share of their common properties in their legal separation. Under these conditions Maria, contrary to the belief that prima donnas are invulnerable, proceeded to fulfil her engagement. At the dress rehearsal she hardly sang, but saved her voice and physical strength.

On the night of 14th May the Paris Opéra was packed with the usual first performance elegant audience. A few seconds before the curtain rose the house manager appeared to announce Maria's state of health. 'Nevertheless Callas will sing, but she begs for your indulgence.' This is the kind of thing that is not uncommon among singers, but for Callas it was uncommon. After a singing career of twenty-six years it was the first time. But she need not have worried. Her singing varied from passable to very good. True much of the fire in the voice was missing, but still she managed to produce several moments of greatness. All in all this was a double victory, for Callas, even when sick, proved that she alone is the Norma of our times.

With medical care Maria soon felt reasonably well, and happily looked forward to the next performance. At 4 p.m. on the day of the second performance, however, quite dramatically her blood pressure dropped alarmingly. At her own insistence Callas, after having coramine injections, went on the stage. It was a most courageous effort, for the *diva* could hardly walk straight; this was due to the after-effects—usually fainting spells—that the injection can sometimes bring. The first two acts were hardly passable, but in the third and fourth acts Callas gathered her strength, and in a superhuman effort won the day. Alas, the improvement proved to be temporary. As there was no understudy—there really is no understudy, particularly for Callas's Norma—Maria under great strain and with superhuman effort carried out the remainder of her six performances, until in the last performance she was unable to appear in the last act.

Surprisingly there was no scandal this time, like the time in Rome in 1958, when Callas abandoned the opera—*Norma* again— after the first act. When it was announced that Callas had been able to get so far with great effort, but now had to abandon the opera, the audience left the theatre in dead silence. This was the way they could show their understanding and sympathy. Amongst the audience there were the Shah of Persia and Empress Farah Diba, who most touchingly expressed their sympathy and best wishes, sending Callas flowers. Maria sadly had this to say: 'I beg Paris to forgive me but I shall return.' The fact was, however, that Maria had a nervous breakdown and a complete rest was ordered by her doctor. A day later in Monte Carlo, embarking on the *Christina* for a month's cruise in the Mediterranean and the Greek islands, Maria, obviously still very much in mind of what had happened, had this to say: 'It was not I who was singing. I thought I was hearing somebody else, unknown to my ears.' There was just a month before her. In London, where she was then expected to appear in *Tosca*, the musical world was already waiting.

A few days later, while Maria was already cruising in Greek waters, a Milan court announced its decision on Meneghini's last action, whereby the public prosecutor, on behalf of Meneghini, had asked the court to put the blame on Maria alone for the breaking of their marriage. The court, however, blamed both Maria and Meneghini, finding Meneghini guilty of having caused considerable 'losses' to Maria's career, and also that at the time of their separation and afterwards he had seriously damaged her personal reputation with his statements to the press. On the other hand Maria's association with Onassis was found by the court to be far beyond the requirements of social life and ordinary friendship.

There was little holiday time before Maria's next engagement at Covent Garden, London, where she was expected to give four performances of *Tosca*, one being a gala performance before the English royal family in aid of the Royal Opera House Benevolent Fund. The rest and the hot Mediterranean sun soon showed how beneficial they can be, and Maria was back in Paris fourteen days before her first London *Tosca*. She looked well and relaxed, quite different from when she left Paris after her last performance in *Norma*. A week later Maria, feeling well and looking very beautiful, went to a ball given by Rothschild, the banker. It was a very pleasant evening, doubly so for Maria, who was above all feeling well and naturally looking forward to her London appearances.

In London, as always, she was eagerly expected. Thousands of people had queued, many of them for five days, for tickets to hear Callas and at prices never paid before at Covent Garden. Maria's recent indisposition and eventual breakdown only a month before at the Paris Opéra did not seem to hold keen opera-goers back.

People seemed to be quite optimistic that Maria would get well—anyway she can always make a superhuman effort. As the day of the first *Tosca* performance was approaching excitement grew, and the black market for tickets soared. Everything was going well until Monday, 28th June, when Maria was expected to arrive in London a week in advance for rehearsals. All day long friends and well-wishers sent flowers to the Savoy Hotel where she would be staying, but Maria did not arrive. In Paris at Maria's home in the Avenue Foch it was only stated that Maria would not leave her flat at present. By Wednesday it was known that Maria had a sudden relapse. It was again a lowering of her blood pressure that can be so crippling physically, and Maria, on strict doctor's orders. had to cancel her performances. No matter how she would try it was decided that nobody under such conditions should or could undertake four performances of any opera. The maximum that the doctors would allow Maria, and that on her insistence, was to undertake just one performance. The public would be greatly disappointed, it is true, but the artist's disappointment must not be overlooked. Maria naturally wanted to sing, otherwise she would not have agreed to do so in the first place, and anyway if she did not she would be, as far as she herself was concerned, the greatest loser. For the moment she could only send her regrets. A statement from Covent Garden said: 'Miss Callas sends her deepest regrets to her many admirers in London and begs them to realize that she would never cancel these performances without real necessity.' Meanwhile Covent Garden announced that Marie Collier, the Australian soprano, would sing in place of the indisposed Callas.

A new dilemma was born, however, as to which performance Callas would sing at, since she could undertake only one. Quite naturally the Royal Gala was chosen. It was a performance to be given for a good cause, that of the Royal Opera House Benevolent Fund. People had paid unprecedentedly large sums of money for tickets, and to a very great extent they did so in order to be able to hear Callas. Also the royal family would be present. Naturally this decision drew a controversy, but the English press were very understanding and did not make a scandal out of it as they could easily have done. A London evening newspaper did try, however. They even remembered Callas's past upsets with the Rome Opera, the Metropolitan, La Scala, Milan and Paris. Apart from the fact that there had been nothing of the kind in Paris, the others were absolutely irrelevant. Also there was a very strong complaint as to why Callas could sing at one (royal) performance and not at the other three.

Maria eventually arrived in London only two days before her performance. She could not even arrange any rehearsals. It was a very silent Maria except for a statement mainly in answer to the press. She said: 'I am deeply grateful for the interest that all the press and my admirers have shown. I have come against my doctor's wishes to do one performance. I had to choose one performance out of the four and I felt it was doing what the English people would have wanted when I chose to sing before their queen. I hope I have not chosen badly. I hope I have not upset too many people.'

On 5th July, before the Queen, the Duke of Edinburgh, the Queen Mother and a glittering audience, Callas sang in *Tosca*. Not surprisingly there was not much volume in her voice, but Callas managed to use her voice most artistically, achieving a triumph entirely by means of inflexion and colour. At the end of the performance Sir David Webster, general administrator of Covent Garden, remarked: 'She sang some things as beautifully as I have ever heard. But it is right—from the physical point of view—that she should sing only one performance.'

Maria wasted no time after London, and almost immediately went to Greece where the climate is so beneficial. For the months that lay ahead there was going to be no work, no singing, and only rest that would with medical attention restore her health. In the autumn Maria went to Monte Carlo and then eventually returned to her home in Paris.

There can be no long period of time without news of Callas. Soon people began to wonder and inquire where and when she would sing again. Callas had no definite plans for the moment. Her health had improved, but naturally more time would be needed to be absolutely certain, within reason, that nothing would happen to her. Of the possible appearances that might materialize, provided she is well enough, are performances of *Traviata* in February 1966 and *Medea* in 1966, both for the Paris Opéra, *Norma* for Covent Garden, a possible return to Epidaurus,

Greece, where the twelfth anniversary of the Athens Festival will be celebrated in the summer of 1966, and a return to the Metropolitan Opera, New York, where Maria was promised a new production at the time she agreed to sing two performances of *Tosca* at the Metropolitan in March 1965.

One piece of information was, however, published. Maria Callas would make a film of *Tosca*. Several times in the past Callas came very close to making a film but always decided against it. Being a very cautious artist she would naturally painstakingly consider such a step. Anyway this time it was more than just a familiar idea that the newspapers exploited. It would seem that Franco Zefirelli, the brilliant producer, had persuaded Callas to make a film, and in fact a screen test was made in Rome at the beginning of September. Everybody concerned, including Maria herself, thought the result to be most successful. As a matter of fact it really surpassed her expectations. Production of the film was therefore arranged to start a little later in Rome. The sound track was already made when Callas recorded *Tosca*, directed by Georges Prêtre, in Paris, in the autumn of 1964. But crisis soon overtook the film project. Another company had already bought the rights for making a film of *Tosca*, and now they wanted a very large sum of money to allow Zefirelli to make the film. Although at first the negotiations were going on well, by the end of November, due to other commitments of the people concerned in the making of the film (and in any case no reasonable agreement had been reached with the rights owners) the project was dropped—for the moment anyway.

Once again the idea of Callas making a film—a wonderful idea, for it would have been for many people the only way of seeing her perform, and for posterity—could not materialize.

Meantime Callas decided not to undertake any performances of *Norma* at Covent Garden, which were intended for the end of November, or *Traviata* in February and *Medea* in May, both the last two to have been at the Paris Opéra. No recordings either. In fact she decided not to sing at all during this forthcoming season, for otherwise it would have been too much of a risk, as Maria, although she was feeling better, could not be reasonably certain yet that she would be well at the actual time of the performances. Low blood pressure just needs its time to be cured.

* D

Maria spent the whole winter resting in Paris and Monte Carlo. In January she paid a visit to Milan. Although she stayed privately it did not take long for the press and the Milanese to know. For a while the Milanese hoped that Callas's visit might mean arrangements for her return to La Scala. It had been a long time since she last sang there and she was missed. La Scala, in spite of the high standard that is usually maintained there, had not really a prima donna who could excite the Milanese. But Maria's visit to Milan was of a very different kind. She still had most of her dresses made by Madame Biki, with whom she also stayed. In any case she was not going to sing for several months.

It had been already two years since she rented her apartment in Paris, and as the contract was expiring Maria moved to a bigger house only a few doors away. She found great pleasure in furnishing her new home and getting settled in her new more comfortable surroundings.

Meanwhile on 6th April news of a different nature was announced. Maria Callas was taking up Greek nationality. She had on 18th March handed in her American passport at the United States Embassy in Paris and signed the necessary papers relinquishing her citizenship. Maria, who had been born in New York of Greek parents, had always held American citizenship even after she had married Meneghini, an Italian, in 1949. Now it was because of her marriage to Meneghini that she was making the change. After seven years of legal separation but no divorce Maria's lawyers discovered a Greek law passed in 1946 which decreed that all marriages contracted by Greeks outside the Greek Orthodox Church did not exist. Therefore, by taking up Greek nationality, Maria's marriage simply did not exist throughout the whole world except in Italy. Maria was now free to marry again, should she want to, and go anywhere she wished except in Italy, where her marriage would be considered bigamous. But no marriage was arranged as yet. Callas had kept a constant friendship with Onassis since her separation from Meneghini in 1959, and several times during this period rumours floated around that they would get married. It was natural now that Maria was free that the question of marriage would come up again. But again nothing came from Maria except her comment: 'Freedom is so very nice.'

Soon rumours were spreading—and there cannot be too long a time without any—that Maria Callas will sing *Medea* in the coming season. Also that she might participate at a gala concert to be given at the Paris Opéra in November. It will be, in a way, her comeback to the stage. On these rumours rest the hopes of so many people for whom a Callas performance is an artistically exciting and incomparable event.

But all this can only be thought of on the condition that Maria will recover her health completely. It cannot be helped at the same time for the sad word 'retirement' to be heard. Every artist has to face it, although few know the correct time. It would be sad, but brave people can take it. On the other hand the hernia, and especially the sinus trouble, which she developed, and which for some time affected her singing, thereby causing a wobble in her voice and a deterioration in her hearing, have been temporary. These were passing troubles, and Callas has overcome them. If the lowering of her blood pressure can be permanently overcome it is quite possible that a new or really the old Callas will reappear all the better with her matured artistry. Also singers around a certain age can go through a temporarily difficult phase. Callas, now at forty-two, has already given twenty-seven years of her life to her vocation. But she is still a young woman and has a long time ahead of her. In short if Maria succeeds to regain her physical strength, that she will continue to sing for a long time yet is certain. Her art *is* her life. Callas cannot but deeply in her heart know this. Some people, it would seem, are born in this world with a specific mission, and however difficult, constantly demanding, and even heart-breaking this mission may at times be, man is destined to pursue it and give it all he can. For this is the reason that the artist has his being.

There are many roles that are waiting for her to re-create and to be given new life: Donizetti's Elisabetta in *Roberto D'Evereux*, which could still be another *Anna Bolena*. Roles like Lucrezia in Donizetti's *Lucrezia Borgia*, *Maria di Rohan*, an opera that demands not only great singing but also great acting, can only really be successful nowadays if Callas appears in them. Then there are Richard Strauss's heroines Electra, Salome, and possibly a return to Wagner's Kundry and Isolde. And there is also *Carmen* and many others. There will still be more sacrifices, heart-breaks and triumphs, until the time comes when she will inevitably take her leave of the operatic stages of the world.

No one can be certain what the future holds for Maria Callas. As a woman she is only human and must be judged as such. As an artist she is sublime, and must be judged by the highest possible standards. This is what she herself would also like us to do.

What is certain is that it will not all have been in vain, although we can never fully estimate the achievement of Maria Callas's artistic mission. Even were she to retire from the world of music tomorrow, she runs no risk of being forgotten. In time everything, both good and bad, about the human being will be forgotten; but the memory of the artist will live for ever.

There will be other great artists, but the present generation will always be proud of its great Maria Callas—Callas La Divina.

III

THE ART OF THE 'DIVINA'

In the creative state a man is taken out of himself. He lets down
as it were a bucket into his subconscious, and draws up something which is normally beyond his reach. He mixes this thing
with his normal experiences, and out of the mixture he makes a
work of art.

E. M. FORSTER

'THE GREAT ART of singing is a thing of the past, and singers of
today are not what they used to be in bygone days; the days
referred to as the golden age of opera.'

One often hears statements such as this, usually from older
people who have heard the great singers of previous generations.
At the end of a performance at the opera one frequently hears
remarks such as, 'Very good, but not like Melba or Caruso,
not like Destinn', and so on. But there have always been such
complaints, sighs and lamentations. Perhaps this is a sign of high
artistic standards. At any rate, it seems that complaints and
comparisons with the past started soon after the beginning of
opera as we know it.[1] Was it not Tosi, the famous Bologna
singing master, who in 1713 could no longer find singers who
were at all comparable with those he had heard in bygone days?

---

[1] Cavalieri's *La rappresentazione di anima e di corpo*, performed in February 1600 in
Rome, and Peri's *Euridice*, performed in October 1600 in Florence, are the first
operas of which the entire music survives.

It has often been wrongly stated that *Euridice* is the first surviving opera, considering *La rappresentazione di anima e di corpo* an oratorio. This may have resulted from the
fact that the work was performed in an Oratory; otherwise it is as much an opera as
Euridice is.

There was an earlier work by Peri, *La Dafne*, produced in Florence in 1597, but
the music is lost.

A hundred years later Rossini found the standard of contemporary singing beneath contempt. And so one could go on—the list is long. Perhaps Verdi's remark about the celebrated *prima donna*, Madame Penco, best illustrates the situation; he said she was singing as they sang thirty years before, whereas he wished her to sing as they would thirty years hence.

However, despite the admiration we cherish for the great singers of the past, I think that if we were to hear them sing today in the style of their period—and by style is meant the conception of a role in its totality—we would in all probability find their performances boring. All the interpretative arts, and the art of singing in particular, are constantly in a state of flux, for they represent the ever-changing habits, customs and outlook of each particular period.

But after all the complaints and regrets have been voiced, we must appreciate the great contemporary movement to revive grand opera, and admit that we have a larger number of opera-goers today than has probably ever existed. And what other age can boast of better operatic productions, an essential part of opera that is now taken seriously and treated with considerable respect? Are we not now acknowledging and, more important still, trying to put into practice the basic principle that opera is drama expressed in music and not just 'vocalization'? This of course is largely due to the great interpreters of our own generation. No doubt our grandchildren will also look back on our generation and admire our operatic ventures and magnificent singers.

Of our generation the figure that stands at the top of the ladder, the figure that has conquered the musical world of today and has given opera new life, is the *prima donna assoluta* (the absolute first lady of opera) of our time, Maria Callas, who has brought to us the 'cult of the prima donna'.

The 'cult of the prima donna' was virtually new to the present generation until the arrival of a real prima donna in the person of Maria Callas. This title which means the first lady, the main soprano in opera, originated in Naples during the beginning of the eighteenth century—*primo uomo* being the equivalent for the first male singer, usually being then a *castrato*. Francesca Caccini was perhaps the first prima donna in the early part of the seventeenth century. Vittoria Archilei, Leonora Baroni and Andriana

Basile were others. Soon, however, the women lost their importance. The great stars of song of the seventeenth and eighteenth centuries became the *castrati*, Farinelli being the greatest of them all. For moral reasons the Church banished women from the stage, and into their places the *castrati*, who were artificially preserved male sopranos and contraltos, stepped in. Their voices were pure, sexless and had an enormous range, as could be expected from a woman's voice produced with the power of a man's chest. These singers, who soon assumed male roles as well, became masters of the florid style, ornamenting their melodic lines with every kind of embellishment, creating a style that is called *bel canto*. Many of the *castrati* later became great teachers of singing, many of their pupils being women, as eventually people preferred to hear women in soprano roles. Psychological differentiation of character became necessary in the musical drama.

Some of the famous prima donnas of the Baroque were Giorgina Maupin and Giulia de Caro. The golden age of *bel canto* offered Faustina Hasse-Bordoni, Angelica Catalani, Giuditta Pasta, Maria Felicita Malibran, Henriette Sontag and Pauline Viardot-Garcìa. Later came Adelina Patti and Nellie Melba, and in more recent times there were Maria Jeritza, Conchita Supervia, Claudia Muzio and Toti dal Monte. Today we have Maria Callas.

The temptation to try to describe the artist Callas is irresistible. The difficulties are, however, immense, and one despairs at one's inadequacy in finding suitable words. Nature has bestowed so many gifts on this extraordinary artist that one does not know how to begin. Indeed there is no beginning, as such, in analysing Maria Callas's art. Not that she is a supernatural phenomenon; on the contrary, she is just a natural human being with all her needs for self-expression completely fulfilled. Hers is the kind of art made of many jewels, and although they may sparkle individually it is only the complete *ensemble* that creates supreme beauty.

The emotion, impression or whatever it is that one experiences at first sight of Maria Callas on the stage, consists simply of her profound musicianship projected to each member of the audience. This she does through her assured personality and great dignity, the ideal qualities we cherish in the great singers of the past.

Personality has always been a most important factor in all the

interpretative arts. I use the word personality advisedly, for today
it is so often wrongly used, implying the superficial behaviour we
usually associate with film stars. Personality in the singer is that
rare quality which enables him to give new life to music with the
help of instinct, vocal quality, technique and conscious knowledge; the kind of quality which enabled Callas to take Donizetti's
music, that singers of this century expressed as nothing more
than a waltz, and make it into a 'liebstod', as an eminent opera
critic once wrote about her Lucia di Lammermoor. Personality,
expressive of its own period, remains the vital factor in opera.
This is what is lacking today; there is certainly no shortage of
beautiful voices as such. Even to those who have never heard her
in person, the mere mention of Maria Callas is enough to arouse
excitement, interest and, at times, high controversy. But whatever
one thinks of her as an operatic artist, one cannot deny the fact
that she has contributed more to Italian opera in our time than
anyone else. Gone are the days when all that was expected was
just the mere beauty of song. Now in the hands of Callas all
the operatic heroines, once so superficially presented—Norma,
Violetta (*La Traviata*), Amina and so many others—have ceased
to be cardboard characters. Instead women of flesh and blood,
adapted to the twentieth century, appear full of human failings
and achievements—something very similar to the revolution that
took place in the world of traditional theatre at the beginning of
the twentieth century, with the creation of Tchechov's women.

Long-neglected operas by Bellini, Cherubini, Donizetti,
Spontini and others are revived for her, and she triumphs in them.
At first sight this may not appear to be quite true, for other
artists have in fact appeared in long-forgotten operas. But the big
difference is that, although at the time these revivals created much
interest, they are now once again buried in libraries. The Callas
revivals on the other hand continue their new lease of life, at least
for as long as she appears in them, because she has resurrected
them by means of her own individual interpretations. Most of
these operas have lain for so long among the cobwebs, forgotten
long before the advent of the gramophone, that not even one
piece of vocal music from these works had been recorded before
Callas. Also, since the composers are no longer alive to explain
points about their work, the performer must rely largely on his

own intuition for the interpretation. One could say in fact that she has personally created these roles for us, and certainly Cherubini, Donizetti, Bellini and Spontini would have been very happy and proud of Maria Callas's ability to bring their masterpieces to life.

Her interpretations of works already in the standard repertory have at times aroused controversy. I particularly remember a Callas performance of *La Traviata* several years ago in Italy. After the performance some of the audience argued so fiercely that they nearly came to blows. Some thought she was marvellous, and others did not like her. I think one must analyse the audience more than the performer to discover the reason for this particular controversy. The people who did not approve of this Violetta were not prepared to admit to themselves that the root of their dissatisfaction was the fact that they did not get what they expected, what in fact they had been getting from so many other artists. In short, the dissatisfied section of the audience pronounced Callas guilty of violating tradition. This is exactly true. Callas has always shown that she does not accept this so-called tradition, which more often than not means a series of errors, exhibitionistic effects and peculiarities irrelevant to the drama in question, committed previously by various interpreters and bequeathed to inartistic performers who repeat them mechanically. Above all Callas's Violetta was every inch a 'Lady of the Camelias'; she understood the character's illness and frailty and expressed them primarily through music with conviction.

Maria Callas will never copy any set model of a performance simply because, for one reason or another, people have come to associate certain conventions with the particular role. She will re-create her own role. This applies to several other roles, especially to the ones that have been performed by the prima donnas of the twentieth century and with whom Callas's singing has very little in common. The Rossini, Bellini, Donizetti and the early Verdi soprano roles were composed for a kind of singer that is very different from the accepted types of twentieth-century sopranos, who have, however, for a long time now made us used to hearing these roles sung with their kind of voice and consequently in their own style. Callas's singing, which is very close to that for which the above composers wrote their music, naturally appeared as anachronistic to its age but bringing to opera its authentic heroines. Her audiences were dazzled and enthused, but there were those who were irritated, even worried, and would not readily accept. Also her means for her purpose could not have been unquestionable to all, and Callas was received controversially. With time more people understood.

But what of the voice itself? Well, the first thoughts that spring to mind are that it is a voice that thrills, a voice that can move one to tears or can sparkle like a jewel. At other times it exercises a powerful hypnotic effect upon the soul of the listener. And yet at other times it can irritate certain types of listeners, those who are looking for just the beauty of a voice that can in particular display loud ringing high notes with accuracy and without any stridency. Callas has a considerable vocal range. She can hit notes with perfect resonance from low G to high E, an exceptional range by any standard, and her low notes have the chesty quality of a true mezzo-soprano. It is an individual voice that does not correspond to any of the categories that voices are divided into today, and yet her voice contains all the categories. In other words her voice cannot be defined as light or lyric or dramatic soprano, the categories that the voices of singers today, and in fact since the beginning of the twentieth century, belong to, though usually one voice belongs to two categories, e.g. 'light-lyric' soprano which applies today to Joan Sutherland or 'lyric-dramatic' which applies to Renata Tebaldi. Light soprano is the voice with weak low notes and brilliant top notes with amazing agility, the whole voice having a low volume, whereas the lyric soprano can produce more solid tone and coloured low and middle notes but with less extension in the high register accompanied also by considerably less agility. The dramatic soprano voice on the other hand, being a voluminous voice but not particularly agile, produces the greatest volume all through its range which usually extends to the high C.

Maria Callas's voice is classified as dramatic *soprano d'agilità*, that is, a voice with an enormous range, capable of the florid style simultaneously accomplished with dramatic accentuations that give it a very moving quality of tone. The voice possesses great virtuosity and tremendous agility, thereby lacking somewhat in volume compared with the volume which a present-day defined dramatic soprano voice would legitimately exhibit. The singing voice of Maria Callas cannot be compared with any living singer's voice. Such a voice does not belong to the present age or even to the whole twentieth century. One can only go back to the time of Giuditta Pasta and Maria Malibran, the time when composers like Rossini, Bellini, Donizetti and the 'young and middle' Verdi were producing their operas for precisely this kind of singer. In those days too the question of volume was not so difficult as it is today. The stages then projected practically half way into the auditorium, and the orchestras were comparatively very small and usually one tone lower compared with present-day large, highly pitched orchestras. The artist could thus project his voice more easily, particularly when less volume was required. The ability to sing mezzo-soprano as easily as soprano—this distinction did not originally exist—also accounts for Callas's successful appearances in so many long-forgotten operas, which demanded a singer of such an extensive vocal range.

Callas sings with more than one voice. Her chest notes and high notes are clean and open with a perfectly controlled cutting edge and exacting pitch, and she can alternate head and chest notes with an amazing degree of technical facility. By using her rapid, pure and sparkling *pianissimo* she can achieve a tonal colouring in her melodic lines that is nothing short of a miracle of emotional revelation, electrifying the listener. It is this rare gift of being able appropriately to colour every passage with imagination and skill that distinguishes Callas's singing. In this she is not, like the majority of present-day singers, handicapped by the use of words. On the contrary she makes words act as a vehicle for the coloration, the consonants helping in articulating and inflecting the notes, the vowels blending the sense of the words with the character of the music.

Her middle register is veiled, a quality that is quite unique among singers of today. It is this quality which Maria Callas uses so superbly in producing the suffocating tone that makes her portrayals of moments of passionate sadness and anguish so unbearably moving. Another extraordinary feature of such a voice is that it possesses many timbres throughout its complete range. This explains Callas's success in completely identifying herself with the great variety of roles she has undertaken. The ability to vary the timbre of the voice can provide a wealth of musical expression, especially when it is fully exploited by the artistry of a great singer such as Callas. Perhaps a short example might help: when Callas sings the same notes in *La Sonnambula* as in *Norma*, she does not sound like the same person, despite the fact that both operas are by the same composer and incidentally were both written for Giuditta Pasta. This superior quality accounts more than anything else for Callas's ability to play such a great variety of roles, from Rossini's *Armida* to Wagner's *Isolde*; from Bellini's *Sonnambula* to Puccini's *Turandot*; a record without precedent.

With Callas *coloratura* is always an integral part of the dramatic context of the music, and not merely an exhibition of technique. Her tonal colouring and expressiveness are as much in evidence in her *coloratura* singing as in everything else. Her *fioriture*, chromatic *glissandi* and arpeggios, not to mention her most expressive descending scales and trills, are never short of fabulous; her roulades and cadenzas possess a flexibility full of the sparkle and freshness that only a stylist like Maria Callas can achieve, whilst doing full justice to the content with her interpretative genius. One cannot help thinking of the many brilliant singers, the light and even the lyric sopranos of the past. One cannot help also thinking how thoughtless they often sounded. Only those who have seen a Callas performance of *Norma* can really understand this, and the point is proved by comparing the way she sings the melodious 'Casta Diva', where Norma appears as a demi-goddess to her people, with her portrayal of the scorned woman, who expresses her anger at Pollione in the unbridled scales of 'Oh non tremare'.

No one can deny that Callas excels in the art of ornamentation, with a unique excellence that very few singers or any other kind of musicians have ever possessed. These embellishments, usually indicated by the composer for use by gifted singers and some-times left to the singer to provide, are in no way redundant. They are just as important as the main melodic line which they supple-ment, intensifying the expression. Callas understands the reason and importance of ornaments, which she treats with no less reverence than the main notes. A scrupulous execution of the ornaments alone is by no means adequate, inasmuch as that of the main notes would not be either, as monotony then takes control.

On the other hand when the ornaments in particular are properly interpreted any possible monotony is banished.

It is true, however, that like all singers Maria Callas occasionally faces difficulties, and in her case they are mainly technical; an unevenness of colour in the timbre or a certain slurring of high notes. A fluctuating *vibrato* is sometimes noticeable on some high notes when sung at full voice, and her tone on these notes is occasionally disagreeable. These faults are naturally more evident on nights when the *diva* is not vocally on good form. But who could always be? The irony is that when Maria Callas *is* on top form, she herself sets the audience such high standards that they inevitably criticize her when she falls short of these standards. The biggest criticism is always the inequality of colour that exists throughout her range and inefficiency of some of her high notes, these actually being considered as Callas's stumbling-block.

This appropriately brings in the two different approaches to singing appreciation. One approach is the love and appreciation of merely a beautiful voice—beautiful in this case meaning agreeable to the ear of the listener, completely even in colour in all its range and with easily achieved high ringing notes completely free of any stridency. The last quality is most essential to listeners whose approach is such. Further, in the question of high ringing notes, it is not important, or even considered such, whether these high ringing notes are in any way an integral part of the musical drama they are supposed to express. To such listeners Callas's singing does not have a great appeal. The other approach is the appreciation of drama expressed in music. Consequently the singer must be fully expressive, and must naturally possess an essentially well-trained voice that is capable of musical exactness, in perfect intonation and rhythm. This approach does not appreciate vocalistic exhibitions when they are made for just exhibition's sake. To such listeners Callas's singing appeals greatly.

This is not meant to praise faults in a voice. But the great voices of musical history, the kind of voices that Giuditta Pasta and Maria Malibran possessed, and the sublime way they used them, also had this unevenness of colour and stridency on some high notes. Verdi's remark, 'In spite of everything Malibran is a very great and marvellous artist', helps to explain the situation.

Callas compensates for these technical shortcomings; she is intelligent enough to be aware of them, and if she finds she cannot correct a fault she makes use of it instead, investing it with a subtle significance, thus making it an integral part of the music and character. In any case, when a voice is always completely even and impeccably accurate throughout its register, the timbre cannot possibly be varied—such perfection must be obtained at the expense of musical expression. How often does Callas masterfully use a slurred high note as a superb expression of despair or loneliness? To listeners of the second approach as described above, her ability to combine both her dramatic and musical talents is so extraordinary that she is quite capable of making the listener either oblivious to vocal blemishes or to regard them as trivial. Faults, when placed in the context of the overall effect and final achievement, are nothing more than drops in a vast ocean. The strength of her artistic realism, like a vast ocean, obliterates technical faults. The faults on the fingers of Michaelangelo's masterpiece, the statue of David in Florence, does not make it any the less of a masterpiece.

Above all Maria Callas has a beautiful voice. By beautiful I do not mean that she has the ability to sing sweetly—which of course she can do when the situation warrants—instead I mean the fruit of intelligent imagination and study as applied to a given piece of music. We must remember that a voice is not beautiful in isolation, but becomes so only when it is properly and correctly adapted to a particular situation. A single example will suffice: compare the cool and beautiful playing of Kreisler on an ordinary violin with that of a merely competent violinist on a Stradivarius. Nothing is more necessary, more vital in an artist, especially a singer, than dramatic expression. However much natural sweetness or beauty a voice may have been endowed with by nature, it will always be inadequate without the power of dramatic expression. Not that beauty of tone is unimportant. It is so when it exists without the right shaping of the music.

As a result of her highly developed vocal ability Callas can sing music so softly, and with such assurance and apparent lack of effort, that she always has enough time to breathe, and so control the tempo, colouring and expression of the music. So the phrases are shaped musically, and although they bring with them all the meaning of their words, they nevertheless remain musical phrases. Often she delivers recitatives in a mezzo-soprano voice, a style which, in her hands, lends a strange reality. Always, and without the slightest exaggeration, the recitatives are both expressive and completely musical, for Callas has discovered the secret of speaking through music, and interprets her music with such impeccable intuition that we never feel that even a single word that she has 'spoken' could be expressed in any other. She makes one feel every time that her way is not only the best way, but the only way. Callas could be considered a consummate actress on singing merit alone, for she acts with her voice. True, her physical presence with her ideal countenance, her overpowering charm and her graceful movements, supplements her artistry greatly, but even so on gramophone records this ability to act with her voice is so powerful that one actually feels her presence. It is almost a physical impossibility to close one's eyes when in her presence, in order to hear without seeing her; such is the power she wields over her audience, holding them all in the very palm of her hand.

Her gestures are grand and surprisingly graceful. She can, on the other hand, freeze into immobility. In tragedy she can suggest horror or terror that so often then culminates in pity and compassion. And in her death scenes she wrings every scrap of emotion from her aria until even her audience is completely exhausted. In comedy she never caricatures, but draws humour from situations with subtlety. The way she uses her beautiful hands is a study alone, for they too seem to sing! She dares gestures which, although perfectly apt for her, would be, and often are, quite ridiculous when used by an artist sufficiently misguided to imitate her. Such misguided artists do succeed in imitating her up to a point, but such imitation in their hands, as it does not spring from an inner source, is reduced to nothing more than mannerism with the disastrous result of caricature as their only achievement.

When watching Maria Callas on the stage, one does not think: 'This is Maria Callas, the consummate actress, acting well.' She does not only act, but lives the part, identifying herself with each of her roles in turn; and so immersed is she in the character she is playing that one suffers with her in moments of despair and rejoices in moments of happiness. Hers is the kind of art that conceals art. For, over and above her accomplished technique, her superb colouring, her expressive *portamento* and her fabulous *fioriture*, she can make her audience take all these technical achievements for granted and believe they were attained with ease. Maria Callas's greatest achievement is making her art conceal art, and it is this which raises her work above the level of mere skill, to the divine heights of eloquent poetry. This is what makes Callas 'La Divina'.

It would be most interesting and helpful to quote a few things the 'Divina' herself has said about acting in opera and the way she works when preparing a role: 'It's the Greek in me that speaks. Nothing to do with tragedy,' says Callas. 'I have done nothing outside the operatic stage. Before I sing I know nothing: it's panic, for I do not remember anything and I feel quite lost. I do not even know with what gestures I should begin, until I go on the stage, then everything comes pouring out, the music, words, gestures—everything.' Instinct then is the main driving force that guides Maria Callas. Nothing that she does on the stage seems to be planned in advance; it is always as though she were doing it for the first time. Even two performances of the same work are often different. The amazing thing about this spontaneity is that each time her gestures and movements seem to be the right and inevitable ones: they harmonize with those of her colleagues and, above all, with the music. There is also a wonderful continuity in all her movements, and as one word leads to another in a beautiful poem, so one gesture is born of another. Much of the improvisation depends of course on the reactions of the other singers, and Callas always takes them into consideration, attempting in her own performance to evoke those reactions from them which will give that thrilling feeling of inevitability.

This does not mean that Callas's mind is in a perpetual whirl and depending for guidance on the inspiration of the moment. She constantly searches for improvements, always penetrating further into new depths that bring some new light. There are certainly always variety and spontaneity, but behind all these there is also a tremendous amount of hard work. In order to communicate the composer's ideas the interpreter must understand them completely, and this can only be done by strict adherence.

Without this, inspiration alone can never achieve much. It is the hard work and detailed study that produce the great spontaneity, and Callas has constantly proved that she believes in this. Even the most passionate scenes that appear to be so convincingly springing from the heart in such an unforced way need meticulous study; in fact all the more so. A look into original manuscripts of great musicians might well be illuminating. It is not altogether a coincidence that the more passionate and seemingly inspiring passages are those with the most corrections and consideration. 'For perfection and truth, precision and exactness, are necessary,' Gluck, the great composer, said.

Callas's first step in studying a role is to compile a summary of the physiological and psychological qualities of the character she is to portray; the age, nationality, period and social class. She then learns the words and an approximate form of the music. Then shutting herself in a quiet room, with as little light as possible, and with the score by her side, she begins to experiment, learning the part musically and rhythmically until she can hear and see the whole opera in her imagination. Rehearsals on stage follow until she begins to feel and react in character through modern sensibility. The stage is now no longer a room with the fourth wall missing, but the place where she lives and sleeps—the place where she exists. She will have become an interpreter and not a performer. Callas most certainly understands that to interpret is to re-create within herself. By putting herself as much as possible back into the same original conditions as those of the work in question, she is able to make the music live again.

My memory takes me back to London a few years ago when Maria Callas was singing Cherubini's *Medea* at Covent Garden. I was watching the performance from a secluded corner in the wings. After the performance had started I saw the lithe figure of Callas coming down the steps just behind the set, her long cloak trailing behind her. She seemed to be going anywhere but on to a stage and her expression was that of an unsure and slightly nervous woman. She suddenly began to pray quietly and crossed herself in the manner that is peculiar to the Greek Orthodox Church. This in itself was a most moving scene. I had already forgotten the performance on the stage, and making myself as small as possible in my corner I was trying to watch unseen. The time approached when Medea at last makes her first entrance on the stage. Callas abruptly sweeps up her cloak and covers her face up to her eyes, as her first appearance demands. She then knocks gently on wood, presumably for luck, and finds her way on to the stage. I watched tensely as she raised her hand to utter the words 'Io Medea!'. The transformation was complete. She was by now Medea.

People often wonder how Callas learned her craft as an actress. There seems to be no answer other than hard work and an intelligent approach to everything she undertakes. Her teacher is none other than her own heart and instinct and her extremely sensitive reactions to the finer nuances of human emotion, the drama her voice contains within the personal drama, continuously purifying her own humanity with an unceasing struggle for artistic perfection, the life 'credo' for which she will always strive.

Each different role she assumes brings new surprises to her audience or gives a novel touch to familiar delights, for she holds the fascinating secret of being able to paint her material in fresh colours and to give new life to old, familiar music. This is due exclusively to her greatness as a singer. It is as though one were hearing the music for the first time, as if the ink had not yet dried on the composer's manuscript when it was so lovingly entrusted to Callas. Her performance surprises, enlightens and delights those who witness it. For through her genius her interpretations go beyond a satisfying of all the aroused expectation. They exalt.

In the last four years there have, however, been considerable changes in Callas's singing: the throbbing *vibrato* is felt more frequently in the top notes and sometimes even a big wobble in the voice is noticeable. Furthermore the volume of the voice is diminished and she needs to work harder to attain her former standards.

Although voices do change with the years, in Callas's case it seems that other reasons are the main cause. The serious sinus trouble which she developed make her unconsciously force her voice, especially in the high notes, as the control of her hearing diminished. In addition the development of a hernia near her appendix weakened her greatly. Fortunately a successful operation, as far as the hernia was concerned, was made, but time was needed to completely restore the damage. It also seems now that the sinus trouble has been overcome, but low blood pressure seems now to be a threat to Callas's health. No doubt medical treatment and enough rest can cure it. It also seems that Callas has been replacing her voice, studying again after her vocal crisis. A rather lyric soprano voice seems to be the kind of voice she uses nowadays, though this is not so exclusively as her recording of Bizet's *Carmen* shows. Although the role is basically mezzo-soprano, Callas's voice to a very great extent displays the regaining of the freedom and quality it had before.

Out of all this story the fact emerges that Callas's trouble has been a physical and not directly a vocal one; that is, there has fortunately not been anything wrong with her vocal chords. Even in her most recent performance of *Tosca* at Covent Garden in July 1965 it was evident that the voice itself was in good form and was most artistically used, displaying at times utmost beauty. Physically, however, there was not much strength. Hence the lowering of the volume. Important though all these troubles may be they seem, with the exception of the low blood pressure, to have already been overcome. When complete health is restored one will be able to appreciate the virtues that the voice has acquired with the years; the new suppleness and lyrical depth to her voice, together with a mature refinement of dramatic expression which springs from an inner source. Consequently, although the resultant effect may be superficially less brilliant, there is a profound sense of poignancy and poetic eloquence.

But, finally, it is not really the voice, the technique, the amazing control and discipline, the extraordinary range, or all the other qualities which compose this great artist with which our whole being is filled as we leave the theatre. We have been held spellbound not only by Callas's performance but by something more mysterious, something virtually divine: 'The melody which echoes in the soul, the melody that lingers on.' For to Callas, priestess of grand opera, 'singing is an act of humility and not an act of pride. It is merely an attempt to rise towards those heights where everything is harmony'. And this she has achieved. For when Maria Callas sings or, more accurately, moulds her voice, she shapes a character now terrifying, now gentle, and one is carried away. Even more breathtaking is her voice when it becomes the sound of a distant, muted violin that touches one's very heart-strings. The images evoked by her singing can be like shooting stars in a stormy sky, an arc ending in a cascading light over her amazed audience; and when the storm is over, gentle sunlight or bright moonlight often follows in a stillness that is scarcely credible. For all this we can only salute the great artist. We should not really applaud her but simply say 'Thank you'.

IV

REFLECTIONS ON THE OPERATIC
REPERTOIRE OF THE ARTIST

The stage but echoes back the public voice,
The drama's laws, the drama's patrons give,
For we that live to please, must please to live.
                            DR JOHNSON, *Prologue*, 1747

IT IS BY no means a small thing to master and re-create over forty
operatic roles in a matter of fifteen years as Maria Callas has done.
This of course does not include the years in Greece but starts with
her Italian début in 1947 at the Arena of Verona. To find a parallel
feat we can look only to Lilli Lehmann. It is really not so much the
number of roles but the kind of roles. Maria Callas's repertoire is
of unequalled variety, a variety that testifies both to her sound
basic vocal training and to her extraordinary musical versatility.

In many cases it is due to her influence and foremost to her
artistic capability that a number of roles were brought back to the
operatic stage after years of neglect. And in many of these roles,
such as in *Norma*, *Medea*, *Anna Bolena*, *Il Pirata* and others, she
seems to have no rivals, good or bad. In the early days of her
career Maria Callas, like Kirsten Flagstad, made a brief excursion
into operetta (Suppé's *Boccaccio* and Millocker's *Bettelstudent*), an
experience which is always enjoyable for the artist with its lightness of approach. Unusually Maria Callas also sang in Wagner's
operas at the beginning of her career. It was a new experience to
see this Isolde, for not only could she sing the great music but she
could also act the great part. No less impressive was her Kundry in

Parsifal, and her Brünnhilde in *Die Walküre*. All her Wagnerian roles were sung in Italian. In fact Callas, at the beginning of her career, was able to sing any role that was given her. She was more or less brilliant in everything she did. But every role then was not necessarily correct for her.

Verismo opera, such as Puccini's works, although it required different degrees of intensity, usually requires a single vocal colour, not, in other words, what Callas's voice can offer at its best. Furthermore as such music has to be sung with exceptional volume and often fiercely, this can easily lead to the damaging of muscles of vocal chords such as Callas possesses. This Callas fortunately understood early on, and with the fame she had acquired people could not dictate to her what she should sing. The happy result was the cutting out of most of these heavy, then unsuited, roles for her, even if she was most successful in them. She was then able to concentrate on *bel canto*, the music of Bellini, Donizetti and Verdi and re-create their heroines in the way they were originally conceived, and this is how Callas came to know the years of triumph. With a big part of her career behind her now one hopes that Callas will one day soon return to Wagner. Especially now that she has matured so much as an artist, it would be a great partnership.

Since her brilliant characterization of Constanze in Mozart's *Die Entführung aus dem Serail*, Maria Callas has, with the exception of some excerpts from *Le Noce di Figaro* and *Don Giovanni* for a recording, sung no more Mozart on the stage and shows no interest in doing so. She could certainly make a great Donna Elvira in *Don Giovanni*. As for Richard Strauss, Callas has until now unfortunately ignored him. In a way she was quite right, as Strauss's kind of music would not have benefited Callas's vocal instrument that was intended for other things. But at the present stage of her career, with her exceptional talents as an actress-singer, she would be an ideal interpreter of Strauss's operas. It will be a great loss to the musical world if Maria Callas, with her outstanding talent, deprives it of the experience of hearing her interpretation of Strauss's music. What a great Electra or Salome she could be!

Maria Callas's extensive repertoire is based mainly on Italian Opera: Rossini, Bellini, Donizetti and Verdi, with occasional excursions to Cherubini, Spontini, Puccini, Giordano and Ponchielli, have been the main composers. In Bellini, Callas has particularly distinguished herself so completely that she is generally accepted as the greatest exponent of his music in this generation. Not surprisingly really since she has just the right kind of voice that Bellini appropriately composed to express the characters of his heroines.

She has also proved an outstanding interpreter of Gluck's stately music. She sang a very touching Alceste, and a tragic Iphigenia in *Iphigenia en Tauride*.

In comedy she has appeared in roles such as Rosina in Rossini's *Il Barbiere di Siviglia* with controversial result. But as Constanze in *Die Entführung aus dem Serail* and, even more so, as Donna Fiorilla in Rossini's *Il Turco in Italia* she was brilliant, and has shown that she can be a comedienne of the first order with a really deeply grained comic quality.

In 1961 a gramophone record was issued with Callas singing arias from French operas. It was a great revelation, for it showed that a new repertoire was open to her. In her 1962 London concert, where she included in her programme Chimène's air 'Pleurez, mes yeux' from Massenet's *Le Cid*, she showed what a poignant and passionate Chimène she would make, with great nobility of style. If, however, one could choose, it would be to hear Maria Callas as Orfeo in Gluck's *Orfeo ed Euridice*. But then there is Saint Saëns's Dalila and Bizet's Carmen and many others.

With the exception of the role of Smaragda in Kalomiris' *Ho Protomastoras*, which Callas sang in the early days in Greece, she has never been persuaded to appear in modern opera. This is not at all surprising, for Callas's conception of opera, that is expressing her characterizations through melody and the beauty of the human voice, is so much at variance with the modern opera composer's intentions.

So far, with the exception of her early appearances in Athens, where she sang in Greek and once in German in *Fidelio*, her entire repertoire on stage has been sung in Italian. (In her 1962 London concert, for the first time in her career she sang Weber's aria 'Ocean! Thou mighty monster' from *Oberon* in its original English version. She later recorded this music.) She has recorded

French opera in French and has also sung in French on the concert platform.

The following is a complete list of Maria Callas's repertoire; it is followed by an analysis of many of her greater roles in opera. The dates and theatres mentioned in the list are those dates and theatres where each particular role was first sung by Maria Callas.

V

ROLES SUNG ON THE STAGE
BY MARIA CALLAS

WORK	ROLE	DATE	THEATRE AND PLACE
Cavalleria Rusticana (Mascagni)	Santuzza	April 1939	Athens (student performance)
Suor Angelica (Puccini)	Angelica	May 1940	Athens (student performance)
Un Ballo in Maschera (Verdi)	Amelia	— 1940	Athens (student performance)
Aida (Verdi)	Aida	— 1940	Athens (student performance)
Boccaccio (von Suppé)	Beatrice	27 Nov. 1940	Athens Opera (first appearance)
Tosca (Puccini)	Floria Tosca	4 July 1942	Athens Opera (début)
Cavalleria Rusticana (Mascagni)	Santuzza	Jan. 1943	Athens Opera
Ho Protomastoras (Kalomiris)	Smaragda	Mar. 1943	Athens Opera (world première)
Tiefland (D'Albert)	Marta	April 1944	Athens Opera
Fidelio (Beethoven)	Leonore	Sept. 1944	Herodes Atticus, Athens
Bettelstudent (Millocker)	Laura	Aug. 1945	Athens Opera
La Gioconda (Ponchielli)	Gioconda	3 Aug. 1947	Arena of Verona (Italian début)
Tristan und Isolde (Wagner)	Isolde	22 Dec. 1947	La Fenice, Venice

E   115

WORK	ROLE	DATE	THEATRE AND PLACE
Turandot (Puccini)	Turandot	Jan. 1948	La Fenice, Venice
Aida (Verdi)	Aida	Feb. 1948	Rovigo, Italy
La Forza del Destino (Verdi)	Leonora	Mar. 1948	Giuseppe Verdi, Trieste
Die Walküre (Wagner)	Brünnhilde	Jan. 1949	La Fenice, Venice
I Puritani (Bellini)	Elvira	Jan. 1949	La Fenice, Venice
Parsifal (Wagner)	Kundry	Mar. 1949	Rome Opera House
Norma (Bellini)	Norma	17 July 1949	Colon, Buenos Aires
Nabucco (Verdi)	Abigail	22 Dec. 1949	San Carlo, Naples
Il Trovatore (Verdi)	Leonora	July, 1950	Mexico City
Il Turco in Italia (Rossini)	Fiorilla	19 Oct. 1950	Eliseo, Rome
La Traviata (Verdi)	Violetta	15 Jan. 1951	Communale, Florence
I Vespri Siciliani (Verdi)	Elena	May 1951	Maggio Musicale, Florence
Orfeo ed Euridice (Haydn)	Euridice	10 June 1951	Maggio Musicale, Florence (World stage première)
Die Entführung aus dem Serail (Mozart)	Constanze	2 April 1952	La Scala, Milan
Armida (Rossini)	Armida	26 April 1952	Maggio Musicale, Florence
Lucia di Lammermoor (Donizetti)	Lucia	10 June 1952	Mexico City
Rigoletto (Verdi)	Gilda	June 1952	Mexico City
Macbeth (Verdi)	Lady Macbeth	7 Dec. 1952	La Scala, Milan
Medea (Cherubini)	Medea	May 1953	Maggio Musicale, Florence

WORK	ROLE	DATE	THEATRE AND PLACE
Alceste (Gluck)	Alceste	4 April 1954	La Scala, Milan
Don Carlo (Verdi)	Elisabetta di Valois	12 April 1954	La Scala, Milan
Mefistofele (Boïto)	Margarita	15 July 1954	Arena di Verona
La Vestale (Spontini)	Giulia	7 Dec. 1954	La Scala, Milan
Andrea Chenier (Giordano)	Maddalena di Coigny	8 Jan. 1955	La Scala, Milan
La Sonnambula (Bellini)	Amina	5 May 1955	La Scala, Milan
Madama Butterfly (Puccini)	Cio-Cio San	11 Nov. 1955	Lyric, Chicago
Il Barbiere di Siviglia (Rossini)	Rosina	16 Feb. 1956	La Scala, Milan
Fedora (Giordano)	Fedora	21 May 1956	La Scala, Milan
Anna Bolena (Donizetti)	Anna	14 April 1957	La Scala, Milan
Iphigenia en Tauride (Gluck)	Iphigenia	30 May 1957	La Scala, Milan
Un Ballo in Maschera (Verdi)	Amelia	7 Dec. 1957	La Scala, Milan
Il Pirata (Bellini)	Imogene	18 May 1958	La Scala, Milan
Poliuto (Donizetti)	Paolina	7 Dec. 1960	La Scala, Milan

ROLES SUNG FOR THE GRAMOPHONE ONLY BY MARIA CALLAS

WORK	ROLE	DATE OF RECORDING
I Pagliacci (Leoncavallo)	Nedda	June 1954
La Bohème (Puccini)	Mimi	Aug. 1956
Manon Lescaut (Puccini)	Manon	July 1957
Carmen (Bizet)	Carmen	July 1964

VI

ANALYSIS OF MARIA CALLAS'S MOST FAMOUS ROLES

LA GIOCONDA

Opera in four acts by Amilcare Ponchielli.
Libretto by Arrigo Boïto based on Victor Hugo's play, *Angelo, Tyran de Padoue*.

Principal Characters

GIOCONDA, a ballad singer	Soprano
LAURA ADORNO, a Genoese lady, wife of ALVISE	Mezzo-soprano
ALVISE BADOERE, a leader of the State Inquisition	Bass
ENZO GRIMALDO, a Genoese nobleman .	Tenor
BARNABA, a spy of the Inquisition . .	Baritone
LA CIECA, blind mother of GIOCONDA . .	Contralto

TIME: 17th century.   PLACE: Venice.

First performed 8th April 1876, at La Scala, Milan, with Maddalena Mariani-Masi as Gioconda and Giuliano Gayarre as Enzo.

Maria Callas first sang Gioconda on 3rd August 1947, at the Arena of Verona. Also at La Scala, Milan, and the Arena of Verona in 1952.

La Gioconda was Ponchielli's greatest success, one which he never repeated with his later works.

It is true that Verdi puts Ponchielli in the shade; but it is equally true that Verdi took many ideas from Ponchielli's concept of grand opera, such as the rapid changes of mood. Nevertheless *La Gioconda* is full of theatrical strokes with hardly a dull moment and, given a good cast, the opera can be most exciting, for Ponchielli possessed an original talent. It was not long afterwards that the opera found the success it deserved. It enjoys a great popularity in Italy up to the present day, always attracting most of the best voices of the age.

Barnaba, a spy of the Inquisition, standing by the Lion's Mouth (a letter-box by means of which one could anonymously denounce an enemy of the republic), sees Gioconda guiding her blind mother, La Cieca, through the crowd of the grand court-yard of the Ducal Palace to church. Barnaba, who is infatuated with Gioconda, presses his love on her but she repulses him.

Gioconda, who is in love with Enzo Grimaldo, a banished nobleman, flees, leaving her mother at the church door. Barnaba retaliates by denouncing La Cieca to the crowd as a witch. Enzo, who was hiding in the crowd, intervenes but La Cieca is arrested. At this moment, however, Alvise, a lord of the Inquisition, and his wife Laura, who is wearing a mask, appear at the palace gate. At the intercession of Laura La Cieca is freed, and in gratitude she gives a rosary to Laura. Laura and Enzo exchange looks as they recognize each other, for Enzo was betrothed to her before he was banished from Venice. Barnaba, who has recognized Enzo, offers to take Laura on board his ship. But he also dictates a letter telling of Laura's elopement, which he throws into the Lion's Mouth. Gioconda, who overhears him, is overcome by Enzo's love for Laura. She hides on Enzo's ship and tries to kill Laura when she arrives. But she sees on her her mother's rosary, and instead sends Laura in a boat safely away before elopement. Enzo sets his ship on fire rather than allow the vessel to be captured, and then he escapes. Alvise, back in his house, accuses Laura of faithlessness and then he leaves, expecting her to take poison before he returns. Gioconda comes to her aid with a sleeping potion with which they replace the poison. Laura takes the potion and when Alvise returns he thinks her dead.

Alvise is giving a sumptuous party when Barnaba enters,

dragging with him La Cieca, whom he again accuses of witch-craft. La Cieca senses that there is a dead person in the house, whereupon Alvise causes the curtains to be drawn back for all to see Laura lying in her burial robes. Enzo, who is hidden amongst the guests, believing Laura to be dead, throws off his mask and tries to stab Alvise, but is arrested. Gioconda during the con-fusion manages to carry off Laura to her house. Then, her love for Enzo greater than her jealousy of Laura, she asks for Barnaba's help to save Enzo. The price of this pact is Gioconda herself.

Gioconda in despair contemplates suicide with the poison she has taken from Laura, when Enzo appears. In a tense scene she tells him that she has removed Laura's body from the tomb. Enzo in his rage attempts to stab her, when Laura awakens. The two lovers then, with Gioconda's help, escape. As Gioconda is preparing to escape too Barnaba arrives to claim his prize; but as he embraces her she stabs herself. In revenge Barnaba shouts at the dead Gioconda that he had strangled her mother the previous night.

Callas in her portrayal of Gioconda is astonishing to say the least. She re-creates one of the most demanding and complex roles in Italian grand opera, and brings it to us with such excitement that the whole thing becomes a revelation rather than a mere performance.

It is not only because of the wonderful expression and infinite variety of colour in Ponchielli's idiomatic music that Callas is so impressive in this role, but also because of her exceptional dramatic gifts, incredible insight and sense of the meaning of every word—gifts that any dramatic actress would envy. In fact one wonders if so many words have ever come across in any other performance of *La Gioconda*. Her singing is tender, passionate and fiery by turns, all of it very exciting. However, vocally it is by no means perfect from the purists' point of view; there are the occasional hard top notes and a slight *vibrato* in some. But who could seriously mind this, the only flaw in a performance which even at its weakest point is thrilling and introduces one to a great historical opera.

At the very beginning of the opera, when Callas comes on to the stage leading La Cieca, her blind mother, we enjoy some excel-lently delivered recitative. Her first utterance, 'Madre adorata'

('Beloved mother'), captures at once our full attention. There is something commanding and very impressive in Callas's appearance, or rather in her controlled movements. Her harsh words to Barnaba in the following scene reveal the fiery side of Gioconda's character, as does her piercing cry, 'Ah! Mia madre' ('Ah! It is my mother'), when she discovers that her mother is accused of witchcraft. Callas uses her hands and eyes marvellously, and her singing is expertly supported by her gestures, such as in 'Il mio destino è questo, o morte o amor' ('This is my destiny, love or death').

In the famous Act II duet, the battle between Gioconda and Laura, beginning with 'E un anatema' ('And a curse'), Callas gives us some thrilling singing, with exquisite phrasing and without resorting to any vocal crudities. Her timing is perfect and the whole scene is one of the highlights of the opera. So also is the scene between Enzo and Gioconda. Callas sings with an intensity and passion that are yet unrivalled, finishing the scene with an impassioned 'E sempre Laura! Ma almen poss' io con te morir!' ('It's always Laura! I at least can die with you!').

The passage that ends Act III, Scene 1, is not exactly inspired music. It becomes so, however, when Callas sings it, beginning with 'O madre mia' ('O my mother') and ending with 'Per lui, per lui che l'ama!' ('For him, for him who loves her!'). The impact that she makes here, especially with the words 'per lui', using only her voice, is simply shattering.

Gioconda's grand scene in the last act is the climax of the opera, and Callas is totally superb. She brings tremendous force and some outstanding phrasing to her recitative 'O pietosi' ('O generous hearts') before the famous aria 'Suicidio! . . . in questi fieri momenti' ('Suicide! . . . in these terrible moments'). This aria has been described as a 'terrible song'. As Callas, seized by despair, takes up the vial of poison, she embarks on a most dramatic and passionate soliloquy. Her low notes in 'Or piombo esausta fra le tenebre!' ('I now sink, exhausted in darkness!') are most telling and the terrible misery that Callas gives to 'Di dormir queta dentro l'avel' ('Quietly to sleep into the grave') is as truly memorable as the middle section of the aria 'E un dì leggiadre volavan l'ore' ('Once upon a time the hours used to fly gaily by') sung in her glorious *mezza-voce*. After this aria Gioconda

contemplates killing Laura, and Callas gives the whole scene from
'No, tentator, lungi da me!' ('No, away, temptation!') a fine
musical interpretation. With great poignancy she sings 'Enzo!
... Sei tu!' ('Enzo!... It is you!') and the duet with Enzo, which
later becomes a trio as Laura wakes from the anaesthetic. There is
a terrible despair when this Gioconda shrieks the words 'No! Io
dissi il ver' ('No! I spoke the truth') and her expressive singing
is enhanced by the dramatic way in which she prostrates herself
before the image of the Virgin in 'Vergine Santa, allontana il
demonio!' ('Drive the devil away, O Holy Virgin!').

The final scene in the opera, with Barnaba, is terrifying. Callas
pretends a fake femininity in 'Vo' farmi più gaia, più fulgida
ancora!' ('I wish to make myself gayer and brighter!'). Her florid
singing is astonishingly brilliant, with a constant dramatic under-
current which alerts one to her grasp of the situation as a whole.

Her final utterances, full of a desperate sarcasm in 'Volesti il
mio corpo, demon maledetto! E il corpo ti do' ('You always
wanted my body, you cursed demon! And my body I now give
you'), just before she stabs herself in the heart, are eternally
memorable.

TOSCA

Opera in three acts by Giacomo Puccini.
Libretto by Giuseppe Giacosa and Luigi Illica, after Victorien
Sardou's melodrama *La Tosca*.

Principal Characters

FLORIA TOSCA, a celebrated singer	Soprano
MARIO CAVARADOSSI, a painter	Tenor
BARON SCARPIA, Chief of Police	Baritone

TIME: June 1800.   PLACE: Rome.

First performed at the Costanzi Theatre, Rome, on 14th January
1900, with Hariclea Darcleè as Tosca, Emilio de Marchi as
Cavaradossi and Eugenio Giraldoni as Scarpia.

Maria Callas first sang Floria Tosca in July 1942 at the Athens

* E

Opera, Greece. Also in Bologna in 1950; in Rio de Janeiro in 1951; in Mexico City in 1952; at the Metropolitan, New York, in 1956 and 1958; at the Paris Opéra (second act only) in 1959; at Covent Garden, London, in 1964; at the Paris Opéra, Metropolitan, New York, and at Covent Garden, London, in 1965.

The comments made by the critics on Puccini's *Tosca*, after its *première*, were unfavourable; in fact the opera was in their opinion very little short of being a fiasco. Although they thought Puccini successful in composing music suitable for matter-of-fact actions and fast dialogue, they found him temperamentally unsuited to composing the music for Sardou's melodrama. The work soon established itself as Puccini's latest success. Today *Tosca* is Puccini's most thrilling work, and remains one of the most popular and most often performed operas in the world.

In the Church of Sant' Andrea della Valle in Rome Mario Cavaradossi, a young painter and republican sympathizer, is painting the picture of Mary Magdalene when Angellotti, an escaped republican prisoner, begs him for help. He responds by giving him the key of his villa where he can hide.

Floria Tosca, a celebrated opera singer and Mario's mistress, arrives on the scene just in time to miss Angellotti. However, she is suspicious and thinks Mario has had an assignation with another woman. She is extremely jealous when she recognizes Countess D'Attavanti's features in the picture Mario is painting. Countess D'Attavanti is Angellotti's sister, who has been coming to pray in the church in the hope of leaving a key for her brother. It was then that Mario saw her, and in his picture blended her blonde features with Tosca's dark ones.

Baron Scarpia, the monstrous chief of police, traces the fugitive to the church, but he is too late for him. He uses this, however, as an opportunity to put Mario out of the way by implicating him in the escape, for Scarpia wants Tosca for himself. Scarpia has Mario arrested and invites Tosca to his apartment at the Farnese Palace, as he has news of Mario for her. Tosca is forced to reveal Angellotti's hiding-place to Scarpia, who will then cease Mario's torture. Once Tosca does this Scarpia tells her that Mario will be shot unless she consents to give herself to him. In that case the execution will be a fake, with dummy bullets. Tosca agrees, but demands a safe conduct via Civita Vecchia. Scarpia writes it, but as he advances to take her in his arms Tosca stabs him. She then hurries to the fortress of Sant' Angelo where Mario is imprisoned awaiting his execution. Tosca tells him of her bargain with Scarpia and that she will stand by to escape with him after the firing squad departs. The soldiers shoot and Mario falls. Tosca waits for them to leave. She then calls to Mario that it is safe to get up, only to find that Scarpia has cheated her to the end: Mario is dead.

Meanwhile Scarpia's murder has been discovered and his men hasten to arrest Tosca, who evades them and throws herself from the battlements to her death in the turgid Tiber below.

Puccini wrote an exciting entry for Floria Tosca and Callas lives up to its demands. From the moment we hear her 'Mario, Mario' offstage we know that this is a highly dramatic Tosca, passionate and very feminine. On her entrance Callas looks at once regal and a woman in love, impulsively torn with doubt. Yet by the way she runs to her lover it is as if her heart arrives even before her hands reach for him. Her movements also indicate her anxiety, but she never forgets to show her extreme piety. In the duet 'Ora stammi a sentir' (And now listen to me') she sings with a tenderness that gives her Tosca great femininity. The actual words 'Non la sospiri la nostra casetta?' ('Do you not long for our secluded cottage?') are delivered with a sensual beauty, which accounts for a sudden display of excessive jealousy a little later, when she recognizes the Countess D'Attavanti's features in the picture Mario is painting. The words 'Aspetta . . . aspetta . . . è l'Attavanti!' ('A moment . . . a moment . . . it's Attavanti!') are sung with a fiery intensity that could come only from an excessively jealous woman. Callas understands this important point very well, for unless we are aware of Tosca's pathological jealousy there seems to be no logical reason for the rest of the plot. Above all in this scene Callas's greatest achievement is her complete embodiment of a woman in love. The way she uses her beautiful hands as she embraces her lover, the way she strokes his hair, are a lesson in love-making. There is nothing here of the kind one gets from the usual Tosca—a caricature of a temperamental prima donna with little else. Instead Callas depicts a human being, capricious, tenderly loving and ready to battle against anyone who would try to harm the man she loves. How disarmingly, with just that right amount of coquettishness blended with simple charm, she tells Mario, as she leaves him, 'Ma falle gli occhi neri!' ('But do make her eyes dark!').

In the scene with Scarpia too she shows a superb ability to project quick changes of mood, especially when Scarpia shows her the fan, with her sudden explosion in 'La corona, lo stemma! E l'Attavanti!' ('A coronet, her coat-of-arms! It's Attavanti's!'). It is here that Callas's Tosca begins to gain our sympathy which so much helps to raise her situation in the second act to great heights of poignancy. This is a scene that brings unusual conviction as Tosca starts, so to speak, to enter the human trap Scarpia is setting for her. 'Traditor! Traditor! Oh mio bel nido insozzato di fango' ('Traitor! Traitor! You have brought mud in my beautiful nest') is sung with deeply felt grief as she wanders with the fan in her hand, having forgotten she is in a church. The jealousy, artfully incited by Scarpia, gives way to rage, when again Scarpia makes her realize she is in church. Humbly and distressed she sings 'Dio mi perdona. Egli vede ch'io piango' ('God will forgive me. He can see my tears'). Although a victim already of Scarpia, still she keeps her distance from his subtle approaches. When she notices Mario's coat lying where he has been painting, her eyes express with rare conviction that feeling of combination of great unhappiness and rage.

Callas reaches her peak in Act II. This is a distinctive and overwhelming performance, highly dramatic and full of emphasis, with an intensity of declamation that is rare among singers today. This is a Tosca of whom not only Puccini would have approved, but for whom Victorien Sardou might have well written the play. This is, unlike the usual conception of a rather unsubtle, haughty and temperamental prima donna, a stunning performance of a study in humanity. The way Callas alternates pleas with contempt in her terrible scene with Scarpia is magnificent by any standards. The vocal climaxes are exciting and so is her plea to Scarpia: 'È troppo soffrir! Ah! non posso più! Ah! non posso più!' ('Do not torment me any more! Ah! I can no more! Ah! I can no more!'). Her low notes in 'Torturate l'anima! . . . sì, l'anima mi torturate!' ('It is I, whom you torture so cruelly') have a warmth and sensuous beauty that are very much in keeping with Puccini's music. Her cry 'Assassino!' ('Murderer!') as she plucks up courage to blast Scarpia carries a permanent stamp that will always echo. Then the voice changes tenderly to 'Voglio vederlo' ('I want to see him'). Nor can we forget Callas's magnificently portrayed bitterness when she coldly asks Scarpia 'Quanto? Il prezzo' ('How much? Your price'). She is well aware already to what depth of cruelty this could go. The stress she puts on the word 'prezzo', together with the slight movement of her hand, carries with it a certain attempt to show that she can meet him on equal ground; that she believes he can be bought with money. The brewing storm as Tosca fences with Scarpia, at once his victim and victor, breaks out when Mario is dragged in from the torture chamber. Like a wild cat Callas jumps on the back of one of Scarpia's henchmen, who has been carrying Mario off to his death, beating him with clenched fists until he throws her on the floor. There she lies like a crumpled heap, helpless, in the end having to plead to Scarpia, 'Salvatello!' ('Save him').

It is in the aria 'Vissi d'arte, vissi d'amore' ('I have lived for art's sake and for love'), Tosca's only aria in the opera, that Callas, as in the murder scene later, brings her own amazing insight and throws new light. One cannot say that her rendering of this aria is the most beautiful ever when judged entirely from a vocal point of view, that is in the way that a voice completely even in colour could give. But then it could not be. What other Tosca can live through this aria more dramatically and express Tosca's moment of great despair so convincingly? The aria is more of a lament, in which Tosca piteously appeals to Scarpia for mercy for her lover by telling him of her pious actions. Here is a frightened and confused human being who finds herself completely and inescapably trapped. Suddenly this apparently imperious woman reveals the vulnerable child inside her. And Callas expresses all these emotions through the medium of her voice. The sounds she emits are like dark honey, yet floating softly. Just before the final phrase she shapes the music with a limpid tone that ravishes not only one's ear but one's heart. For a moment we are with her out of this world. Callas ends the aria on the words 'Ah, perchè me ne rimuneri cosi?' ('Why, oh why, my God, have you abandoned me thus?') in a *pianissimo* which is tender and immensely moving. What wonderful expression she gives to everything she does, even when she is not singing. In the hands of Callas the assassination scene is not an act of murder as such but more a terrifying insight of personal fear for self-preservation. Even though we know that Tosca is going to kill Scarpia, yet Callas always, in every performance, takes us by surprise. She never searches for the knife, but it seems that the knife finds her at just the right moment. While Scarpia is writing the supposed safe conduct for her she drinks some wine to fortify herself, when suddenly through the glass she sees the knife on the table, slightly magnified. We know what plan is forming itself in her mind, but nevertheless we don't think she will carry it out. Her eyes are riveted to the knife, having forgotten the glass in her hand which slowly, unbearably slowly, finds its way on to the table. Before anybody realizes what she is doing her arm shoots up and the knife is plunged into Scarpia as he approaches her. Her 'Questo e il bacio di Tosca' ('This is Tosca's kiss') is full of revenge while standing above him waiting for him to die in 'Muori dannato! Muori! Muori! Muori!' ('Die damned! Die! Die! Die!'). And then when the deed is done we realize together with her the full magnitude of Tosca's action; 'E morto! Or gli perdono!' ('He is dead! Now I forgive him') is sung in a tone that expresses fatalism, after which she intones 'E avanti a lui tremava tutta Roma!' ('And before him all Rome trembled') in a most convincing and unexaggerated way, free from any grotesquerie, and with deep feeling in every word of it. Overtaken by hysterical sobs she places candles on either side of the corpse.

In the short last act Callas gives us her best pure singing in the opera. She brings a wonderful lyricism to the fragmentary duet with Mario, and she is quite superb in the scene where, bringing out the actress in Tosca, she tells him not to laugh as the firing squad appears. Believing it to be a mock execution she tells Mario to fall lightly and not rise until she calls him 'Yes, like what Tosca does in the theatre'. In a voice that suggests utmost admiration she sings 'Là! Muori! Ecco un artista!' ('There! Die! What an artist!') when Mario falls, only to find that Scarpia has cheated her to the end. Her despair over the dead Mario is completely heart-breaking, making what follows a matter of logical conclusion. Her final cry 'O Scarpia, avanti a Dio!' ('Oh, Scarpia, we shall meet before God!') as she springs on to the parapet to throw herself to her death, is full of the drama one expects from this great singer-actress.

Although it is more difficult to identify Callas with conventional opera, her incursion into such works as *Tosca* has nevertheless added something new: probably the realism the opera so essentially needs. True there is the occasional sour note, especially in more recent years, but surely this is a drop in a vast ocean, for the final achievement of purpose is as vast as an ocean. Even bearing this in mind Callas's portrayal of Floria Tosca is a major contribution to twentieth-century Italian opera.

TURANDOT

Opera in three acts by Giacomo Puccini.
Libretto by Giuseppe Adami and Renato Simoni after Gozzi's Chinese fable.

Principal Characters

THE PRINCESS TURANDOT	Soprano
CALAF, the unknown prince	Tenor
LIU, a young slave girl	Soprano
TIMUR, the exiled king, CALAF's father . .	Bass

TIME: Legendary times.   PLACE: Peking.

First performed at La Scala, Milan, on 25th April 1926, with Rosa Raisa as Turandot, Miguel Fleta as Calaf and Maria Zamboni as Liu. Conductor, Arturo Toscanini.

Maria Callas first sang Turandot in January 1948 at the Teatro La Fenice, Venice; also at the Arena of Verona in 1948; at the San Carlo, Naples, and the Teatro Colon, Buenos Aires, in 1949.

Turandot, Puccini's last opera, was unfinished. Alfano finished the opera, following some outlines of the concluding duet, which were found after the composer's death. Alfano's tactfully arranged conclusion, however, cannot compensate for what would obviously have been the great climax of the work, and really after Liu's death scene the opera does not mean very much.

This opera is a fantastic fairy-tale, a blend of tragedy and comedy, expressed with an unusual grotesqueness, and stands apart from anything else that Puccini has written. This is mainly due to the subject. The music, although it retains all earlier Puccini characteristics, shows a definite development. It was a most unfortunate and ironical fate that Puccini never finished the final duet for which he had reserved all his creative powers. It might be that he could not finish it. Whatever the reason, had Puccini lived to finish the opera *Turandot* would undoubtedly have been his masterpiece.

Turandot—the name of the cruel ice-cold princess of ancient Peking. The princess slays all those who love her by setting them riddles, the penalty for failing to answer them correctly being death. But if they can answer the prize is herself and the throne of China.

Calaf, a young prince in disguise, thought to have been killed in battle, tries to win Turandot. In the crowd he meets his aged and blind father Timur, the exiled king of Mongolia, who is accompanied by a devoted slave girl, Liu. Nobody can dissuade the young prince from his perilous task.

Turandot appears and first tells that her bitter war against mankind is to avenge her ancestress, Lo-u-ling, who many years ago was betrayed by a foreign conqueror and carried into exile, where she died of grief. She then warns the stranger that the riddles are three, but there is only one death. The first riddle is asked: 'What is the phantom that is born every night to die in the morning?' Calaf answers: 'It is what now inspires me—hope.' Turandot proceeds: 'What is it that at times is like a fever, yet grows cold when you die; that also blazes up if you think of great deeds?' 'Blood' is the answer. Turandot, desperate now, asks the last riddle: 'What is the ice that sets you on fire?' Calaf, who at first seems to be at a loss, finally answers: 'It is Turandot.' He has won.

Turandot, defeated, pleads with her father to prevent the stranger from possessing her. Calaf now generously sets a riddle to Turandot—to guess his name and origin by morning—and then he will release her from her pledge and be ready to die. Turandot orders that none shall sleep in all Peking until someone finds out the name of the stranger. She then interrogates Liu and Timur. Liu's devotion is so great that when she can no longer bear the torture she seizes a dagger and stabs herself. Turandot faces the stranger who, despite her protests, boldly embraces and kisses her. She returns the kiss and admits that she loves him too. At the appointed time, before the crowd, Turandot declares the stranger's name: 'It is love.' Her icy heart has melted and the reign of terror is at an end.

Even those who are only slightly familiar with Callas's art would expect Turandot to be a 'Callas role'. This may be so because of certain exciting qualities in the character which one has learned to expect from her art. It is the great authority with which she invests the character of the cruel and cold Princess Turandot, with just that right blend of imperiousness and cold-ness that makes her performance thrilling and a great theatrical experience. She may lack a little of the steely and powerful voice and the steadiness in the extremely taxing upper ranges that the role so often demands, but I certainly doubt whether any other Turandot—and there have been many good ones—has ever made this role more completely memorable. Callas's Turandot has just that extra something, the something which is infinitely aristocratic and individual in her voice, and which adds a certain strange reality to everything she sings.

Callas's first singing appearance, when she delivers Princess Turandot's great address 'In questa reggia, or son mill'anni e mille' ('Within these regions, thousands and thousands of years ago') is a superb piece of theatre as well as also being vocally exceptional. She sings 'E quel grido, traverso stirpe e stirpe' ('Cry of anguish that is heard down the ages') with tremendous intensity and employs a most wonderful *mezza-voce*, a rather rare thing for *Turandot* interpreters, in the words 'Princepessa Lo-u-ling' ('Noble Princess Lo-u-ling').

The voice is a little hollow in her cry 'Quel grido e quella morte' ('That cry, that dying cry') but the phrase is held with a terrifying intensity and sweeps upwards, though somewhat unsteadily, in a thrilling way with 'No, No! Mai nessun m'avrà' ('No, No! They will not have me').

It is her telling facial expressions as well as her vocal

interpretation that make the 'Straniero! Non tentar la fortuna!' ('Stranger! Do not challenge your fortune!') so appropriately menacing. Also it is in the repeat of 'Gli enigmi sono tre, la morte è una' ('The riddles are three, there is one death'), when Turandot sings with Calaf, that Callas makes her point and chills one as she so thrillingly sails to a top C.

The riddle scene is excellently realized. There are one or two parts in which a slower pace would have been more effective, but again it is the excitement and drama of the whole situation that overwhelms us. How expertly does Callas, with the minimum of movement, make her impact! It is a moment to remember when she comes half way down the staircase and nervously sings 'Si! La speranza che delude sempre!' ('Yes. It is hope that falsely makes you go on!'). And when she is eventually defeated she tries to get out of it with fear, anger and a feminine iciness. The scene between the Princess Turandot and the slave girl Liu is marvellously played with great subtlety. Turandot asks 'Chi pose tanta forza nel tuo cuore?' ('What is it that gives you this power of resistance?').

This is where the composer left off. What follows is Puccini's—and yet it is not. Alfano finishes the opera after a fashion, but the dramatic interest diminishes so substantially that it is practically lost. All that remains is for Callas to apply her own interesting and intelligent personality, and this, together with her fine musicianship, raises the stature of the concluding scenes. There is a definite melting of the ice in the princess. Callas changes the tone of her voice and her 'Del primo pianto . . . Ah!' ('Ah! I have never wept before') is admirable. So is her 'Il suo nome è . . . Amor!' ('His name is . . . Love!').

One wonders what the last scene would have been like had Puccini been able to finish the opera in the way he hoped. One wonders also what Callas would have made of it then.

AIDA

Opera in four acts by Giuseppe Verdi.
Libretto by Antonio Ghislanzoni from the French of Camille du
Locle, scenario by the French archaeologist August-Édouard
Mariette Bey.

Principal Characters

AIDA, an Ethiopian princess, now slave of AMNERIS	Soprano
RHADAMÈS, an Egyptian general . . .	Tenor
AMNERIS, the Pharaoh's daughter . .	Mezzo-soprano
AMONASRO, King of Ethiopia . . .	Baritone
THE KING OF EGYPT	Bass

TIME: The time of the Pharaohs, probably during the period of
the Nineteenth Dynasty, 1230 B.C.
PLACE: Memphis and Thebes in Egypt.

First performed at the Teatro Khediviale, Cairo, on 24th
December 1871, with Antonietta Anastasi-Pozzoni as Aida,
Eleonora Grossi as Amneris and Pietro Mongini as Rhadamès.[1]
Maria Callas first sang Aida in Rovigo, Italy, in 1948. Also at
the Terme di Caracalla, Rome, in 1948; at the Teatro Colon,
Buenos Aires, and in Rome in 1949; at La Scala, Milan, at
Brescia, and the San Carlo, Naples, and in Mexico City, in 1950;
in Mexico City, in 1951; at Covent Garden, London and at the
Arena of Verona in 1953.

Verdi was commissioned to write *Aida* by Ismail Pasha, Khedive
of Egypt, for the newly built opera house in Cairo. *Aida* ranks as
one of Verdi's greatest operas, written on a grand scale yet full of
unbroken melodies which are highly expressive of the excellent
libretto.
In *Aida* Verdi showed a more mature style, and the opera is far
better constructed than any of his previous works. At its *première*

[1] The *première*, which was originally planned for January 1871, was delayed by the
Franco-Prussian War (scenery and costumes which were designed and constructed
in Paris could not leave the besieged city).

it was extremely successful. When a few months later it had its European *première* at La Scala, Milan, its reception was sensational. *Aida* today remains one of the grandest and most popular operas in the world.

Rhadamès, a young Egyptian general, is chosen by the goddess Isis to command the armies of Egypt against the Ethiopians. Amneris, the Pharaoh's daughter, is in love with Rhadamès, but he is unresponsive to her advances, for he is in love with Aida, a slave of Amneris. Aida is the daughter of the Ethiopian king Amonasro, but her identity is unknown to the Egyptians. She is torn between her love for the Egyptian Rhadamès and her love for her country. Amneris shows friendship towards her slave girl but is really very jealous of her. While Amneris is waiting for the victorious Rhadamès, suspecting Aida as her rival, she tricks her into confessing she is in love with Rhadamès. Rhadamès returns victorious, and the Pharaoh, as a reward, offers him the hand of Amneris. Aida recognizes her father Amonasro amongst the Ethiopian prisoners, but they both keep their identities secret. The king agrees to free the prisoners of war but Aida's father is kept as a hostage. Rhadamès appeals for mercy for the Ethiopian prisoners.

By the banks of the Nile Aida is waiting for Rhadamès, whom she is to meet for the last time, as on the next day he is to marry Amneris. Amonasro, however, who has eluded his guards, comes first and, cunningly making use of Aida's feelings, forces her to trick Rhadamès into telling her the way the Egyptians are to march again against the Ethiopians. Reluctantly she consents, and when Rhadamès arrives she succeeds in persuading him to flee with her to Ethiopia where they will be safe. She asks him, 'By which path can we avoid meeting the Egyptian army?—The path chosen by our troops will be deserted until tomorrow.' The Napata gorges is the answer. Rhadamès is tricked and Amonasro, who has overheard everything, reveals his presence and, after he declares himself as the King of Ethiopia, tries to make Rhadamès fly with them. But the delay is fatal, for Amneris, who was praying in the nearby temple, surprises them. Amonasro and Aida flee, whilst Rhadamès, realizing he has betrayed his country, surrenders his sword to the priests. Amneris tries to win Rhadamès's love by promising to save his life if he will renounce Aida. He refuses and chooses to die. The priests formally condemn him to death. Beneath the floor of the Temple of Phtha Rhadamès is to be buried alive. When the last stone seals the tomb he discovers that Aida has concealed herself in the tomb. The lovers die in each other's arms, while above Amneris laments the tragedy she has brought about and prays for Rhadamès's soul.

Vocally the role of Aida is not a 'natural' for Callas. Yet her ability to see the role as a whole, together with the dramatic intensity and pathos she brings to it, make her one of the greatest Aidas. She fully realizes Aida's position as a princess-slave who is torn between love and patriotism. This is a gripping performance, very much in the grand manner, and constantly reveals new points of interest and delight. But it is the way Callas explores Aida's human predicament in the wonderful series of dramatic duets that Verdi's inexhaustible melodic inspiration has so masterfully contrived for her, that this Aida conquers our hearts. Callas accords Verdi's musical and emotional climaxes all their full value.

Her entrance in Act I and her first aria 'Ritorna vincitor!' ('Return victorious!') is nothing short of a *tour de force*. One must mention that she sometimes sacrifices a smooth line, even a tonal change of vocal colour, but for a dramatic expression for which one can forgive almost anything in the evidence of such results. What other Aida today can express her conflicting emotions with more conviction in such forceful music? And what other Aida can sing as Callas does the superb lines in the aria 'Ah! Non fu in terra mai da più crudeli angoscie in core affranto!' ('Ah! Never on earth was a heart torn by more cruel anguish!') The prayer section of the aria beginning with 'Numi, pietà del mio soffrir!' ('Gods, have pity on my suffering!') is sung with extraordinary beauty, exquisite style and phrasing.

It is in moments such as Aida's duet with Amneris, in Act II, that Callas always scores a great success. Her restraint is excellent when she suddenly realizes that she is acting like a princess instead of a slave girl in 'Mia rivale! Ebben sia pure . . . Anch', io son tal!' ('My rival! Well, even so . . . I also am such!'). She expresses superbly her hopelessness at the end of this scene when she repeats 'Numi, pietà del mio soffrir. Numi, pietà!'

In the finale of the triumphant scene in Act II Callas's superb acting and general artistry are unrivalled. One can never forget her expression, her singing, everything about her at the moment when she recognizes her father amongst the prisoners. There is an anxiety full of emotional intensity in her words 'Che veggo? Egli? Mio padre!' ('What do I see? Him? My father!'). Not even wild horses could have stopped this Aida from meeting her father. In the ensemble singing that follows Callas's thrilling voice rides gloriously over all. 'Ma tu, re, tu signore possente' ('But you, O King, you powerful lord') is sung with a touching beauty. The scene ends with the chorus 'Gloria all Egitto' ('Glory to Egypt'), above which we hear Callas's superbly managed cry 'Qual speme, o mai più restami? A lui la gloria, il trono, a me l'oblio' ('What hope now remains for me? For him, glory and the throne. For me, oblivion').

Act III, the Nile scene, is one of Verdi's great creations. Indeed this act is one of the most powerful in all opera. With the exception of some vocal shortcomings Callas surpasses herself in her aria 'O patria mia, mai più ti rivedrò' ('O my country, I shall not see you any more'). She breathes memories of her fatherland with all the beauty and nostalgia that Verdi intended. Some notes, however, and especially the final one of the aria, are not so steady and sweet as one could have wished; a partial failure in an otherwise perfect whole. In the duet that follows between Aida and her father Amonasro, Callas gives an exciting performance that is simply greatness, both vocally and histrionically. Even her excessive weight (that she had during the time when she was singing Aida on the stage) does not seem to matter, for she always employs a certain economy of movement that is most expressive. Of course there is always the most assured vocal delivery with which she sweeps all before her. Her dramatic outburst 'Un giorno solo di sì dolce incanto, un' ora, un' ora di tal gioia, e poi morir' ('One day of such enchantment, one hour, one hour of such joy, and then I would die') is a moment when Callas's greatness wins us completely. Her cries of horror in 'Orrore! Che mi consigli tu? No! No! Giammai!' ('Horror! What are you asking? No! No! Never!'), when Amonasro finally makes his demands, are like the cries of a wounded tigress. To the grandeur and sensitivity that she brings to phrases like 'Ancor tua figlia potrai chiamarmi della mia patria degna sarò' ('You will still call me your daughter . . . I shall be worthy of my country'), with 'degna sarò' she adds a strange realism in her wonderful low notes. And then, in a tone that contrasts strongly with Amonasro's savage imprecation, she whispers loudly 'O patria, patria, quanto mi costi' ('O my country, my country, how much you cost me').

The duet with Rhadamès, which ends the act, provides further feats of enchantement. As she begins with 'Là tra foreste vergini' ('There, in virgin forests') Callas becomes most feminine and uses a tone charged with seductive rapture. The whole scene becomes exotic by the final lines, when Aida tricks Rhadamès into betraying his country.

In the tomb scene which ends the opera, Callas caresses the section beginning with 'Vedi? di morte l'angelo radiante' ('Do you see? Death's radiant angel') and enchants one with her beautifully managed downward *portamento*. In the final duet, 'O Terra, addio' ('O Earth, farewell'), her singing has a muted passion and a stillness that leave us equally ecstatic.

I PURITANI

Opera in three acts by Vincenzo Bellini.
Libretto by Count Carlo Pepoli, after the play *Têtes Rondes Et Cavaliers*, by François Ancelot and Saintine.

Principal Characters

ELVIRA, daughter of LORD WALTON . . .	Soprano
LORD ARTHUR TALBOT, of the Cavaliers . . .	Tenor
LORD GAULTIERS WALTON, of the Puritans . .	Bass
SIR RICHARD FORTH, of the Puritans . . .	Bass

TIME: During the wars between Cromwell and the Stuarts.
PLACE: Near Plymouth, England.

First performed at Théâtre des Italiens, Paris, on 24th January 1835, with Giulia Grisi as Elvira and Rubini as Arturo.
Maria Callas first sang Elvira in January 1949 at the Teatro La

Fenice, Venice. Also in Rome in 1949; in Mexico City and Rome in 1952; at the Lyric Theatre, Chicago, in 1955; and at Covent Garden, London (mad scene only) in 1958.

I Puritani was Bellini's last work. He died in the autumn of the same year as its *première*. In this opera he tried to develop his style rather than change it, and also paid more attention to orchestration than in any of his previous works. The opera was successful at its *première*, but was not to enjoy the fame of *Norma* or *La Sonnambula*, the other two Bellini operas which together form the wonderful trilogy of Bellini's more mature works. In the autumn of 1835, the year of the opera's *première*, the opera was again given in Paris to open a new season. A few hours later the same singers were taking part in Bellini's funeral service, singing the tenor melody from Act III, arranged as a Lacrymosa.

Lord Walton, the Roundhead governor of Plymouth, plans to wed his daughter Elvira to fellow Roundhead Sir Richard Forth. Elvira is, however, in love with a Royalist, Lord Arthur Talbot (Arturo), of whom her father at first strongly disapproves, but eventually agrees to the marriage.

Queen Henrietta, widow of Charles I of England, who is under sentence of death, is kept a prisoner in Plymouth castle. While Elvira, who has, according to custom, dropped her veil at the door, waits at the altar, Lord Arthur learns that Queen Henrietta is a prisoner at the castle. He seizes the opportunity and, throwing the bridal veil over the queen, the Royalist soldier helps her to escape to France. Lord Arthur is forced to hide as, in his efforts to help the queen, he is banished as a traitor.

Elvira, believing herself to have been deserted at the altar steps, loses her reason. Later, on meeting him she regains her sanity, but Arthur is captured and condemned to death, only to be saved by the timely defeat of the Roundheads. With great rejoicings the happy couple are united.

As Elvira, Callas gives a performance much to her advantage. Vocally she is astonishingly at home with the music Bellini gave to his last heroine. One wonders whether the quasi-recitative passages have been sung before with so much expression; a gift which only Callas, amongst present-day singers, seems to possess. Her performance is one that has a brilliance and vividness coupled with a virtuosity that would compare favourably with any other. Like so many other Bellini roles, which she has resurrected and re-established in the way that they were originally conceived by the composer, *I Puritani* is no exception. Indeed in this opera Callas has infused her portrayal of the frail and gentle Puritan maiden with much more personal insight than we are ever aware. Elvira becomes a more convincing, more 'living' character. Bellini would have found in Callas's feat of virtuosity and *coloratura* agility that never fails to be an integral part of the drama, an artist who could do full justice to his aims. No wonder then the great Bellini revivals; for, with the right interpreters, the music of Bellini can easily cast its magic spell.

We first hear Callas's voice offstage floating in the prayer 'La luna, il sol, le stelle' ('The moon, the sun, the stars'). This makes her first entrance more anxiously anticipated. Her first aria 'Sai come arde in petto mio' ('Well you know a fond emotion') is sung with such simplicity that Elvira is immediately endeared to us.

In the duet that follows between Elvira and her uncle she brings out all the passionate frailty and anxiety that are now associated with Elvira. Her singing of the Polonaise 'Son vergin vezzosa' ('I am a blithesome maiden'), apart from a slight tendency to scoop on crescendos, is brilliant and sparkles with gaiety. The florid passages are accurate and the initial note 'Ah', with which Elvira enters, is very exciting. There is a concealed anxiety, as if something tragic is about to happen, in her wonderful entrance, dressed in her bridal gown. When she screams 'Alas!' it is easy to see that Elvira has lost her reason. All the innocent hilarity of the loving girl vanishes, as though insanity has suddenly attacked her. The approach of madness was evident in the simple yet expressive way she tore Arthur's bracelet from her neck. Her cries 'Arturo! Tu ritorni?' ('Arthur! Why don't you return?'), when she imagines she sees Arthur, are both lyrical and mournful. Her aria 'Oh, vieni al tempio' ('Oh, come to the altar') is a masterpiece of expressive vocalization, and so is her lamenting 'Qual febbre vorrace m'uccide!' ('What a fever is raging inside me!') when her voice rides over the chorus.

Again we first hear Elvira approaching offstage, singing at the beginning of her big scene 'O, rendetemi la speme o lasciate, lasciatemi morir' ('Ah, restore in me the faith or let me, let me die!'). This is one of the loveliest and most musical mad scenes in the whole history of opera. It finds Callas at the summit of her powers, both as a vocalist of extraordinary ability and a great artist of vocal interpretation. Each note, each word, each syllable is part of a wonderful whole; the actual aria 'Qui la voce sua soave' ('Here, his voice so tender') is sung with a marvellous *legato*. She achieves a melancholy beauty and pathos which create almost unbearable tension, yet she handles everything with loving delicacy and care. And how well she uses her hands that so simply say so much, achieving a dramatic effect that blends superbly with the expression of the music. There are countless little details, like the catch in her voice on the word 'morir' in 'lasciate, lasciatemi morir' ('Let me, let me die'), as if she were choking. There is not a single phrase that is not filled with an amazing eloquent significance. There are minor vocal faults, however, such as a tendency to scoop on some notes in some of the rising major sixths. The recitative that follows with her uncle is so obviously delivered by a true musician that one does not feel the slightest discontinuity in this big scene. Only a great actress could have spoken to herself with so much convincing naïvité the words 'E gli piange, forsè amò?' ('He is weeping—is it for love?'). The brilliant cabaletta 'Vien diletto, è in ciel la luna' ('Come beneath the moon and sky') is breathtaking. Callas never treats it as a mere exhibition piece, and easily puts singers of the past in the shade. We find yet again in her a most thoughtful singer, a rare quality. Her descending scales are incomparable. There is nothing purely mechanical about them, for they are all sung with such musicianship that they are completely integrated with the drama.

In the final duet, restoring order, Callas's impassioned singing carries a spark that convinces us of her restored sanity.

NORMA

Opera in two acts by Vincenzo Bellini.
Libretto by Felice Romani, based on Alexandre Soumet's tragedy
Norma.

Principal Characters

NORMA, Druid high priestess . . .	Soprano
ADALGISA, a virgin of the temple . .	Mezzo-soprano
POLLIONE, Roman Governor . . .	Tenor
OROVESO, Druid chief priest, father of NORMA	Bass

TIME: Around 50 B.C., during the Roman occupation.
PLACE: Gaul.

First performed at La Scala, Milan, on 26th December 1831,
with Giuditta Pasta as Norma, Giulia Grisi as Adalgisa and
Domenico Donzelli as Pollione.

Maria Callas first sang Norma on 17th June 1949 at the Teatro
Colon, Buenos Aires. Also in Rome, Venice and Mexico City in
1950; in Palermo and Teatro Bellini, Catania, and in Rio de
Janeiro in 1951; at La Scala, Milan, Covent Garden, London, and
Rome in 1952; at Trieste in 1953; in Chicago in 1954; at the
Metropolitan, New York, and in Philadelphia in 1956; at Covent
Garden, London, in 1957; in Rome (first act only) in 1958; at
Epidaurus, Greece, in 1960; in Paris in 1964 and 1965.

In spite of the magnificent cast that was assembled the first
performance of *Norma* was a '*fiasco fiaschissimo*', to use Bellini's
own words. This had nothing to do with the merits of the opera,
but was due entirely to the machinations of the patroness of
a rival composer, Giovanni Paccini, who arranged for a hostile
audience to be present on the opening night. Later on, during the
summer of 1832, at Bergamo, *Norma* won the success it deserved.

Norma is a work of great lyrical and dramatic beauty, and the
structure of the music that expresses the dramatic action is
virtually of epic scale with a constantly rising dramatic climax
culminating to the divine finale of the opera.

The role of Norma has been called the most difficult in the operatic repertoire, for unless the Norma herself is absolutely first rate the opera disintegrates. In the 130 years of its existence, famous Normas have been very few and far between. Giuditta Pasta, Maria Malibran, Giulia Grisi, Lilli Lehmann,[1] Teresa Titjiens and Rosa Ponselle, the last of the great Normas who sang the role in the twenties, complete the short list.[2]

The opera begins with the Druids awaiting the arrival of Norma, the high priestess of the Druids and a demigoddess to her people, to advise them when they should rebel against the Romans, their cruel oppressors. Norma, however, has long broken her vows and fallen in love with Pollione, the Roman Governor, their greatest enemy, by whom she has secretly had two children. The Roman is faithless, and he has now fallen in love with Adalgisa, another Druid priestess, with whom he is planning to elope to Rome. Adalgisa confides in Norma that she is in love with a stranger and begs her to relieve her of her sacred vows. The stranger is none other than Pollione, and when Norma learns this, in her rage, she decides to kill her two children.

Unable to bring herself to do the actual deed, Norma begs Adalgisa to take them and go away with Pollione. Adalgisa, on the other hand, says she will go to Pollione only to persuade him to return to Norma. But Adalgisa fails in her mission and Pollione, who has tried to carry Adalgisa by force, on entering the sacred temple is arrested and brought before Norma to be judged. Norma declares war against the Romans. Pollione is to be the sacrificial victim and Norma is expected to strike the fatal blow. But first Norma pleads with him to leave Adalgisa. He refuses. Then Norma says that with him his two children will die, to say nothing of the thousands of Romans who will perish. The Roman then asks her to kill him alone, but Norma cannot bring herself to do it for, in spite of everything, she still loves him. Norma confesses her own guilt, tearing off the sacred wreath, and asks her father, Oroveso, who is the high priest of the Druids, to spare

[1] Lilli Lehmann always considered the role of Norma more demanding than the three Brünnhilde roles in Wagner's *Der Ring des Nibelungen*.

[2] The great Pauline Viardot-García (Malibran's younger sister), who had sung Norma several times during her career, knew that somehow the part was beyond her. The last word that she uttered, at the age of ninety, before she died was 'Norma', the role in which complete success had just eluded her.

her two children. Pollione, recognizing Norma's greatness, feels his love for her return and together they ascend the funeral pyre, the penalty for sacrilege, to die united and purified.

It is a great moment in *Norma* when Callas first appears on the stage, for one is expecting a demigoddess, and this Norma not only looks like a demigoddess, but she also sings like one. She begins her recitative 'Sediziose voci' ('Seditious words') just before her prayer, the celebrated aria 'Casta Diva' ('Chaste Goddess'), most authoritatively: her people are completely subjected to her. There is an unusual beauty in her singing of 'E il sacro vischio io mieto' ('And I cut the sacred mistletoe'), to a splendid *diminuendo* on 'io mieto' just before the 'Casta Diva'.

'Casta Diva' is at once lyrical and full of mystery. The veiled tone in Callas's voice is sensitively used to begin this aria. But the real mystery of her sacred nature is expressed when she reaches the *passagio* in F; by some mystifying alchemy the voice seems to become effortless in the *coloratura* part of the aria, and even more so in the vocally formidable cadenza at the end.[1]

In the short recitative between the aria and the cabaletta, Callas gives us a glimpse of the more mortal side of Norma's character, as she dismisses the Druids from the sacred ritual with 'Cadrà . . . punirlo io posso; ma punirlo il cor non sa' ('He fall? Yes, I can kill him, but my heart cannot'). The cabaletta 'Ah! Bello a me ritorno' ('Ah! My first love would return') which follows with its chromatic *glissandi*, holds no terrors for Callas; the *coloratura* singing is not only breathtaking but also, as it should be, an integral part of the dramatic expression in the music. The whole scene in such capable hands, with such an infinite variety of contrasting and consenting expressive elements, maintains a rare agreeable unity.

In the second act we find this Norma womanly, worried by doubts and tender, as she embraces her children in the privacy of her house. And when Adalgisa confesses her own illicit love, with beauty and simplicity, Callas sings 'Oh, rimembranza!' ('Oh,

[1] Callas has in many performances of *Norma* (Covent Garden in 1953, La Scala in 1955, etc.) sung 'Casta Diva' in the original G major key as well as the two Norma-Adalgisa duets in the original higher key. Giuditta Pasta, the creator of Norma, sang 'Casta Diva' a tone down, from G major to F major; a transposition that all published scores, except the autograph score, show.

what remembrance!') as she nostalgically relives the emotion of being loved by Pollione. Then suddenly the change to the vindictive woman, the wronged mother, the woman who senses she is lost, as she finds out how Pollione has so utterly betrayed her with another woman, her friend Adalgisa. 'Tremi tu? È per chi?' ('You tremble? And for whom?'), as she faces Pollione at her doorstep, is terrifying and full of contempt. What a difference from her lyrical 'Casta Diva' to her biting scorn at Pollione in the trio 'Oh, di qual sei tu vittima!' ('Oh, how you became the victim!') which closes the scene with Norma's reproachful 'Va! Va!' ('Go! Go!') as she orders Pollione out of her house.

In the second scene of Act II Norma is alone, contemplating killing her children. Callas, in her singing, lives through a wide range of emotion: from the ferocious 'Di Pollion son figli' ('You are the sons of Pollione') to the tender but choked cry 'Ah, no! Son miei figli' ('Ah, no! They are my sons'). The duet 'Mira, O Norma' ('You see, O Norma'), that follows between Norma and Adalgisa, is probably the most celebrated duet in all Italian Opera. It is sung in thirds, and it is essential that both ladies should sing absolutely perfectly on pitch. Of all the Adalgisas who have sung together with this Norma Ebe Stignani and Giulietta Simionato have been the best. 'Mira, O Norma', and the rondo 'Sì, fino all ore' that follows, express the reconciliation of the two women and, when sung as superbly as this, the duet truly deserves its fame.

In the last act we find Norma waiting, clutching her last hopes. In 'Ei tornerà!' ('He will return!') she gives to her voice a very feminine tone that expresses hope and doubt at the same time, only to change to rage when she finds that Pollione will not return to her. For a while again she becomes the demigoddess to her people as she ferociously strikes the shield of Irminsul that brings the Druids to hear her declare war on the Romans. 'Guerra! Strage! Sterminio!' ('War, pillage and death!') is sung with rage that is underlined with despair. Callas's hands, as always, play a great part in this. It seems that, as she raises her hand, she tries to obtain authority from this gesture in order to hide her despair.

There is a world of meaning in 'Sì, Norma' ('Yes, it is Norma') when she sings it, as Pollione, a prisoner, is brought before her; as if she were only then realizing the true magnitude of her situation. The duet 'In mia man' alfin tu sei' ('You are in my hands at last') is nothing short of perfection, and shows us Callas both as a singer and an actress of the highest imaginable rank. Her bitterness, especially in the opening of the duet, is a feat of vocal expression. The sadness in the colour she suddenly employs in the second verse of the duet 'Pel tuo Dio pei figli tuoi' ('For your God's sake, your children') sung in *mezza-voce* superbly expresses her conflicting passions. The *diminuendo* on 'Son io' ('It is I') that diminishes from the greatest intensity to the smallest, so full of dramatic expression when she makes her confession of guilt, admirably personifies in the hands of an artist of Callas's calibre the complete collapse of a human being who knows that death is the only absolution.

From 'Qual cor tradisti' ('The heart, you have betrayed') on her singing assumes a rare beauty and forms yet another fitting climax to the opera. And when Pollione tells her that his love is reborn for her Callas momentarily becomes all woman, expressing a satisfaction within herself that she, however, knows is a hopeless case. Her pleadings with her father, who repels her, to forgive her achieve a pathos that builds to sublime heights in 'Deh! Non volerli vittime' ('Oh, do not make them victims') when she remembers her children. The way she sings 'di lor pietà' with a shriek of despair, without ever straying from the music, or the arpeggio that she spins out in 'Ah, padre, un prego ancor' ('Ah, father, my last prayer'), will always remain in the memory of those who have heard it as a deeply felt human drama. Divine is the only word to describe the heights of eloquence and harmony that are reached in the infinitely moving finale of the opera where Callas, using her hands as if to express her heart and her voice to express her soul, hangs on her father's shoulders in 'Padre, ah, padre! Tu mei prometti?' ('Father, ah, father! You promise me?'), begging him to spare her children.

Callas's interpretation of the tragic Druid priestess, that brings the personal drama with so much conviction, is the major achievement of a genius.

True there are vocal flaws here and there (for that matter no singer could be flawless in this role. The greatest of Normas, including Pasta, the creator of the role, we know were not at all flawless), such as forcing of tone, an unevenness in certain notes or a high note that might end unevenly. But with what compensations!

Just as our grandfathers would tell us of an earlier great Norma, so we shall tell our own grandchildren of this great Norma, *the* Norma of our generation.

IL TROVATORE

Opera in four acts by Giuseppe Verdi.
Libretto by Salvatore Cammarano, completed after his death by L. E. Bardare, based on Antonio Garcia Gutierrez's play, *El Trovador*.

Principal Characters

COUNT DI LUNA, a young nobleman of Aragon	Baritone
MANRICO, a young chieftain under the Prince of Biscay, reputed son of AZUCENA . .	Tenor
LEONORA, lady-in-waiting to the Princess of Aragon	Soprano
AZUCENA, a wandering gipsy of Biscay . .	Mezzo-soprano
FERRANDO, a captain of COUNT DI LUNA's guard	Bass

TIME: During the civil war in the fifteenth century.
PLACE: Biscay and Aragon, Spain.

First performed at the Apollo Theatre, Rome, on 19th January 1853, with Rosina Penco as Leonora, Carlo Baucardè as Manrico and Emilia Coggi as Azucena.

Maria Callas first sang Leonora in Mexico City in June 1950. Also at the San Carlo, Naples, in 1951; at La Scala, Milan; Covent Garden, London; Arena of Verona and in Rome in 1953; and at the Lyric Theatre, Chicago, in 1955.

In spite of the absurdities of its libretto, *Il Trovatore* is one of the most popular and most often performed operas in the world. It seems that the uninterrupted melodiousness that is to be found in the music, a melodiousness that is full of vitality and passion, with hardly a boring moment, and which is by no means without

Cherubini: *Medea*

Callas as the Barbarian Colchian Princess achieved a characterisation
that is classic, unique in its infinite variety and utterly unchallengeable.

The end of a triumph. Thanks from both sides of the footlights.

(Callas as Medea at La Scala, Milan)

ABOVE. Cherubini: *Medea*. All Medea's anguish, jealousy, pride and vengeance; the woman who became a curse to humanity.
BELOW. Puccini: *Tosca*. The beginning of Scarpia's bargaining with Tosca; at once his victim and victor. Maria Callas with Tito Gobbi.

Puccini: *Tosca*

A memorable Tosca that both Puccini and Sardou would have
approved.

Rossini: *Il Turco in Italia*

Callas in Dona Fiorilla possibly found her best comic characterisation.

Ponchielli: *La Gioconda*

Callas as Gioconda made her Italian début in 1947, an event that was
destined to change the operatic world.

Bellini: *La Sonnambula*

The role of Amina fitted Maria like a glove.

Bellini: *La Sonnambula*

Maria created a wonderful Amina in Visconti's production. Here she is seen with
Nicola Zaccaria in La Scala's 1955 production

dramatic significance, accounts for its popularity. One reason for the inadequacy of the libretto is that a considerable part of the story is supposed to have happened before the curtain goes up. Also the play *El Trovador*, on which the libretto of *Il Trovatore* was based, is a lengthy melodrama based on historical fact, and in which a complicated series of plots take place against a backcloth of one of the Spanish civil wars. The reduction of this lengthy play into a relatively shorter opera libretto stripped it of its political background. The compression resulted in a series of episodic scenes, which are largely governed by possible improbabilities, since the background explains the actions of the principal characters. On its first production the opera was enthusiastically received, an enthusiasm prompted almost entirely by its wonderful melodies. The same enthusiasm continues, for today *Il Trovatore* is staged in practically every opera house in the world.

The opera begins with Ferrando, the captain of the guard, relating to his men, who are keeping watch in the guard-room of the palace of Count di Luna, the story of the count's brother. The old Count di Luna, now dead, had two sons of about the same age. One of these sons was stolen by a gipsy girl, Azucena, in revenge for the burning of her mother by the count. Years later the stolen child, Manrico, who was brought up by Azucena, becomes a troubadour and is in love with the beautiful Duchess Leonora. Count di Luna, who is also in love with Leonora, catches Manrico serenading Leonora, and in a fight wounds him, but he escapes. Leonora, thinking Manrico dead, decides to take the veil. The count tries to carry Leonora off by force to prevent her from becoming a nun. Manrico interposes and takes Leonora himself to Castellor, where they are besieged by the count's forces. Manrico receives news that Azucena has been captured and is to be burned at the stake, as one of the courtiers recognized her as the gipsy who stole the count's brother. Manrico makes a heroic sortie, but is captured and thrown in the same cell as Azucena. Leonora, to save Manrico, consents to become the count's wife. She goes to Manrico in his cell and announces his release. He is, however, horrified, for he suspects the price Leonora has paid for this. But Leonora, who never intended to carry out her bargain

F

with the count, has already taken poison and now falls dead in Manrico's arms. The count enters and, on seeing Leonora dead, orders Manrico's immediate execution. As the count exclaims 'It is over,' Azucena screams 'That was your brother, O Mother! You are avenged!'

The role of Leonora is one which reveals the degree to which Callas's art is a major contribution to Italian Opera. She has given to this often performed opera new life and understanding. Just as it should be, her presentation is basically that of an aristocratic lady. She understands and conveys, with all the formality that is demanded of her, Leonora's passionate humanity. Also she gives the role all the Spanish fervour it requires, at the same time revealing countless little suspected dramatic subtleties in her masterly portrayal.

In her singing she approaches a rare perfection. Her musical phrasing can only be compared to that of a master virtuoso violinist playing on a Stradivarius. Her voice amazes us in scene after scene. One feels that one is hearing all those marvellous trills, the scales and the arpeggios for the first time. They were always there before, when other good sopranos sang them, but they were somehow not the same; now they take on a new meaning. Her inflections on the long phrases are exquisite, no less so her *portamentos* and, above all, the fine musicianship that brings grandeur to Verdi's melodies.

Her first recitative is tellingly delivered with a sense of the meaning of every word. In her aria 'Tacea la notte placida' ('The night was calm and peaceful') Callas gives us a highly and subtly romantic kind of singing, with a most exciting crescendo on the words 'dolci s'udiro e flebili' ('touched by an unseen hand'). There is an extraordinary intensity and excitement when she sings 'Versi di prece ed umile qual d'uom che prega Iddio' ('It was like a humble prayer to Heaven, devoutly made'). It is in the rapid and difficult cabaletta that follows, 'Di tale amor che dirsi' ('In my heart there is a raging flame'), that Callas comes entirely into her own, and her best is *the* best. Her *coloratura* singing here is absolutely impeccable, both vocally and histrionically, leaving nothing more to be desired. The act ends with a very exciting trio 'Un instante almen dia loco' ('Stay for a moment and let me implore you'), in which she pleads with intensity and excitement, yet still remaining very much the great lady. There is a great humanity in Leonora's final words, 'Te amar non vuol-nè-può, no non può' ('My heart will never claim you, will never claim you'), when she swoons, as Manrico and the count rush off to fight their duel. Callas's excellent instinct and insight make this a memorable scene.

In the convent scene Callas does not come off quite so spectacularly as expected; good though she is, she does not reach to the high standards she has led us to expect. 'E deggio . . . e posso crederlo?' ('Can I really believe my eyes?') is slightly imperfect, slightly lacking in the expression of amazement. She, however, in this scene sings 'Perchè piangete? O dolci amiche' ('Why are you weeping? Oh, sweet friends') most touchingly.

Callas excels most in her big scene of Act IV; here she is perfection itself. Her recitative 'Timor di me? Sicura presta è la mia difesa' ('This poisoned ring will, if necessary, defend me') is most expressively delivered with perfect timing and tonal colour. She truly distinguishes herself in the aria that follows, 'D'amor sull'ali rosee' ('Borne on the rosy wings of love'). Whatever ovation she receives after this aria, it is never more than she deserves. This is singing very much in the grand manner. The actual spanning of the phrases, the trills, especially those on the words 'rosee' and 'dolente', that so touchingly express Leonora's anxiety and sorrow with such an ardently pathetic colour, are effects to be wondered at. Surely one had not heard them before in our generation—yet they must have been in the music all the time. And what marvellous expression, with a kind of ethereal beauty, does Callas's fine musicianship contribute to this beautiful aria Verdi wrote for Leonora. The final phrase 'le pene, le pene del mio cor' could only be compared yet again with the playing of the finest virtuoso violinist.

The 'Miserere' scene, beginning with Leonora's 'Quel suon quelle preci' ('The prayer for the dying'), is so expertly sung that, hackneyed though this piece of music may be, it comes to us fresh and rejuvenated, and again we feel as if we are hearing it for the first time, with all its dramatic accents, that only a dramatic *soprano d'agilità* could give, especially after a lyrical aria such as 'D'amor sull'ali rosee'. Her wonderfully warm low notes sound lovely in 'Sull'arrida torre ochi! par che la morte' ('I hear in the darkness the angel of death'). One wonders whether 'Tu vedrai che amore in terra mai del mio non fu più forte' ('You will see that no woman has ever loved with more passion') has ever been sung with such intensity, yet at the same time vocalized so perfectly, without a single note thrown out of balance.

Her scene with the count that follows is no less admirable. She lives every moment of it, astonishing us with her dynamic phrasing. The echo of her plea to the count in 'Salva deh! salva, salva il Trovator!' ('Save, oh save, save the Troubadour'), and especially the way she utters the word 'Conte' as she clings to him, is most moving. Her florid singing in the cabaletta 'Vivrà! Contende il giubilo' ('He lives! Oh, God, I now thank you') is breathtaking and completely in character.

Leonora's death scene is beautifully touching, as Callas, poisoned, soars to the words 'Prima che d'altri vivere, io volli tua morir' ('Rather than live as someone else's bride, I would have died as yours'). And then, as she utters 'Manrico, addio, morir' ('Manrico, goodbye, I die') she seems to touch our very hearts.

IL TURCO IN ITALIA

Opera in two acts by Gioacchino Antonio Rossini.
Libretto by Felice Romani.

Principal Characters

SULTAN SELIM, the Turk	Bass
FIORILLA	Soprano
DON GERONIO, a wealthy and elderly husband to FIORILLA	Bass
ZAIDA	Mezzo-soprano
NARCISSO	Tenor
PROSDOCIMO, the poet, in search of a plot .	Baritone

TIME: The eighteenth century.   PLACE: Naples, Italy.

The opera was first performed on 14th August 1814 at La Scala,

Milan, with Maffei-Festa as Fiorilla, Filippo Galli as Selim and
Giovanni David as Narcisso.

Maria Callas first sang the role of Fiorilla at the Teatro Eliseo,
Rome, in October 1950, and at La Scala, Milan, in April 1955.

The opera at its *première* at La Scala, Milan, was very coldly
received. There was nothing wrong with Rossini's music. The
trouble was that the Milanese audience thought the opera devoid
of any individuality, and a poor copy of Rossini's earlier work
L'Italiana in Algeri, which he very successfully wrote for Venice,
Milan's rival city. The whole thing was considered by the Milanese
as a personal insult. Rossini could have done this for any other
theatre, but for La Scala, the greatest temple of melodrama,
surely this was too much.

Four years later, however, the opera was revived in Milan, and
this time it was triumphantly successful.

From 1855 to 1950 the opera was not heard in Italy at all, and it
was largely due to the presence of Maria Callas that the opera was
revived and re-established. *Il Turco in Italia* is a most delightful
opera. True it may not have the perfection of Mozart's comic
operas, but nevertheless it is full of deliciously funny things, all
expressed in sparkling tunes.

Prosdocimo, the poet, visits a gipsy encampment near Naples
in search of material to write a comedy for his patron. Among the
gipsies there are two Turks, Zaida and Albazar, who have fled
from their country. Don Geronio arrives in search of a gipsy to
tell him his fortune. He hopes that in his fortune the gipsy will
give him hope that with time and patience he will succeed in
curing the deranged mind of his very much younger wife,
Fiorilla.

Fiorilla, the gay and extremely flirtatious wife of Geronio, is
telling her friends of her stormy love life, and preaches in favour
of infidelity. Soon afterwards Selim, a Turkish prince, arrives,
and Fiorilla, who already has a husband and a jealous young
lover, loses no time in attracting the Turk's eager attention.

Prosdocimo, the poet, is delighted, for he has found the plot he
was looking for, and in fact everything is turning out much
better than he had ever expected.

Fiorilla asks the Turk to her luxurious house, where she will offer him coffee—and possibly much more. Geronio angrily surprises them, but Fiorilla soon takes control of the situation, and in fact makes her husband, much to the disgust of Narcisso, Fiorilla's other lover, be over-polite to the Turk.

The poet advises Geronio, who sadly realizes his mistake in marrying someone so much younger than himself, to be firmer with his wife. This Geronio tries but finds impossible. Fiorilla counter-attacks by feigning tenderness and saying how unhappy he is making her, to the point that Geronio even apologizes to her. Once Fiorilla disarms him she then declares that for his punishment she will take a hundred lovers and have pleasure night and day.

Fiorilla and the Turk plan to elope. The Turk goes to the gipsy camp to have his fortune told. There he meets Zaida, who is no other than his long lost love. Fiorilla, veiled, arrived on the scene with Geronio and Narcisso, and nearly comes to blows with Zaida about who is to have Selim, the Turk.

Prosdocimo, the poet, is the only one pleased with the situation. His plot is developing wonderfully.

Sultan Selim, the Turk, and Don Geronio meet at an inn. Selim tries quite bluntly to persuade Geronio to sell Fiorilla. Geronio is furious and threatens to kill Selim should he persist.

Fiorilla and Zaida are now getting ready for the deciding battle, but Zaida, feeling humiliated, withdraws. The poet steps in and announces to Geronio and Narcisso that there is to be a masked ball, and advises Geronio to disguise himself as a Turk, and that Zaida will appear dressed as Fiorilla. The whole thing is further confused by Narcisso turning out as a Turk, making three Turks and two Fiorillas. Fiorilla pairs off with Narcisso, and Geronio with Zaida. But Selim eventually departs with Zaida, thinking her to be Fiorilla. Fiorilla, repentant and quite ashamed of her behaviour, makes it up with her husband and remains his enchanting but hardly changed wife.

The poet is completely satisfied with his plot.

From her very first entrance Callas, as though returning casually from a walk, captivates us. In her first bravura aria 'Non si dà follia maggiore dell'amore un solo oggetto' ('There cannot be a greater folly than to love only a single object') she is already coquettishly boasting, and her acting is very vivid when she tells her friends simply about her unhappy love life and, above all, that she is in favour of infidelity. Her *coloratura* singing is clean-cut and bright and one feels she does not miss a single detail, singing always as if, like her audience, she is herself enjoying every minute of it. Surely this must be one of the most important factors for the success of Rossini's comedy.

Her eyes sparkle mischievously and she uses her voice well when she sings 'Che bel Turco! Avviciniamoci' ('What a handsome Turk! Let me see better'), and then 'Vo'parlargli' ('I'd better speak to him') as if she has already contrived to do something rather naughty. It is in the quartet 'Siete Turchi non vi credo, non vi credo' ('You, the Turks? I do not believe you. I do not believe you') that Callas really comes into her own, and gives a triumphant characterization of Rossini's heroine. Even in the phrases 'Ola tosto il caffè . . . sedete' ('Now . . . coffee is coming . . . do sit down'), that precede the actual quartet, she re-enacts every word, and her every movement, her rolling eyes, are all done superbly, with tremendous vitality, gusto and finesse. She is so deliciously provocative, and her hands alone play the whole game admirably. She is very funny, and her timing is perfect when her husband appears to interrupt her *tête-à-tête* with the Turk: 'Vi calmate è mio marito' ('Do not worry, it's nothing. It is only my husband'). One literally finds oneself remembering many of her phrases—more accurately the way she delivers them—for hours afterwards. The lightening of her voice, with the excellent coloration she gives it, is a constant delight and she makes every repeat—and there are quite a number—sound just that little bit different every time. There is great subtlety in the way she rejects, on the surface of course, the Turk's advances, actually feeling more hopeful that her pretexts would be rejected instead. Equally so is her subtle reproach in 'Le comprate, le vendete quando spento è in voi l'ardor' ('You buy and you sell your women when your ardour is spent') at its every repeat that is filled with a suggestive hint by her underlying expression. Her asides to her husband 'Me la godo son conpiti' ('Serve him well too, be polite') are hilarious. The duet that follows with her husband, Geronio, together with the previous quartet, are really highlights of

Callas's infectiously frivolous performance. The husband-wife exchanges in the duet 'Per piacere alla signore' ('Well, so tell me what the conditions are') are given with the best possible vocal acting. Callas is coy and spiteful in turn, when she tells her husband of her conditions in 'Voi dovete ognor tacere mai di nulla sospettar' ('You must have no suspicions and just play your part silently'). Her singing in this particular scene is most enjoyable and extremely accurate. And when she pretends she is offended, her disdainful 'Mi lasciate' ('Do not touch me') and then her 'crocodile tears' in 'Senza aver di me pietà' ('You scorn me and scold me without pity'), and the change, when she henpecks her husband again, is a triumph of both singing and acting. One cannot help smiling for hours afterwards on remembering her 'Per punirvi aver vogl'io mille amanti ognor d'intorno for la pazza notte e giorno divertimi in liberta' ('I shall therefore punish you with a hundred lovers with whom night and day I shall go mad'). In the disguise scene she sings her music beautifully, with a dash of melancholy, but her unfriendly exchanges with Zaida, 'Sei tu sola la civetta' ('Indeed you are such a flirt'), are quite spiteful.

Her aria 'Che Turca inpertinente osa a Fiorilla l'amante disputar' ('That impertinent Turkish woman dares to be the rival of me, Fiorilla') is sung with spite and feminine confidence. The quintet 'Oh! guardate che accidente non conosco più mia moglie' ('Oh, see how disastrous—I can no longer even recognize my own wife') is wonderfully sung in the true Rossinian style. Callas in this quintet sounds like a muted violin, but a very feminine one.

Dona Fiorilla remains possibly the best comic characterization that she has undertaken. That she has real seeds of comedy in her is certain, and both her voice and acting are beautifully adjusted. If we find anything missing—and this is judged on the highest standards (we have no other standards to go by as far as Callas is concerned)—and perhaps if there was something more we would have liked in her performance, is it just a little more spontaneous charm?

LA TRAVIATA

Opera in three acts by Giuseppe Verdi.
Libretto by Francesco Maria Piave, based on Alexandre Dumas's play *La Dame aux Camélias*.

Principal Characters

VIOLETTA VALERY, a courtesan	Soprano
ALFREDO GERMONT, her lover	Tenor
GIORGIO GERMONT, ALFREDO's father . . .	Baritone

TIME: 1840–50   PLACE: Paris and vicinity.

First performed at Teatro La Fenice, Venice, on 6th March 1853, with Fanny Salvini-Donatelli as Violetta, Lodovico Graziani as Alfredo and Felice Varesi as Germont.

Maria Callas first sang *La Traviata* on 15th January 1951 at the Teatro Communale, Florence. Also in Mexico City, São Paulo and Rio de Janeiro in 1951; at the Arena di Verona, La Fenice, Venice and in Mexico City in 1952; in Rome in 1953; at the Lyric Theatre, Chicago, in 1954; at La Scala, Milan, in 1955; at the Metropolitan, New York, in 1956; at the San Carlos, Lisbon, Covent Garden, London, and the Dallas Civic Opera in 1958.

'Last night *Traviata* was a fiasco. Is the fault mine or the singers'? Time will tell,' Verdi wrote to a friend after the *première* of the opera.

Poor casting was not alone responsible for the failure, though the tenor was hoarse, the baritone sang carelessly and the soprano herself, a far too fat prima donna, was laughed off the stage in the last act, when she was supposed to be dying from consumption. But the most important reason for the failure was that *La Traviata* was for the 1853 audience a picture of contemporary life and the first Italian opera that offered realism in a bourgeois environment, and had as protagonist a consumptive courtesan. But time has told. *La Traviata* is today one of the most popular operas, both with musicians and the general public; a success that seems to

*F

derive from the perfect union of music and drama which expresses the emotional life beneath the surface of the people concerned.

The opera begins with the fête of Violetta, a consumptive courtesan.

Alfredo, who is in love with Violetta, is introduced to her, an event that she treats with outward indifference, though deeply she is touched by his devotion and concern for her. Alfredo and Violetta sing a brilliant drinking song 'Libiamo, libiamo ne'lieti calici' and in the waltz that follows Violetta is seized by a fit of coughing. Alfredo goes to help her, and in the duet 'Un dì felice, eterea' pours out his love for her. The guests leave and Violetta, lost in contemplation, in a long aria 'Ah fors'è lui che l'anima' thinks of the very recent events. She of all people, and in spite of herself, has fallen in love.

Violetta deserts her gay life, and establishes herself with Alfredo in the country. She is slowly selling her jewels to enable her to keep herself and her lover. When Alfredo discovers this he rushes to Paris to raise money. During his absence Alfredo's father, Germont, visits Violetta to demand from her that she should give Alfredo up, for the sake of his career and his sister, whose chances of a good marriage are being ruined by Violetta's scandalous liaison with Alfredo. Violetta eventually consents to make the sacrifice and leaves Alfredo, to return to Paris and her former mode of life.

At a party given by Flora Bervoix, Alfredo meets Violetta, who loyally pretends she is in love with another, richer man. Alfredo, beside himself, calls the guests to witness as he throws the money he has just won gambling at Violetta's feet in payment for the pleasures she gave him in the past.

A few months later Violetta is dying from consumption. As she listens to the sounds of the carnival in the street she reads a letter from Alfredo's father, which tells her that Alfredo, who has now learnt the truth about her sacrifice, is returning to her. Alfredo does return, but it is too late. Violetta dies in his arms just as the elder Germont comes to take her to his heart as his daughter.

In the first act Callas presents a gay, highly strung and restless Violetta. It is in the spirited drinking song 'Libiamo, ne'lieti

calici' ('Let us drink from the winecup overflowing') that she
begins to suggest the tragedy of Violetta. For, in spite of everything, she is a doomed woman. The way she sighs 'Oh qual
pallor' when she looks at herself in the mirror, after she has been
seized with a fit of coughing, is the moment of truth. We realize
with her that she is a dying woman.

Her *coloratura* in the duet 'Un dì felice, eterea' ('One unforgettable day') has a naturalness of suggestion which is all too rare.
She at once expresses the carefree life of the courtesan she is, and
at the same time reveals a sensitive heart. But it is in the long
scene that follows that Callas exposes the whole of Violetta's
personality: she begins her aria 'Ah fors' è lui' ('Perhaps my soul
has found him') in a soft, melting tone, making her voice sound
very beautiful, a perfect example of the way she can make an aria
both lyrical and dramatic as it should be. Suddenly she changes,
giving you the feeling that her dreams of lasting love are too much
to expect. As she sits on a table, throws her slipper off and dashes
into the brilliant 'Sempre libera degg'io folleggiare di gioia in
gioia' ('Ever free shall I still hasten madly on from pleasure to
pleasure'), we become aware of her conflict. Only a true dramatic
soprano d'agilità—that is the kind of voice Callas possesses—can
express Violetta's character through Verdi's musical intentions,
using the flexibility of her voice to express the frivolity of the
character. The timing of her ascending and descending scales,
when she hears Alfredo's voice, is impeccable. And when she
cradles her face in her hands and utters from the depths of her
heart 'Oh, Amore', we know, just as much as she does, the truth.
Violetta is in love, and cannot help herself.

It is the second act of the opera, however, that provides the
triumph of Callas's vocal and histrionic art. Her long duet with
Germont is the kind of music in which she excels. The way she
sings the long sustained B flat and the beginning of 'Dite alla
giovine' ('Say to your daughter') is an unforgettable moment,
both musically and dramatically. In some mysterious way her
poetic magic performs a miracle by making that note remain
suspended in mid air in the auditorium; and this so meaningfully,
yet so effortlessly, and without any trace of mannerism. In the
writing of the note, and in her *addio* to Alfredo, she achieves an
almost unbearable intensity. The way she goes down on her knees

embracing Alfredo as she opens up her voice in the impassioned 'Amami, Alfredo' ('Love me, Alfredo') makes us believe that her heart is truly breaking. Even the smallest gestures and little details seem to become important in the way she uses them. For her nothing is of minor importance. Her rebuke to Germont, 'Donna son'io, signore, ed in mia casa' ('I am a woman, sir, and I am in my house'), to the 'Silenzio; va all instante' to Annina, her maid, are words which might have been delivered by the most consummate actress. In the second scene of Act II Callas gives her singing, especially in the great ensemble that closes the act, a quality of fatalism. Violetta can no longer fight the world.

In the last act her singing is that of a tragedienne of the first order. She makes us believe that she has indeed been ill in that bed for months and months, dying, abandoned and forgotten. The way she drags her weak body from bed to sit once more at her dressing-table, her arms useless, is extremely realistic.

Her reading of the letter 'Teneste la promessa' ('You have kept your promise') is so quiet and touching that it is comparable only to Claudia Muzio's performance of the same scene a generation ago. And, as she senses the approach of death, she looks in the mirror and sings 'Addio del Passato' ('Farewell to bright visions') so movingly that it is no longer merely an aria, but a sigh from the depths of a once frail but now purified soul. Then comes the desire to live, when Alfredo returns to her; her hands touch Alfredo's face, as if to make sure it is he, and then comes the actual death scene. There is something inhuman in the final phrases, 'Rinasce, rinasce . . . m'agita insolito vigor!' ('My pulse is beating and my strength is returning!') which is not of this world. This Violetta does not fall but, upright in her death, held by father and son, is horrific and at the same time beautiful.

All through the opera Callas's tone is that of a woman dying of tuberculosis. It is true, however, that some notes, especially in the first act, are sometimes uncertain and slightly strident. But these are unimportant, considering the overall effect of her profound understanding of Verdi's loveliest female character.

Callas makes us fall in love with her Violetta with which no other contemporary interpretation can compare. In this role she approaches the quality of a Sarah Bernhardt.

LUCIA DI LAMMERMOOR

Opera in three acts by Gaetano Donizetti.
Libretto by Salvatore Cammarano after the novel by Sir Walter
Scott, *The Bride of Lammermoor*.

Principal Characters

LUCIA . . . . Soprano
SIR EDGAR RAVENSWOOD (EDGARDO) . . . Tenor
LORD HENRY ASHTON, LUCIA's brother (ENRICO) . Baritone

TIME: The end of the seventeenth century.   PLACE: Scotland.

First performed at Teatro San Carlo, Naples, on 26th September
1835, with Fanny Persiani as Lucia and Gilbert-Louis Duprez as
Edgardo.

Maria Callas first sang Lucia di Lammermoor in June 1952 in
Mexico City. Also in Florence in 1953; at La Scala, Milan, and the
Lyric Theatre, Chicago, in 1954; in Berlin in 1955; in Vienna and
at the Metropolitan, New York, in 1956; at the Metropolitan,
New York, and at the Dallas Civic Opera in 1958.

Lucia di Lammermoor, generally considered Donizetti's finest
tragic opera, was an immediate success. The originality and inexhaustible invention of melody make this opera one of the most
popular, provided of course that it is properly sung. Even the
very ornate passages in the score are basically essential to the
expression of the drama.

The role of Lucia has always been an inspiration and a great
incentive to many singers. Its demands are extremely severe. Only
a true dramatic *soprano d'agilità* voice can be made the vehicle to
justify Donizetti's artistic achievement. It is precisely through this
florid music that Lucia has to go through madness. Then the
rewards are immense.

The story of Donizetti's *Lucia di Lammermoor*, though simple,
ends in great tragedy, with Lucia's mad scene as the climax of the
opera.

Henry Ashton, Lord of Lammermoor, having dissipated his family fortune, and having been placed in a perilous situation due to his political activities against the king, as a means of re-establishing his position wishes to wed his sister Lucia to the rich Lord Arthur Bucklaw.

Lucia, however, is secretly in love with Sir Edgar Ravenswood, between whose family and her own there is a raging feud, for Henry wrongfully holds Edgar's estates. Lucia meets Sir Edgar in a secluded place in the castle grounds. He tells her that he must leave for France, to take up arms for Scotland.

Edgar's letters to Lucia are intercepted by Lucia's brother. Lucia fights against all her brother's arguments but eventually succumbs to his pressure and reluctantly agrees to the marriage with Bucklaw, believing Sir Edgar to be unfaithful to her. The marriage ceremony is taking place when Sir Edgar returns. He demands his avowed bride, but it is too late, for Lucia has already signed the marriage contract. When he asks Lucia herself to confirm her signature she does. In his rage Sir Edgar curses her and the House of Lammermoor.

Lucia, on entering the bridal chamber, goes mad and kills her bridegroom. Sir Edgar, who wanders amidst the tombs of the Ravenswoods, musing on his misfortune, on learning of Lucia's madness and eventual death, stabs himself.

To begin with Callas's Lucia is unique, because it is not merely a lyric soprano using a *coloratura* technique, like the artists of the twentieth century who generally sing this role. She makes Lucia a tragic heroine of the greatest magnitude. This is an interpretation of creative genius, a truly classical interpretation expressed in Callas's dramatic soprano voice, which is also capable of an extraordinary crisp and superbly articulated *coloratura*.

No one besides Callas could invest her Lucia in the opening phrase 'Ancor non giunse' ('He still has not come'), when she is waiting for Edgar, with such simple pathos so full of meaning. She relates the story of the fountain, in 'Regnava nel silenzio' ('There was silence everywhere'), touchingly and convincingly, and the cabaletta that follows, 'Quando rapito in estasi' ('Then, fast in ecstasy'), is sung with superb articulation: Lucia's one hour of happiness in the whole opera. How subtly her voice hints at her brief joy. And in the duet, 'Verrano a te sull'aure i miei sospiri ardenti' ('My sighs will come to you on the breeze'), when she bids farewell to Edgar, how beautifully she seems to caress the music.

Both scenes in Act II are after Callas's heart. As she listlessly enters her brother's apartment we begin to feel that Lucia's tragedy is beginning with the dramatic duet 'Il pallor funesto, orrendo' ('The horribly deathly pallor') with her brother. Her reading of the forged letter—Callas shaking as if from an inward tremor—is unforgettable. And the touchingly moving 'Soffriva nel pianto' ('I suffered in tears') that follows in a way that brings all the melancholy and suffering of Lucia's sensitive character. It does even more. This is the moment when Lucia can no longer offer resistance to the madness that is creeping on her. She sounds completely lost, and grief turns to despair in the way she sings 'La tomba, la tomba a me s'appresta!' ('It is the tomb, the tomb that awaits me!') when her brother tells her that the marriage bed with another awaits her. In the wedding scene Callas gives the impression that she is going through everything mechanically. Nothing means anything to her any longer. She sings brilliantly in ensemble, shown in the famous sextet 'Chi mi frena in tal momento' ('What keeps me back at such a moment') when her voice of despair floats above all the others.

The great mad scene, the climax of the opera, takes over the whole of Act III, Scene 2. This is an elaborate scene, full of wonderful melodies, but when sung by Callas we become aware of their exceptionally strong dramatic significance.

Her entrance in this scene is haunting. She is now a mentally deranged young woman, her hair dishevelled and her dress stained in blood after she had killed her husband. Unusually Callas does not appear still clutching a dagger. Instead she uses her hands to describe, as if in retrospect, the murder that had taken place and for which, it would seem, her hands know more about than she herself does. It will be a long time before we shall forget her glassy stare as she stands at the top of the staircase, both physically and mentally exhausted. One feels the imminence of death. In 'Il dolce suono mi colpi di sua voce' ('On my ear softly falls his sweet voice') she lets her demented mind carry her back to happier times. She now believes Edgar is with her and goes through an imaginary wedding scene. She sings the *coloratura* aria 'Ardon gl'incensi' ('The incense is burning') superbly. How full of meaning she makes 'Alfin son tua, alfin sei mio' ('At last I am yours and you are mine'), which, tenderly sung and subtly coloured, is also invested with an innocence and simplicity that convey Lucia's temporarily overwhelming joy—a joy that enhances the situation's poignancy. In the fiendishly difficult *coloratura*, with the flute *obbligato* that ends the first part of the mad scene, whose transparence demands perfect pitch, Callas has an opportunity to show us the fluency and flexibility of her voice. However, she never lets it become merely an exhibition piece, but applies to it a dramatic intensity which is of paramount importance in her portrayal of Lucia's mental derangement. Here, and in the scene as a whole, her singing is nothing short of a *tour de force*. But however adroit her singing may be, it is really something in the magnificent simplicity of her total performance (her art that conceals art) that conveys a sense of the tragedy of Lucia, especially in the way a human mind can go in and out of eclipse.

The emotion in 'Spargi d'amaro pianto' ('Shed a bitter tear of sorrow') is reminiscent of Ophelia, and Callas's limpid and deeply affecting tone is followed by a rapid *stretto* to conclude this greatest of operatic mad scenes. In Callas's performance there are vocal imperfections here and there, such as the insecurity of the D sharp trill in 'Regnava nel silenzio' and the high C in the cabaletta 'Quando rapito'. But what of the great gifts of this artist: hear the superlative way she sings the recitatives. All the great Lucias of the last few generations doubtless sang brilliantly, but can we even begin to compare them with Callas's unique interpretation, or her intelligence, with which she so vividly colours her phrases, or the tragic overtones with which she miraculously invests her Lucia?

There it is again, one can say. *Lucia di Lammermoor* is restored in its original conception, and we can witness the work in the way Donizetti intended it and the way the great singers sang it during the composer's lifetime.

Our generation will be proud to add Callas's name to the list of the great interpreters of this role.

MACBETH

Opera in four acts by Giuseppe Verdi.
Libretto by Francesco Maria Piave, after Shakespeare.

Principal Characters

LADY MACBETH	Soprano
MACBETH, a general	Baritone
BANQUO, a general	Bass
MACDUFF, a Scottish nobleman	Tenor

TIME: A.D. 1040–57   PLACE: Scotland.

First performed at the Teatro della Pergola, Florence, on 14th March 1847, with Marianna Barbieri-Nini as Lady Macbeth and Felice Varesi as Macbeth.

Maria Callas sang the role of Lady Macbeth at La Scala, Milan, on 7th December 1952.

Macbeth had at first a fairly good reception. Politics of the time, however, did not permit Verdi's opera, which had neither a political nor a religious theme, to stand on artistic grounds alone.

In 1865 Verdi revised *Macbeth* for its Paris *première* at the Théâtre Lyrique, a revised form which replaced the original. The most important additions were Lady Macbeth's excellent aria, 'La luce langue', and her duet with Macbeth which ends Act III, as well as the addition of the very moving chorus for the Scottish exiles, which opens Act IV.

The exceptionally difficulty leading roles, and the expensive production that the opera requires, have prevented it from being often performed. Although the libretto follows Shakespeare, in the opera it is Lady Macbeth who is explicitly the protagonist, with Macbeth remaining the central figure of the tragedy. The opera, in spite of its lack of success during Verdi's lifetime, remained a favourite of his.

The witches greet Macbeth, a general, as Thane of Cawdor the King of Scotland, and Banquo as the father of kings. As the witches vanish a messenger arrives from Duncan to announce that Macbeth has become Thane of Cawdor.

In the castle of Cawdor, Lady Macbeth reads a letter from her husband that tells her of his meeting with the witches. In her aria 'Vieni! t'affretta' Lady Macbeth expresses her doubts as to whether her husband has enough ambition to gain the throne, but, as she hears that Macbeth and Duncan, the King of Scotland, will spend the night at the castle, in the cabaletta that follows 'Or tutti sorgete ministri infernali' ('All you infernal ministers now arise'), she calls for the help of the Gods of Evil to enable her to carry out her aims. When Macbeth arrives, Lady Macbeth persuades him that they must murder the king. During the night Macbeth murders the king and, as he comes down the stairs with a bloodstained dagger in his hands, he meets Lady Macbeth, who urges him to return the dagger to the king's chamber and smear the king's grooms with blood. Macbeth, terrified, is unable to do so, but Lady Macbeth replaces the dagger herself and then hurries Macbeth away to wash the blood from their hands.

Macduff, a Scottish nobleman, discovers the murder and wakes up the whole household.

Lady Macbeth further persuades Macbeth, now the king, that the deaths of Banquo and his son are necessary to their scheme, for they both know too much. In a park Banquo dies in the hands of hired assassins, but his son escapes.

At a banquet Macbeth sees Banquo's ghost and, losing his nerve, he practically confesses his guilt. The banquet breaks up in disorder. Macbeth again consults the witches, who tell him to beware of Macduff. Various apparitions appear, ending with a procession of kings who all look like Banquo. As Macbeth faints Lady Macbeth arrives. They both decide to murder Macduff and his family.

Near the border Scottish exiles lament for their sufferings. Macduff, who is among them, learns of the savage murder of his family. Meanwhile Malcolm, with an English army, marches on Macbeth's castle. At the castle the haunted Lady Macbeth sleep-walks, reliving the night of the murder of Duncan, and in her aria 'Una Macchia' she seeks in vain to wash her blood-stained hands. Macbeth, in another part of the castle, still hopes to defeat Malcolm and Macduff. He learns of Lady Macbeth's sudden death. Immediately after the English army storms the castle. Macduff slays Macbeth and the young Malcolm is rightfully acclaimed king.

The role of Lady Macbeth is one of Verdi's finest for a singer who is also a good actress—i.e. a role *par excellence* for Callas.

Verdi gave very meticulous instructions as to how this opera should be performed, and wrote that Lady Macbeth must be wicked, ugly and possess a voice that can be hard, stifled and dark —in fact the voice of the very devil.

In Lady Macbeth's opening scene Callas is unexpectedly not quite effective enough in the reading of the letter 'Nel di della vittoria io le incontrai' ('I met them on the day of victory'). But soon she finds herself in the recitative 'Ambizioso spirto, tu sei Macbetto' ('Macbeth, an ambitious spirit is yours'), which she invests with authority and determination. The aria 'Vieni! t'affretta! accendere' ('The path of power is full of misdeeds') and the following cabaletta 'Or tutti sorgete ministri infernali' ('All you infernal ministers now arise') are sung with the ferocity of a tigress. Already Callas's singing has the demonic qualities that Verdi explicitly demanded. Further proof of this is the way she, addressing hardly any words directly to Macbeth, arranges the murder of the king. There is a world of meaning in the way she intones 'Risponde il gufo al suo lugubre addio' ('The owl is answering to his sad goodbye').

In the duet between Lady Macbeth and Macbeth, after Macbeth has murdered the king, Callas reaches a tremendous climax both as singer and actress: intoxicated with ambition, she launches her music with the voice of the devil. 'Le sue guardie insanguinate . . . Che l'accusa in lor ricada' ('Smear the guards with blood . . . The blame then will fall on them') is terrifying and spine-chilling. Altogether this is a magnificent duet, of great importance to the whole opera, and she makes all her points with a demonic spontaneity.

In Act II Callas sings her superb aria 'La luce langue' ('The light wanes') with a gloomy grandeur, colouring every phrase. 'Nuovo delitto! . . . E necessario' ('A new crime! . . . Yet it is necessary') is at once full of intensity and a haunting beauty. In the drinking song 'Si colmi il calice' ('Fill the goblet to the full') in the banqueting scene, Callas assumes a nervous gaiety, totally devoid of grace, contributing immensely to the powerful effect of the whole scene. Her assurances 'Chi morì tornar non può' ('The dead do not return') when, pretending that nothing is really amiss, she attempts to reassure the horror-stricken Macbeth, are also made with a kind of nervous energy.

The opera reaches its climax with Lady Macbeth's sleep-walking scene. Callas accordingly reaches the zenith of her interpretative and creative powers, both as a singer and a consummate actress. Her every move, her every note, is nothing short of perfection. There are a freedom of movement and an expressiveness in her performance that rise not only to Verdian poetic heights, but also to poetic heights matching the Shakespearian masterpiece. During the orchestral introduction, that creates the haunting atmosphere of this scene, Callas enters sleep-walking. She stops for a while and rubs her hands as if to wash them; the hands seem to express anything Callas wishes. She then begins with a fabulous *pianissimo* 'Una macchia è qui tuttora' ('Still there is a stain there') singing darkly, and as though through clenched teeth, which gives the impression that she is actually speaking in her sleep. Her counting of the hours in 'Una ... due ... gli è questa l'ora' ('One ... two ... this is the hour') is unearthly. She stresses the word 'immaginar' beautifully, a stress that is underlined with despair, in the famous line 'Chi poteva in quel vegliardo tanto sangue immaginar?' ('Who would have imagined there was so much blood in that old man?'). And there is a dark intensity in 'Arabia intera rimondar sì piccol mano' ('All the perfumes of Arabia cannot clean this little hand'). She closes the scene with the softest voice, the merest trace of a voice, which rises to D flat, to drop an octave on the final note, yet is perfectly audible in the ascending and descending arpeggio on 'Andiam, Macbetto, andiam' ('Let us go, Macbeth, let us go') as she quietly sleep-walks away.

Thus Callas portrays Lady Macbeth. It is an electrifying performance which, like Callas herself, is incomparable. She is Verdi's ideal Lady Macbeth.

MEDEA

Opera in three acts by Luigi Cherubini, with recitatives, to replace the original spoken dialogue, by Franz Lachner. Libretto in French by François-Benoît Hoffman, in Italian by Carlo Zangarini after Euripides' drama.

Principal Characters

MEDEA, a Colchian princess . . . Soprano
JASON, leader of the Argonauts . . . Tenor
CREON, King of Corinth . . . . Bass
GLAUCE, daughter of CREON . . . Soprano
NERIS, servant of MEDEA . . . . Mezzo-soprano

TIME: The fifth century B.C.   PLACE: Ancient Corinth.

First performed at the Théâtre Feydeau, Paris, on 13th March 1797, with Madame Scio (Julie Angélique Legrand) as Medea.

Maria Callas first sang Medea in May 1953 at the Maggio Musicale in Florence. Also at La Scala, Milan, in 1953; Rome in 1954; at the Dallas Civic Opera in 1958; at Covent Garden, London and at the Dallas Civic Opera in 1959; at Epidaurus, Greece, and La Scala, Milan, in 1961.

Medea is Cherubini's greatest operatic achievement. The opera was not a success at its *première* and it was not in fact to be revived in Paris before 1963, when again the performance failed to make an impact. This was due to the miscasting of the title role.

It was in Germany and Austria, a few years after the *première*, that it found success. It has a grandeur of its own which remains unsurpassed in its own field. Both Beethoven and Puccini declared *Medea* a masterpiece.

Medeas have always been rare. The merciless length of the title role, with its tremendous demands upon the voice and energy of

the performer, account for this. There is indeed a story that
Madame Scio, the creator of this role, died from consumption
brought about by her singing in this opera.

Jason, with the help of Medea, the Colchian princess, is able to
capture the Golden Fleece. He promises marriage to Medea, who
has fallen in love with him and borne him two sons. Jason and
Medea, on their way to Thessaly, are pursued by Aeëtes, the
Colchian king and father of Medea. Medea has her young brother
dismembered and throws him into the sea, knowing that her
father will stop to collect his remains and bury them. Medea also
causes the death of Pelias, the usurper king of Thessaly and
Jason's uncle. Jason then takes his sons and flees away to
Corinth, where he is about to marry Glauce, the daughter of
King Creon.

The opera begins on the eve of Jason and Glauce's wedding.
Glauce has premonitions of Medea's vengeance, for she is
reputed to be a sorceress. Medea comes to prevent the marriage,
and begs Jason to return to her, the mother of his two children.
But Jason is not at all swayed. Instead, Medea is to be banished
from Corinth and her children, a prospect which grieves and
infuriates her. She begs Creon to allow her to spend one day with
her children, and then she will depart. Creon, touched by Medea's
concern for her children, generously grants her wish. Meanwhile
the wedding ceremony takes place. Medea is now thinking only
of vengeance. She sends Glauce a diadem and cloak as wedding
gifts. These have been dipped in poison, and upon contact with
the flesh they will cause Glauce's death. Glauce dies in agony.
Medea is then about to slay her children. Jason rushes to prevent
her but it is too late; Medea has murdered her children and set the
temple on fire. All disperse in terror.

It is a devastating moment when Callas, with her face covered
up to the eyes, makes her first entrance. From the terrible moment
when she discloses herself to the faithless Jason and the Corin-
thians in her thunderlike cry 'Io Medea!' ('I, Medea!') she brings
life to the barbarian Colchian princess, the wronged and dangerous
sorceress. For from this moment on she *is* Medea. It will be
difficult to forget the way she fixes her gaze and sings with great

assurance 'Perchè Giasone è mio' ('Because Jason is mine'), when she claims her husband.

Medea has little time and very few opportunities of gaining our sympathy. Callas succeeds in this in the way that only she can, and, in spite of ourselves, we cannot help but feel for this terrible woman who has become a legend and a curse to humanity. The metamorphosis is exquisite, when she becomes all tenderness in her last efforts to regain Jason, and there is very subtle womanly tenderness in the way she lets the notes flow in 'Ricordi il giorno tu, la prima volta quando m'hai veduta?' ('Do you remember the day when you first saw me?') just before she begins pleading with Jason.

She uses her hands superbly, as she goes down on her knees to begin the beautiful aria 'Dei tuoi figli la madre' ('You see the mother of your children') with a fine musicianship and exquisite phrasing in this cruelly difficult vocal part. And when she gets no response from Jason she suddenly abandons all traces of softness, to become a menacing and wounded tigress in the electrifying duet with him 'Nemici senza cor' ('Heartless enemies'). She attacks this duet with the force of an explosion, underlining it with despair, the despair of a wronged woman who is fighting for her rights.

As the orchestral introduction to Act II, suggesting suspense, finishes, we find Medea in a state of great agitation. When Creon arrives Medea pleads with him. Here Callas is masterful.

There seems to be no limit to the various colorations that her voice is capable of producing. She is no less resourceful in her movements; the way she kneels and kisses Creon's foot, in order to persuade him to grant her, in spite of his better judgment, leave to stay one more day. And then, after Creon's exit, she falls so naturally on to the steps of the palace, deeply absorbed in a reverie that seems to last an eternity. It must be at this moment that Medea plans her crimes. But as yet they are too monstrous, even for her.

Callas's greatest moment in the opera, in Act II, is when she again pleads with Jason, this time not as a woman, but as a mother. It will be long before one can forget the glow of hatred and triumph in her face in 'Caro pagar dovrai il mio falso dolor!' ('For my false grief, you will pay dearly!'), when she discovers that Jason still loves his children. It is as though she is now sure of what she must do. And then the bitter smile, so full of gratitude, as Jason looks at her.

In the last act Callas becomes Medea the sorceress. She grovels and rages like a fatally wounded panther, as she calls for the infernal gods to come to her aid in 'Numi, venite a me, inferni Dei' ('Infernal gods, come to my aid'). This, and indeed the whole of Act III, must contain some of the most appallingly difficult and exacting vocal music ever written.

The audience shudders at the terrible moment when Callas feels for her dagger and then draws it to slay her children. But she then becomes tender and loving in 'O miei tesor, o miei tesor!' ('Oh, my treasures, oh, my treasures!') when she cannot for the moment bring herself to kill them, as though suddenly shaken by an earthquake of remorse, only to change again and complete the deed in the last scene of the opera, when she appears in a carriage drawn by serpents, her slain children lying at her feet. Her singing of 'Eran figli tuoi' ('They were your children') sounds as though it is sung by a murderess who is already a living ghost. Her final phrase to Jason 'A sacro fiume io vo' colà t'aspetta l'ombra mia' ('I go now to the Styx, the sacred river, where my shade will await you') is spine-chilling.

Again we are aware that, vocally, Callas is not always perfect. However, she always makes use of all her resources, her gestures and movements, all adding to her classic interpretation of the barbarian Colchian princess, unique in its infinite variety and utterly unchallengeable.

LA VESTALE

Opera in three acts by Gasparo Luigi Pacifico Spontini. Libretto in French by V. J. Étienne de Jouy based on J. Wincklemann's *Monumenti antichi inediti*.

Principal Characters

GIULIA, a vestal virgin	Soprano
LICINIUS, a young general	Tenor
CINNA, his friend	Baritone
THE HIGH PRIEST	Bass
THE HIGH PRIESTESS	Mezzo-soprano

TIME: The 269th year of the Roman Empire   PLACE: Rome.

First performed at the Paris Opéra on 16th December 1807, with Branchu as Giulia and Lainè as Licinius.

Maria Callas sang Giulia in *La Vestale* on 7th December 1954 at La Scala, Milan.

La Vestale at its *première* was a resounding success. The Parisians considered the opera a large and serious work, full of impressive melodies and the grand spectacles which it requires, abounding in dramatic stage effects. *La Vestale* was equally successful all over Europe, until Weber's *Der Freischütz* and his other romantic operas made Spontini's music sound outdated. Spontini was never to tighten his grip on the public again. Since his death there have been very few revivals of *La Vestale*, the most notable being in 1924 at the Metropolitan Opera, New York, for Rosa Ponselle, and the 1954 La Scala revival for Maria Callas.

Giulia, the daughter of an aristocratic Roman family, fell in love with Licinius, a young soldier, but Giulia's father forbade the marriage. Licinius then sought glory in the wars, and Giulia, following her dying father's wish, became a vestal virgin.

The opera begins five years later with the triumphant return of Licinius, now a young general. He confesses to his friend Cinna his unhappiness in finding Giulia a vestal virgin, but he swears that, in spite of all religion, he will still win her.

The high priestess of the Temple of Vesta announces to Giulia that she has been chosen to bestow the hero's wreath on Licinius in the forthcoming triumphal ceremonies. The high priestess also warns Giulia that she must beware of falling in love; by the laws of the Vestal Virgins she would then have to die. Giulia, who still loves Licinius, when left alone, prays to the gods.

In the triumphal scene that follows Giulia performs the ceremony, and when she is near Licinius he informs her that he will meet her at the temple that night and they will escape together. That night Giulia, who is guarding the everlasting vestal fire, prays for guidance. She is torn between love and duty. Licinius enters the forbidden temple and urges her to fly with him when the fire goes out; a sign that Vesta is angry. They are horrified as they hear the crowd shouting outside. Giulia refuses to fly, as this will mean the death of Licinius too. Licinius rushes out as the high priest arrives. He denounces Giulia and demands to know the name of the man who was with her. Giulia admits only her own guilt. Her vestal ornaments are removed and she is condemned to be buried alive.

Licinius with his men is standing by to rescue Giulia. He pleads for her with the high priest but all is in vain. Giulia and her family are brought in by other vestal virgins. Her veil is hung upon an unlit altar. Should Vesta pardon her, then the veil will be ignited. As Giulia is lowered into the tomb Licinius arrives with his men. Suddenly the sky darkens and, as a storm breaks out, a ball of fire strikes the altar and the veil bursts into flames.

The high priest declares Giulia pardoned by grace of the goddess Vesta. Giulia is released from her sacred vows and the lovers are united.

La Vestale is another of the so-called 'Callas operas'. It was mainly due to her influence and her ability to sing this role that the opera was revived. But, like so many other roles that she has re-created, they survive for only as long as she continues to sing in them. It may be that only she is able to re-create them in the style that a present-day audience finds acceptable.

We first see Callas meditating while the other priestesses are praying. In the duet 'Che si vuole da me?' ('What do you wish of me?') with the Grand Vestale, she already shows us how she can manipulate Spontini's music, which requires so much formal pathos. Her outburst 'E l'Amore un mostro, un barbaro; e nemico a Vesta Amor' ('And love is a monster, a barbarian; and an enemy of Vesta') is superbly managed, without upsetting the balance of the music. Her recitative 'Oh di funesta possa invincibil commando' ('Oh, distressing day. I have no power to control') is marvellously delivered, with an authority that adds to the stature of the music. And as she passes the sacred fire in the triumphant scene, her superbly whispered 'Sostenetemi, o Numi!' ('Restrain me, O Gods!'), loud and intense, conveys all Giulia's inner emotions.

It is in Act II that Callas finds her greatest opportunity in the opera; in the aria 'Tu che invoco, con orrore Dea tremenda, alfin m'ascolta' ('I appeal to you tremendous Goddess, to hear me') she gives us all that could be desired. The melody, grave and superbly sculptured like a Renaissance statue, the perfect phrasing and style that this cantilena requires are all within Callas's ability. In addition to all these she gives the maximum intensity and mystery to all her words, especially in the section where Giulia realizes that her prayers are not heard. In the tender phrases that follow she excels with rare magnificence: passages such as 'Ma Licinio e colà . . . posso mirarlo' ('But Licinius is there . . . unable to see').

The aria 'O Numi tutelar degli infelici, Latona, di i miei prieghi' ('O Gods protect all the unhappy that pray') where Giulia prays for Licinius's identity not be be discovered, is another delightful feat. The crescendo on the word 'Latona' is marvellously accomplished.

In the last scene Callas touches us with a tenderness devoid of any sentimentality, making her aria 'Caro oggeto, il di cui nome proferir non m'e concesso' ('Dear object, the name which I utter without permission') all the more effective. She makes us believe in Giulia, in this lovely farewell to all that is mortal.

Only a great singer-actress could have thus uttered the words 'Qual voce' and 'Dove son io?' when she hears Licinius's voice as she ascends the tomb.

LA SONNAMBULA

Opera in two acts by Vincenzo Bellini
Libretto by Felice Romani.

Principal Characters

AMINA, an orphan	Soprano
TERESA, mill owner and foster mother to AMINA	Mezzo-soprano
ELVINO, a young landowner . . .	Tenor
COUNT RODOLFO	Bass

TIME: Early nineteenth century.   PLACE: A Swiss village.

First performed at the Teatro Carcano, Milan, on 6th March 1831, with Giuditta Pasta as Amina, Rubini as Elvino and Mariani as Rodolfo.

Maria Callas first sang Amina on 5th March 1955 at La Scala, Milan; at La Scala, Milan, in Cologne, Germany, and at the Edinburgh Festival in 1957.

'Last night, at the Carcano, my opera was a resounding success,' Bellini wrote to a friend, the day after the *première* of *La Sonnambula*. He was commissioned to compose *La Sonnambula* by a group of noblemen and merchants of Milan, who were, in 1830, sponsoring an unusually interesting opera season at the Teatro Carcano, in Milan. It was during the same season that Donizetti's *Anna Bolena* was commissioned and produced by this same group.

The opera, which was an immediate success, a masterpiece of the florid style, has proved with time to be as delightful today as ever; given of course singers who can do justice to Bellini's music. All through its life *La Sonnambula* has attracted and is always attracting the greatest singers of the generation.

Amina, an orphan, and the adopted daughter of Teresa, the mill owner, is to be married to Elvino, a young and prosperous landowner. Lisa, the proprietress of the village inn, is very jealous, for she is herself in love with Elvino.

Count Rodolfo, the handsome lord of the nearby castle, has been away since he was a child. Now, a grown man, he returns unrecognized. His compliments to Amina, whom he finds attractive, enrage the jealous Elvino. As it is late Rodolfo decides to spend the night at the village inn. Lisa, who is by now aware of Rodolfo's identity, is flirting lightly with him, when suddenly they hear a noise at the window of the bedroom. Lisa flees, in her haste dropping her handkerchief. Amina, in her nightdress, sleep-walking, enters, muttering to herself about the events of the previous day. She falls asleep on Rodolfo's bed. The villagers, who have learned that the stranger is none other than Count Rodolfo, come to greet him. On seeing a woman asleep in his bed they are about to leave, when Lisa returns with Elvino and denounces the sleeping Amina to him. The noise awakens Amina to find that Elvino has cast her off. Elvino, caught on the rebound, is now going to marry Lisa. Rodolfo tries unsuccessfully to testify to Amina's innocence. His explanations of the psycho-physical manifestations of somnambulism are completely un-comprehended by Elvino, who remains adamant.

Amina, who is sleeping in the nearby mill—sleep-walking again—emerges through a window and, carrying an unlighted lamp, walks along a fragile bridge. As she crosses the bridge a plank breaks and her lamp falls into the water below. Still walking in her sleep she approaches the gasping villagers and Elvino. In her sleep she speaks of the ring Elvino has taken from her. She then prays that Elvino may love her again. Elvino, now convinced of her innocence, replaces the ring on the finger of the still sleeping Amina. To the rejoicing of the villagers Amina awakens in Elvino's arms. All she sees is joy around her, and Elvino waiting to lead her to the altar.

One does not need to wonder very much whether Bellini and the librettist Felice Romani would have approved of the poetic, spell-binding interpretation that makes Callas's Amina so absolutely charming and utterly delightful. Though much of the joy lies in watching Callas embody this exquisite young creature, it is basically her treatment of Bellini's simply lyrical music which reaches the greatest heights of poetry.

It is particularly appropriate to quote the librettist himself on how he visualized his heroine: 'The role of Amina in *La Sonnam-bula*,' Romani wrote, 'although at first sight may seem easy to portray, is probably more difficult than many other roles which are considered more important. It calls for an actress who can be playful, ingenuous and innocent, and at the same time passionate, sensitive and affectionate. Furthermore she must have a cry for sorrow as well as a cry for joy, and different timbres in her voice for reproof and pleading. Amina should show in every movement, in every glance, in every sigh, that elusive combination of the stylized and the realistic, the kind of element one perceives in certain of Theocritus's idylls. Finally, the actual singing must be extremely simple, yet full of adornment, spontaneous, yet scrupulously controlled, technically perfect, yet indicating no sign of study.' Thus was the way that Giuditta Pasta, for whom the role was written, sang. Even more perfect was Maria Malibran's Amina, which in fact became Bellini's favourite. And this is the way Maria Callas performs the role, coming very close to perfection. Yes, I feel both Bellini and Romani would have approved.

It is very striking how Callas renders evocative every word, every note, not least the recitatives. From the very moment she makes her first entrance, gracefully walking down from the mill house to the village square, she colours Amina's every word and note. Her first words 'Care compagne, e voi teneri amici' ('Dearest and sweet friends') make us begin to understand what kind of a person Amina is. She has already won our hearts. The aria 'Come per me sereno' ('How brightly shining is for me') is beautifully sung, and Callas is careful to keep the melodic line impeccably accurate. The elaborate decorations are expertly managed, yet the overall effect is that of a simple haunting melody, although the actual voice is not always quite perfect—the final note of the aria being sharp and slightly unsteady. In the duet of her betrothal scene with Elvino, 'Prendi, l'anel ti dono' ('Take the ring I give you'), Callas's singing has a limpid and liquid tone that one can only describe as delicious. All the innocence and charm of Amina's character emerge when she begins her part in the duet 'Sposi! Oh, tenera parola' ('Married! Oh, what a sweet word').

It is in the second act that we first meet Amina, the sleep-walker.

As Callas sleep-walks her way through the window into Rodolfo's bedroom in the village inn, she speaks of her approaching marriage to Elvino. All through this scene she sings as if there was a veil covering her voice, and this effectively gives the impression that she is singing in her sleep. The timing, colouring and control of 'Oh, Madre mia, m'aita' ('Oh, my mother, help me') with Rodolfo are something to wonder at. So is her last phrase 'Elvino, abbracciami! Alfin sei mio' ('Elvino, embrace me! At last you are mine'), which she delicately suspends, as she falls asleep on Rodolfo's bed. Callas has the 'cry for sorrow'. The tone and expression in the way she starts the quartet 'D'un pensiero, e d'un accento' ('Not in the remotest regions of thought'), when she awakes to find herself in a compromising and damning situation, are perfectly apt to the situation.

In the forest scene with Elvino she shows us in 'M'odi, Elvino' ('Hear me, Elvino') and in 'Innocente io son, tel giuro' ('I am innocent, I swear it'), how expertly she can colour and modulate her tone to express passionate pleading.

In the last act Callas reaches the pinnacle of her performance in this opera. Her first utterances in the big sleep-walking scene 'Oh! se una volta sola' ('Oh, at least for once'), and then the recitative 'L'anello mio . . . l'anello, ei me l'ha tolto' ('My own ring . . . my ring . . . it has been taken away from me'), come straight from her heart to wring our own hearts. She then embarks on the beautiful aria 'Ah, non credea mirarti, si presto estinto, o fiore' ('Oh, flowers, is it possible that you would wither so soon?'). The way Callas begins this evokes the sound of rippling water, accompanied by sighing zephyrs. Her singing is exquisite. One cannot define it technically, for it appears completely spontaneous and simple. One would hardly wish a single syllable sung differently. The long-drawn notes especially, where the only accompaniment is a viola, seem endless—they simply die away peacefully. Probably her greatest achievement is that we are always made to believe, by her expert use of the 'veiled' tone in her voice, that she is really living the whole scene, that she *is* singing in her sleep and her *fioriture* in the end express the right conclusion of the built-up emotion. 'Viva Amina', cry the villagers, and Amina awakens. In the final rondo 'Ah! non giunge uman pensiero al contento ond'io son piena' ('Ah, nobody can understand the happiness I feel') Callas embellishes the music—especially the second verse—brilliantly, and with a musicianship that is incomparable. She is very much the virtuoso, but she does, however, sometimes sound a little laboured on some phrases. But again, shortcomings are overwhelmed by the colour and expression we have come to expect from her.

Our generation should be happy to have heard an artist such as this, singing both *La Sonnambula* and the completely different role in Bellini's *Norma*. (Incidentally both these roles were also written for Giuditta Pasta, who triumphed in them.) If there are no more Bellinis today to create roles for Callas, we can at least be grateful for the great roles of the past which she can resurrect.

IL BARBIERE DI SIVIGLIA

Opera in two acts by Gioacchino Antonio Rossini.
Libretto by Cesare Sterbini founded on Beaumarchais's first play of his trilogy of *Figaro* comedies, *Le Barbier de Séville*.

Principal Characters

FIGARO, the barber of Seville . . . Baritone
COUNT ALMAVIVA . . . . . Tenor
ROSINA, a ward of BARTOLO . . . Mezzo-soprano
or soprano-leggero
DOCTOR BARTOLO . . . . . Bass
BASILIO, a singing teacher . . . Bass

TIME: The seventeenth century   PLACE: Seville, Spain.

First performed on 20th February 1816 at the Teatro Argentina, Rome, with Gertrude Giorghi-Righetti as Rosina, Zamboni as Figaro and M. Garcìa as Count Almaviva. Conductor: Rossini.

Maria Callas first sang in *Il Barbiere di Siviglia* on 16th February 1956 at La Scala, Milan.

It is to a great extent due to the excellent libretto that Rossini's masterful *opera buffa* owes its great success. It is also due to the extremely gay and sparkling music that Rossini used to bring to life those immortal characters of the Commedia dell' Arte.

Il Barbiere di Siviglia was, however, a spectacular failure on its first production in Rome. The Roman audience compared it unfavourably with Paesiello's version of the same work. The second performance, however, was a resounding success. The Roman public again compared Rossini with Paesiello—but this time favourably.

Il Barbiere di Siviglia remains today one of the comic master-pieces of the operatic stage, comparable to the comic operas of Mozart. Its popularity is universal, not least so amongst the Roman audience, and it is one of the most often performed Italian operas.

Rosina, the beautiful and wealthy ward of old Dr Bartolo, is serenaded by Count Almaviva. The young count, a Grandee of Spain, having encountered Rosina in Madrid and fallen desperately in love with her, has followed her to Seville, where he disguises as a student under the name of Lindoro.

With the help of Figaro, the barber of Seville, the general factotum and busybody of the town, Lindoro plots to bring about an introduction to Rosina. Figaro is also the barber of Doctor Bartolo, who is keeping a strict eye on Rosina, for, since she is as rich as she is beautiful, he could not do much better than to marry her himself. He suspects though that Rosina is returning the affection of the count. In this he seeks the help of Bassilio, the music master. Bassilio comes out with a brilliant idea. By subtly organized calumny against the Count Almaviva, whom they have recognized, the count's presence in Seville might easily be greatly embarrassed. Meanwhile Rosina is delighted on learning her admirer's name.

With Figaro's resourcefulness the count, disguised as a drunken soldier, forces his way into Rosina's house and manages to have a few words with her. Doctor Bartolo, however, sees through the count's disguise and has him arrested. He is, however, released as soon as he secretly shows the officer his order as a Grandee of Spain.

The count's ruse having only been partly successful, he now embarks on a more ambitious one. With Figaro's aid he disguises

G

himself as a music teacher sent by Bassilio, who is supposedly ill, to give Rosina her music lesson. Rosina, far from being deceived, is very pleased with this unexpected opportunity. Further the count, in order to obtain Bartolo's confidence, produces Rosina's letter to himself and offers to persuade Rosina that the letter was given him by a mistress of the count.

During the actual music lesson the lovers plan a midnight elopement and a private marriage, which is arranged for them by Figaro. Suddenly, however, Bassilio appears, but they persuade him, with the help of a purse slipped into his hand by the count, that he really is ill and must therefore go to his bed.

Figaro begins to shave Bartolo, who, however, becomes suspicious, and catches the two lovers in a compromising situation. The count, together with Figaro, leaves, and Bartolo shows Rosina the letter she wrote to the count and tells her that it was produced by a mistress of the count. Rosina is piqued and promises to marry Bartolo. But just in time Figaro and the count appear and explain everything. The lovers are reconciled, and are married by the notary whom Bartolo had procured for his own marriage. When Bartolo enters he is too late. He is easily reconciled, however, and, when promised that he shall receive the equivalent of Rosina's dowry, blesses the happy couple with all the grace he can muster.

Rossini's famous *opera buffa Il Barbiere di Siviglia* does not entirely depend on its music for its success, sparkling and gay though it may be. Much depends on the visual counterpoint; the little gestures of the hands and head and the rolling of the eyes—things which cannot be fully expressed by the voice alone.

With the agility that Callas possesses in the upper register of her voice, and her rich and most telling lower tones, the part of Rosina lies comfortably within her vocal range. All her recitatives are positively superb. They are obviously studied, yet sound perfectly spontaneous, with an exhilarating variety of *bravura* and outstanding virtuosity.

The ever versatile Callas plays the role of Rosina with gusto and a great sense of fun. She can be funny, mischievous, flirtatious, and at the same time sound quite blithe if not always with enough simple charm. Yet, in spite of all these, Callas is not wholly successful as Rosina. She indeed can 'play a thousand tricks to have her way', to use a phrase from the opera. But her personality proves too powerful to be completely concealed, and the result is that Callas fails to present a convincing *ingénue*. Furthermore her very outstanding acting abilities, together with her naturally impressive voice, make far too individual a Rosina. And, with the slightly overpowering excitability that she displays, she steals the show to the point of distracting attention from Figaro, who is after all the central character of the plot.

Callas's comic characterization, however musically and dramatically rewarding and enjoyable it may be, does not make one feel that it really represents her great dramatic art at its most convincing. Another point is that it is strange that, except for the singing lesson scene, there is never a touch of melancholy in the characterization of such a person. But this is rather Rossini's fault than Callas's.

On her first entrance Callas gives us a delicious 'Una voce poco fa' ('A little voice I heard'). To the passage 'Io sono docile', where she is gentle, humble and obedient—as long of course as no one crosses her path—she brings a subtle brilliance full of mischief, that is rare amongst present-day singers. Here Callas uses her hands playfully, especially in 'Ma se mi toccano' ('But if you cross my path'). Her *fioriture* in this most famous *cavatina* are clear cut and again, as always, they are not merely for exhibition purposes, but form an integral part of the opera. 'Sì, sì, la vincerò' ('Yes, yes, I will succeed') which follows finds her on top form, as indeed she is in all the recitatives, a most important component of this particular opera.

In her duet 'Dunque io son—tu non m'inganni?' ('Can it be I am his love—dare I believe you?') with Figaro Callas is exquisite. This and the singing lesson scene which comes later in the opera are her best scenes. In the duet she is both flirtatious and calculating, without ever throwing the music out of balance. This is a delightful piece of musical dialogue, and her perfect timing is a constant surprise. In the lesson scene Callas does not sing the music which is usually substituted for Rossini's song, but sings the original—'Contro un cor che accende amore' ('When a heart is glowing with love').[1] She sings beautifully and with every repeat seems to give the aria further meaning. Similarly the repeats in the terzetto 'Ah, qual colpo' ('Ah, what rapture'). All of Callas's entries and exits in the *ensembles* are never less than masterly.

ANNA BOLENA

Opera in two acts by Gaetano Donizetti.
Libretto by Felice Romani.[2]

Principal Characters

ANNA BOLENA, the queen (Anne Boleyn) .	Soprano
ENRICO VIII, the king (Henry VIII) . .	Bass
GIOVANNA SEYMOUR, ANNA's lady-in-waiting (Jane Seymour)	Mezzo-soprano
LORD RICHARD PERCY	Tenor
SMEATON, a page	Mezzo-soprano
ROCHFORD, ANNA's brother . . .	Bass

TIME: A.D. 1536.

PLACE: Windsor Castle, and the Tower of London, England.

First performed on 26th December 1830 at the Teatro Carcano, Milan, with Giuditta Pasta as Anna, Elisa Orlandi as Giovanna Seymour, Rubini and Galli.

Maria Callas first sang Anna Bolena on 14th April 1957 at La Scala, Milan. Also in 1958.

It was *Anna Bolena* that established Donizetti as an operatic

---

[1] It had been the custom for every prima donna to sing practically anything she chose in her music lesson scene. The choice ranged from songs like 'La biondina in gondoletta' and 'Home, Sweet Home' to operatic scenes like the mad scene from *Lucia di Lammermoor*, 'Ah! non giunge' from *La Sonnambula*, etc.

The music lesson that Rossini composed—thought to have been lost together with the actual overture to the opera—exists and is now almost always sung in performance.

[2] The source of Romani's libretto is unidentified. Certainly it is not Shakespeare's *Henry VIII*.

composer, bringing him international fame. The opera, Donizetti's first success, was for a long time considered his masterpiece.
Although the music is modelled on Haydn's, there is a definite
originality of style. It is dramatically effective and often very
beautiful. The libretto is extremely well constructed, and the
characters of the drama are drawn quite realistically. One cannot
expect historical accuracy, but in any case the facts of the tragedy
of Anne Boleyn are uncertain. Romani presents Queen Anne as
being basically innocent.

After its initial success the opera soon fell into neglect. One of
the most important reasons for this is that *Anna Bolena* requires
the very grandest of settings and the finest cast for its success.
When the opera was first produced it had all these components.

The opera begins in the queen's apartments at Windsor Castle.
Anna can hardly conceal her anxiety while waiting for the king
(Enrico VIII). It is no secret amongst the courtiers that the king
is no longer interested in the queen but has fallen in love with
Giovanna Seymour, Anna's beloved lady-in-waiting.

Giovanna Seymour enters, fearing that Anna is aware of her
relations with the king. Anna asks Smeaton, her minstrel page, to
sing for them. Young Smeaton, who loves the queen deeply,
sings a song about a maiden's first love. Anna warns Seymour of
the pitfalls of a throne. Seymour, when left alone, is tormented
with repentance. But the temptation is too great. The king arrives
through a secret door and Seymour, although at first she tries to
break off with him, yields to him as he promises to make her
queen.

Percy, Anna's youthful love, is pardoned by the king and
returns from his banishment. He meets Rochford, Anna's brother,
at Windsor Forest. The king and Anna arrive at Windsor Forest
with a hunting party. Anna is perturbed on seeing Percy, and the
king, who notices this, instructs Harvey to watch them both for
any incident which might give him an excuse to divorce the
queen.

The opportunity soon comes. Smeaton, who is secretly in love
with Anna, hides himself behind a curtain as Rochford persuades
Anna to receive Percy. Percy tries to make love to her, but when
she repulses him, fearing that if their love was renewed it would

G*

be impossible to hide from the king, he tries to kill himself. Smeaton emerges from hiding to prevent him; at the same time Rochford enters hurriedly as the king and his court arrive unexpectedly. The king accuses Anna of misconduct.

Giovanna Seymour, torn between her loyalty to the queen and her genuine love for the king, pleads with Anna to confess her guilt. For if she confesses the king will merely divorce her. If not she will die. Anna refuses and curses her rival. Seymour confesses that she herself is the rival, and begs Anna for forgiveness. Anna forgives her, an act, however, that increases Seymour's remorse.

Harvey informs the king that Smeaton has confessed, claiming to be the adulterer in the hope of saving Anna. Anna pleads innocence, and Percy, who believes her, says that she had been his wife before she married the king. Anna, however, does not confirm this. The peers find Anna guilty and, together with her accomplices, Rochford, Percy and Smeaton, is condemned to death.

Seymour, together with the courtiers, begs the king to show mercy. The king offers reprieve to Percy and Rochford only, but they both refuse the king's clemency.

Anna, imprisoned in the Tower of London, loses her reason. She cannot recognize her three supposed accomplices. As they are taken to the scaffold she falls dead.

The role of Anna in Donizetti's *Anna Bolena* calls for an artist with a voice and temperament that are suited to tragedy in the grand manner. That is, it calls for an artist of the calibre of Callas. This is a 'Callas role' *par excellence*, and Callas surpasses all expectations. It is, after all, entirely due to her presence that La Scala embarked on its triumphant revival of this wonderful but neglected work.

From the moment Callas, dressed in a rather dark and sombre manner, with a white Quaker head-dress, makes her entry down the long and impressive staircase in Windsor Castle, she commands our full attention. Every little gesture, every look, is particularly apt. Callas is always confident, every gesture is made at the right moment, and in the most economical manner possible. Only a great actress could interrupt Smeaton's little song about 'first love' in such a touching way. She prepares her audience artfully as she walks slowly to the footlights, lost in a world of sweet remembrances, to begin her aria 'Come innocente giovane' ('How young and innocent'). This is a vocal triumph for Callas, for the *cavatina*, with its Bellinian melodic line, might have been written for her.

In the duet between Anna and Seymour Callas gives an outstanding performance. She is very much the woman who knows she has lost her husband to, of all people, her beloved lady-in-waiting and friend, but she never abandons the dignity that is expected of her as Queen of England. When Anna warns Seymour of the pitfalls of a throne Callas comes up to all expectations. She is never less than superb, for she identifies herself with the person of Anna Bolena so convincingly that the whole opera gains immeasurably from this extra acquired realism.

In the hunting party scene at Windsor Forest she conveys her anxiety and perturbation at unexpectedly seeing Percy with great simplicity, yet fully and realistically.

Her mood changes in the recitative passages when Anna, with tremendous intensity, yet fully maintaining her queenly dignity, sings 'Giudici! Ad Anna! Giudici!' ('Judges of Anna! Judges!'), at the end of Act I. (Incidentally the opera in this performance is divided into three acts.)

In the final scene, which takes place in the Tower of London, the opera reaches its greatest climax. And so does Callas. For here, in this great scene, we find her at the summit of her amazing powers both as a tragedienne of the first order and as one of the greatest of singers.

All through this scene, as in the whole opera, Callas's tone is regal and dignified—a tone which is the foundation of her master characterization of the 'Tragic Queen' of England, the 'Rose without a thorn'.

Anna, distraught by her many sufferings, and lost in illusions which verge on insanity, begins her aria 'Ah! dolce guidami castel natio' ('To the sweet native castle guide me') full of tender recollections. She imagines this to be her wedding day, and that the king awaits her.

Callas phrases this melody in an unforgettable manner. The long-drawn phrases, the finest of trills, the tenderness, are all here. We could not have wished for more.

A roll of military drums is heard and Sir Harvey, the captain of the guard, enters, and as he orders the other prisoners to be brought out Anna is temporarily restored to sanity, and realizes the gravity of her situation. She forgives Smeaton, her page, and slowly drifts once more into forgetfulness. Here her forgetfulness is beautifully expressed in the lovely aria 'Cielo, a' miei lunghi spasimi' ('Heaven, where my long suffering')—a melody reminiscent of 'Home, Sweet Home'.[1] It seems that Donizetti thought it suitable for an English queen.

Another sound interrupts. It is that of cannon and bells acclaiming the crowning of the new queen, Giovanna Seymour.

In the final outburst, a *tour de force*, Anna denounces the guilty couple. Callas sings the forceful cabaletta 'Copia Iniqua' with style and flexibility. As she soars so remarkably in trills that rise from B flat to F sharp, Callas, the queen of opera, reveals that she is unrivalled in dramatic *coloratura* singing.

IL PIRATA

Opera in two acts by Vincenzo Bellini.
Libretto by Felice Romani.

Principal Characters

ERNESTO, Duke of Caldora	Baritone
IMOGENE, his wife	Soprano
ADELE, her lady-in-waiting	Soprano
GUALTIERO, Count of Montalto	Tenor
GOFFREDO, a hermit	Bass

TIME: The thirteenth century A.D.   PLACE: Caldora in Sicily.

First performed at La Scala, Milan, on 27th October 1827, with Henrietta Méric-Lalande as Imogene, G. Battista Rubini as Gualtiero and Antonio Tamburini as Ernesto.

[1] Henry Bishop first published the song as a Sicilian folk-song and again in 1823 used it as his own—a fact he successfully established in a law court after Donizetti had used it in *Anna Bolena*—in his opera *Clari, or The Maid of Milan*. Nevertheless, in the absence of international copyright law at the time, Donizetti did not have to cut the aria from his opera.

Maria Callas first sang Imogene on 18th May 1958 at La Scala, Milan. Also at Carnegie Hall, New York, and Washington, D.C. (concert version), in 1959.

Il Pirata was Bellini's third opera and the first work that established him as an operatic composer. In *Il Pirata*, although there is evidence of Rossini's influence, there are also signs of new individual elements, which were to develop in future works, and which in their turn were to influence Verdi. At its *première* the opera was a resounding success, a success that was soon repeated elsewhere in Europe. It also marked the beginning of an artistic collaboration between Bellini and the librettist Felice Romani. This collaboration proved very successful and produced seven operas in the six years that followed.

Goffredo, a hermit, recognizes Gualtiero, Count of Montalto, whose tutor he had once been among the survivors of a shipwreck on the coast of Caldora.

Ten years before, on the death of King Manfredi, Gualtiero was, for political reasons, exiled by Ernesto, Duke of Caldora. Gualtiero's banishment was also due to the fact that in him Enesto saw a more favoured rival for the love of Imogene, with whom Ernesto was in love.

During the years of exile Gualtiero has become the leader of a band of pirates, but has never given up hope of returning to his native land, where he would be reunited with his beloved Imogene. Imogene, however, in order to help her dying and imprisoned father, becomes Ernesto's wife.

The hermit hides Gualtiero in order to avoid his meeting with Imogene. But she asks to see the sailor who has been given asylum. Gualtiero at first evades her searching questions, but eventually reveals his identity. Their joy in finding each other soon vanishes as Imogene tells him she is Ernesto's wife. Gualtiero, seized with grief and the desire for revenge, tries to stab the young boy whom he recognizes as Imogene's and Ernesto's son. Only Imogene's anguished cry saves the boy. Gualtiero tries to persuade Imogene to fly away with him, but she refuses and declares herself to be resigned to her unpleasant destiny. Ernesto surprises Imogene and Gualtiero in one of their meetings. This leads to a duel in which Ernesto is killed by Gualtiero, who is arrested and is to be tried by the Council of the Knights. During the trial Imogene loses her reason and imagines she sees Ernesto calling their son to him. Gualtiero is condemned to death, and as Imogene in her imagination sees before her a scaffold for his execution, she despairingly entreats the sun to hide, away from the horrible sight.

To describe Callas's interpretation of the role of Imogene is easy: one can say, without the smallest trace of doubt, that this is a flawless performance. There has probably never been a singer whose means of expression were better suited to Imogene in *Il Pirata*. Bellini himself would have been only too happy to have composed the role for Callas, so perfectly does the artist-interpreter complement the composer. It is Bellini's *and* Callas's Imogene.

In the first act Callas establishes the character when she relates a dream to Adele: 'Lo sognai ferito, e sangue in deserta, ignuda riva' ('I dreamed he was wounded, lying in blood, alone'). Her scene with Gualtiero in 'Stranier . . . la tua tristezza' ('Stranger . . . your sorrow') possesses all the restraint and expressiveness that only Callas could give it. It is, however, in the last scene of the opera, the mad scene, that both Bellini and Callas reach their peak. Even before she begins to sing, from the moment she advances, holding her son by the hand, we are aware of her grief —and destiny. Her hands contains a whole world of expression. With tears in her eyes and voice she kneels to sing 'Oh, s'io potessi dissipar le nubi che mi aggravan la fronte!' ('Oh, help me to remove the cloud that is oppressing me!'), her hand at the same time conveying to us that something terrible is about to happen, and gesturing as though to send it away. Imogene has now lost her reason, and as she waits for Gualtiero to be tried imagines that her dead husband is calling her son to him. The words 'E desso Ernesto . . . ei parla . . . ei chiama il figlio' ('And now, Ernesto . . . speak . . . and call your son') are sung with a force that fully expresses Imogene's passionate grief.

Callas sings the beautiful slow section, 'Col sorriso d'innocenza collo squardo dell'amor' ('With an innocent smile and a look of love'), exquisitely. Here her great gifts—her outstanding ability for mood painting—are very much in evidence. The long-drawn phrases have all the yearning and musicianship that are so essential for this kind of music. The notes fall like audible tears, the *pianissimo* seems to be effortless, always superbly articulated with a coloration that gives it a haunting reality. And after the fanfare on the brass, which announces that Gualtiero has been condemned to death, we see in Callas all of Imogene's despair. Her visions as she imagines a scaffold for Gualtiero's execution are expressed vocally in the difficult cabaletta 'O Sole, ti vela di tenebre oscure'! ('O Sun, quickly cast a darkness!'). One cannot easily forget her look when she desperately sings the words 'La vedete! Il palco funesto, ah!' ('Behold! the fated scaffold, ah!'), using those fabulous low notes with their chesty quality, which add to the excitement of the whole thing. The second verse Callas embellishes with perfectly marvellous *fioriture*.

VII

MARIA CALLAS ON THE
CONCERT PLATFORM

WHAT IS A THEATRE? 'Wherever I perform becomes a theatre,'
Sarah Bernhardt once said to her critics on the occasion when she
acted in a shop. The same can be said for Maria Callas in a concert
hall: 'Wherever she sings becomes an opera house.'

The idea of Maria Callas on a concert platform might sound like
a waste of her talents to someone who has not actually heard her
give such a performance. Not so, however, for she brings her
vocal and acting powers to bear on the concert platform. And
when the lights are dimmed it is possible to be carried away, and
believe that one is, in fact, watching a full-scale opera.

Here there are no stage trappings or costumes to help to create
the appropriate atmosphere. Yet in a Callas concert one sees the
various heroines she wishes to embody. Her gestures and movements in general are not those of the operatic stage. They are more
subdued, and each point is made in a simpler and more economical
way. On the concert platform Callas has to rely mainly on her
singing, and consequently more attention is concentrated upon
the quality of the voice, thus exposing flaws which would otherwise pass unnoticed. A concert appearance by Maria Callas at her
best can be a unique experience, such as no other contemporary
artist can give. Here we do not get merely a few arias as is usual
from any other artist, however brilliantly sung; instead there are
scenes in which Callas becomes the character whose music she is
singing.

It was on 2nd June 1958 that I first heard Callas in a concert,
one which took place in a London television studio before a live
audience. Callas sang 'Vissi d'arte' ('I have lived for art') from

Puccini's *Tosca*. She evoked all the drama in the opera, and made one completely forget the very different atmosphere of a television studio. Even one relatively short aria was enough to make us see Floria Tosca momentarily before our eyes, and it was only a few minutes later that a complete transformation took place: Callas, still in the same dress, became Rossini's heroine, Rosina, from *Il Barbiere di Siviglia*. Into her aria 'Una voce poco fa' ('A little voice I heard') she was able to evoke all of Rosina's frivolity, with its subtle brilliance. Physically she relied entirely on using her expressive hands, or rather just one finger, and of course her beautiful, playful eyes.

It was in 1959, in her first London concert at the Festival Hall on 23rd September, that I fully realized Callas's great concert-hall art. On this occasion she began with Elizabeth de Valois's big scene 'Tu che le vanita' ('You who know that in vain'), from Verdi's *Don Carlo*. In the prelude to the scene Callas stood motionless, and, using only facial expressions and an occasional gesture with her hands, she lived through the whole of Elizabeth's anxiety and, in the actual aria, her sad meditation on the happiness she once had in loving Don Carlo. But a few minutes later Callas again changed completely, this time suggesting the maidenly innocence of Ophelia in the mad scene from Ambroise Thomas's *Hamlet*. The features hardened and the voice became dark; for a while Lady Macbeth stood before us. Callas here surpassed herself. Vocally and histrionically it was a memorable performance. She proceeded to live through the whole of Lady Macbeth's sleep-walking scene, 'Una macchia è qui tuttora' ('Still there is a stain there'). The voice was veiled and, together with the appropriate facial expression, Callas gave one the impression that she was actually sleep-walking. At the end of her song she in fact sleep-walked off the stage so as not to break the effect she had so marvellously created. The concert ended with the final scene from Bellini's *Il Pirata*. The beautiful phrasing, the excitement and, above all, the way Callas literally lived through the gamut of emotion, made one feel one had really seen the whole opera—indeed four operas—in the same evening.

Callas appeared on the concert platform early in her career. It was as far back as 1945, when she was the famous young prima donna of the Athens Opera, that she gave her first recital at the

Rex Theatre in Athens. After her Italian début it was in 1949 that she sang in a radio concert in Turin. Incidentally this concert was recorded to produce her first gramophone records. Since then Callas has appeared quite extensively in concerts in North and South America, Germany, France, England, Holland, Belgium, Greece, Spain and Denmark. Her repertoire in these concerts consisted of many scenes from her operatic stage repertoire, such as *Aida*, *Norma*, *I Vespri Siciliani*, *Fidelio*, *I Puritani*, *Macbeth*, *Anna Bolena*, *Il Pirata*, *Il Trovatore*, *Don Carlo*, *Mefistofele*, *La Vestale*, *Il Barbiere di Siviglia*, *La Traviata*, *La Forza del Destino*, *Tristan und Isolde*, *Lucia di Lammermoor*, *La Sonnambula*, *Die Entführung aus dem Serail*, *Armida* (Rossini), *Nabucco*, *Madama Butterfly*, *Turandot* and *Alceste* (Gluck) and also from operas she has not yet sung on stage, such as *La Bohème* (Puccini) (both Mimi's 'Mi Chiamano' and Musetta's waltz), *Gianni Schicci*, Ophelia's mad scene from *Hamlet* (Thomas), *Lakmé*, *Louise*, *Dinorah*, *Le Cid* (Massenet), *Manon*, *Werther*, *Carmen*, *Oberon* (Weber), *Ernani*, *Cenerentola* (Rossini), *Semiramide* (Rossini), and Dona Anna's arias from *Don Giovanni*.

VIII

CONCERTS GIVEN BY
MARIA CALLAS

THE following is a list of concerts that Maria Callas has given
to date:

1942	Aug.	Salonika	Concert performances of scenes from Italian operas
1943	Aug.	Salonika	Two recitals
1945	July	Athens	Recital
1949	Feb.	Turin	Radio concert
	Oct.	Milan	Concert
1951	April	Trieste	Concert
	Sept.	Rio de Janeiro	Benefit concert
1952	May	Rome	Radio concert
1953	May	Italy	Radio concert
1955	May	Italy	Television concert
1957	Jan.	Chicago	Concert
	June	Zürich	Concert
	5 Aug.	Athens (Herodes Atticus Theatre)	Concert
	21 Nov.	Dallas, Texas	Concert
1958	22 Jan.	Chicago	Benefit concert
	24 Mar.	Madrid	Concert
	2 June	London	Television concert
	10 June	London	Concert (Covent Garden Centenary)
	11 Oct.	Birmingham (America)	Concert (benefit, Alliance Française)
	14 Oct.	Atlanta	Concert
	17 Oct.	Toronto	Concert
	21 Oct.	Montreal	Concert
	25 Oct.	Dallas	Concert

1958	15 Nov.	Cleveland	Concert
	18 Nov.	Detroit	Concert
	22 Nov.	Washington, D.C.	Concert
	26 Nov.	San Francisco	Concert
	29 Nov.	Los Angeles	Concert
	19 Dec.	Paris	Concert (benefit, Legion of Honour)
	31 Dec.	Rome	Television concert
1959	11 Jan.	St Louis	Concert
	24 Jan.	Philadelphia	Concert
	27 Jan.	New York (Carnegie Hall)	Concert version of *Il Pirata*
	29 Jan.	Washington, D.C.	Concert version of *Il Pirata*
	2 May	Madrid	Concert
	5 May	Barcelona	Concert
	15 May	Hamburg	Concert
	18 May	Stuttgart	Concert
	21 May	Munich	Concert
	24 May	Wiesbaden	Concert
	11 July	Amsterdam	Concert
	14 July	Brussels	Concert
	17 Sept.	Bilbao	Concert
	23 Sept.	London	Concert
	23 Oct.	Berlin	Concert
	24 Oct.	London	Television concert
	28 Oct.	Kansas City	Concert
1961	30 May	London (St James's Palace)	Concert (benefit, Edwina Mountbatten Trust)
1962	27 Feb.	London	Concert
	12 Mar.	Munich	Concert
	16 Mar.	Hamburg	Concert
	19 Mar.	Essen	Concert
	23 Mar.	Bonn	Concert
	19 May	New York (Madison Square Garden)	Concert (44th birthday anniversary of President Kennedy)
	4 Nov.	London	Television concert
1963	17 May	Berlin	Concert
	20 May	Düsseldorf	Concert
	23 May	Stuttgart	Concert
	31 May	London	Concert
	5 June	Paris	Concert
	9 June	Copenhagen	Concert

IX

REFLECTIONS ON THE RECORDED
REPERTOIRE OF THE ARTIST

ONE OFTEN reads about the great singers, actors and artists of the past, of their wonderful achievements, and of course of their various shortcomings. In many cases we are fortunate in having recordings that more or less demonstrate their voices, style and technique. In other cases we vainly speculate about them. Just what tone and coloration Giuditta Pasta or Maria Malibran employed we shall never know. The advent of the gramophone was after their time. It is true that contemporary descriptions can tell us a lot, but the handicap here is that we again cannot ascertain with enough accuracy exactly what the highest standards of the time were.

If the gramophone had not been invented Maria Callas would have the reputation of a famous prima donna, but people of future generations would vainly speculate about her actual voice. And what boundless pleasure this great singer has given us through the gramophone! The more one hears this artist the more qualities one discovers.

It is true, however, that Maria Callas's recordings do not do her full justice, judging of course by the highest imaginable standards. Often her good points are minimized and more often still her flaws exaggerated. This does not always apply, however, for although half the joy lies in watching this great lady, it is possible within the limitations of recorded sound to feel that one is not only hearing her, but actually feeling her presence. Maria Callas's outstanding gift of acting with her voice is never more evident in any other medium than it is on the gramophone. Here we have no

stage or costumes to see and, after all, we cannot physically see
Maria Callas. We must rely on the voice alone, and it does not fail
us.

It was in February 1949 that the first records of Maria Callas
were made. She was making her first radio broadcast in Turin. It
was a remarkable recital, doing justice to her incredible versatility. She sang 'Casta Diva' from *Norma*, 'Qui la voce' and 'Vien
diletto' from *I Puritani* and the 'Liebstod' from *Tristan und
Isolde*. Italy's great recording company Cetra issued these arias on
three twelve-inch, 78 r.p.m. records, which travelled far, and laid
the foundations of fame of the already remarkable Maria Callas.

In October 1951 Cetra offered Maria Callas a contract which
provided for three complete operas, all to be recorded during
1952. Only two were, however, recorded—*La Traviata* and *La
Gioconda*. On 21st July 1952 Maria Callas signed a contract
exclusively with the British recording company, E.M.I. (Electric
and Musical Industries Ltd), who had just completed a contract
for about ten years with La Scala. So Maria Callas's recordings
would be made in the La Scala Theatre itself with its wonderful
acoustics and, more important still, La Scala's outstanding
chorus, conductors and other singers who would be her associates. (*Il Barbiere di Siviglia*, the second *Lucia di Lammermoor* and
some recitals were in fact recorded in London.)

Opera after opera followed what became an outstanding
recording career, which took the voice and art of Maria Callas to
practically all the civilized countries of the world. Some of the
operas recorded, such as *I Puritani*, *Il Turco in Italia* and *Medea*, are
the first recordings of the works ever to be made, due largely to
her influence and her ability to sing these difficult roles. The
recording catalogue provides complete recordings of most of
Callas's greatest roles. However, only some excerpts exist from
Anna Bolena, *Il Pirata*, *Macbeth*, *La Vestale*, *Nabucco*, *Don Carlo*,
Alceste and *Iphigenia en Tauride*, and nothing at all from her
memorable portrayal of Giordano's *Fedora*, of her amazing
Armida (Rossini), her brilliant Constanze in Mozart's *Die Entführung aus dem Serail*, Donizetti's *Poliuto* and of her Euridice in
Haydn's *Orfeo ed Euridice*, a role she has after all created. Of the
three Wagnerian roles that she undertook at the beginning of her
career, Kundry in *Parsifal*, Brünnhilde in *Walküre* and Isolde, only

Isolde's 'Liebstod' is recorded. One would have liked to have also her Kundry.

The complete operas which Maria Callas has recorded, and not sung on stage, are Puccini's *La Bohème* and *Manon Lescaut*, *I Pagliacci* and *Carmen*. These recordings only sharpen one's desire to see Callas embodying these heroines on the stage, particularly Carmen, for she seems to have all the qualities—so difficult to find in the same person—that are required.

So far, except for two recital recordings of arias from French operas, Ophelia's mad scene (from *Hamlet* by Ambroise Thomas) and the complete *Carmen*, which are sung in the original French, and the aria 'Ocean! Thou mighty monster', which is sung in the original English, all her other recordings are in Italian, including Isolde's 'Liebstod'.

X

RECORDINGS

The following is a list of Maria Callas's recorded performances:

La Traviata (Verdi)
> Recorded in September 1952, issued on LPC 1246.
> Maria Callas as Violetta, with F. Albanese, U. Savarese.
> Orchestra and chorus of the Turin Radio, conducted by Gabriele Santini.

La Gioconda (Ponchielli)
> Recorded in September 1952, issued on LPC 1241.
> Maria Callas as Gioconda, with G. Poggi, F. Barbieri, P. Silveri.
> Orchestra and chorus of the Turin Radio, conducted by Antonino Votto.

Lucia di Lammermoor (Donizetti)
> Recorded in February 1953, issued on 33CX 1131–2.
> Maria Callas as Lucia, with G. di Stefano, T. Gobbi.
> Orchestra and chorus of the Maggio Musicale Fiorentino, conducted by Tullio Serafin.

I Puritani (Bellini)
> Recorded in March 1953, issued on 33CX 1058–60.
> Maria Callas as Elvira, with G. di Stefano, N. Rossi-Lemeni.
> Orchestra and chorus of La Scala, Milan, conducted by Tullio Serafin.

Tosca (Puccini)
Recorded in August 1953, issued on 33CX 1094–5.
Maria Callas as Floria Tosca, with G. di Stefano, T. Gobbi.
Orchestra and chorus of La Scala, Milan, conducted by Victor
de Sabata.

Norma (Bellini)
Recorded in May 1954, issued on 33CX 1179–81.
Maria Callas as Norma, with E. Stignani, N. Rossi-Lemeni,
M. Filippeschi.
Orchestra and chorus of La Scala, Milan, conducted by Tullio
Serafin.

I Pagliacci (Leoncavallo)
Recorded in June 1954, issued on 33CXS 1211–2.
Maria Callas as Nedda, with G. di Stefano, T. Gobbi.
Orchestra and chorus of La Scala, Milan, conducted by Tullio
Serafin.

Cavalleria Rusticana (Mascagni)
Recorded in June 1954, issued on 33CXB 1182–3.
Maria Callas as Santuzza, with G. di Stefano, R. Panerai.
Orchestra and chorus of La Scala, Milan, conducted by Tullio
Serafin.

La Forza del Destino (Verdi)
Recorded in August 1954, issued on 33CX 1258–60.
Maria Callas as Leonora, with R. Tucker, C. Tagliabue, E.
Nicolai, N. Rossi-Lemeni.
Orchestra and chorus of La Scala, Milan, conducted by Tullio
Serafin.

Il Turco in Italia (Rossini)
Recorded in September 1954, issued on 33CX 1289–91.
Maria Callas as Fiorilla, with N. Rossi-Lemeni, N. Gedda,
M. Stabile.
Orchestra and chorus of La Scala, Milan, conducted by
Gianandrea Gavazzeni.

Madàma Butterfly (Puccini)

Recorded in August 1955, issued on 33CX 1296–8.

Maria Callas as Cio-Cio San, with N. Gedda, M. Barriello, L. Danieli.

Orchestra and chorus of La Scala, Milan, conducted by Herbert von Karajan.

Aida (Verdi)

Recorded in September 1955, issued on 33CX 1318–20.

Maria Callas as Aida, with R. Tucker, F. Barbieri, T. Gobbi, N. Zaccaria.

Orchestra and chorus of La Scala, Milan, conducted by Tullio Serafin.

Rigoletto (Verdi)

Recorded in September 1955, issued on 33CX 1324–6.

Maria Callas as Gilda, with T. Gobbi, G. di Stefano, N. Zaccaria.

Orchestra and chorus of La Scala, Milan, conducted by Tullio Serafin.

La Bohème (Puccini)

Recorded in August 1956, issued on 33CX 1464–5.

Maria Callas as Mimi, with G. di Stefano, R. Panerai, A. Moffo, N. Zaccaria.

Orchestra and chorus of La Scala, Milan, conducted by Antonino Votto.

Il Trovatore (Verdi)

Recorded in August 1956, issued on 33CX 1483–5.

Maria Callas as Leonora, with G. di Stefano, F. Barbieri, R. Panerai, N. Zaccaria.

Orchestra and chorus of La Scala, Milan, conducted by Herbert von Karajan.

Un Ballo in Maschera (Verdi)

Recorded in September 1956, issued on 33CX 1472–4.

Maria Callas as Amelia, with G. di Stefano, T. Gobbi, E. Ratti, N. Zaccaria.

Orchestra and chorus of La Scala, Milan, conducted by Tullio Serafin.

Il Barbiere di Siviglia (Rossini)

Recorded in February 1957, issued on 33CX 1507–9 (Mono); SAX 2268 (Stereo).

Maria Callas as Rosina, with T. Gobbi, L. Alva, N. Zaccaria.

The Philharmonia Orchestra and chorus, conducted by Alceo Galliera.

La Sonnambula (Bellini)

Recorded in March 1957, issued on 33CX 1469–71.

Maria Callas as Amina, with N. Monti, N. Zaccaria, E. Ratti, F. Cossotto.

Orchestra and chorus of La Scala, Milan, conducted by Antonino Votto.

Turandot (Puccini)

Recorded in July 1957, issued on 33CX 1555–7.

Maria Callas as Turandot, with E. Fernandi, E. Schwarzkopf, N. Zaccaria.

Orchestra and chorus of La Scala, Milan, conducted by Tullio Serafin.

Manon Lescaut (Puccini)

Recorded in July 1957, issued on 33CX 1583–5.

Maria Callas as Manon, with G. di Stefano, G. Fioravanti, F. Calabrese.

Orchestra and chorus of La Scala, Milan, conducted by Tullio Serafin.

Medea (Cherubini)

Recorded in September 1957, issued on 33CX 1618–20 (Mono); SAX 2290–2 (Stereo).

Maria Callas as Medea, with M. Picchi, G. Modesti, M. Pirazzini, R. Scotto.

Orchestra and chorus of La Scala, Milan, conducted by Tullio Serafin.

La Gioconda (Ponchielli)

Recorded in September 1959, issued on 33CX 1706–8 (Mono); SAX 2359–61 (Stereo).

Maria Callas as Gioconda, with P. M. Ferraro, F. Cossotto, P. Cappuccilli.

Orchestra and chorus of La Scala, Milan, conducted by Antonino Votto.

Lucia di Lammermoor (Donizetti)

Recorded in February 1959, issued on 33CX 1723–4 (Mono); SAX 2316–7 (Stereo).

Maria Callas as Lucia, with F. Tagliavini, P. Cappuccilli.

The Philharmonia Orchestra and chorus, conducted by Tullio Serafin.

Norma (Bellini)

Recorded in September 1960, issued on 33CX 1766–8 (Mono); SAX 2412–14 (Stereo).

Maria Callas as Norma, with F. Corelli, C. Ludwig, N. Zaccaria.

Orchestra and chorus of La Scala, Milan, conducted by Tullio Serafin.

Carmen (Bizet)

Recorded in July 1964, issued on AN 140 (Mono); SAN 140 (Stereo).

Maria Callas as Carmen, with N. Gedda, R. Massard, A. Guiot.

L'Orchestre du Théâtre National de l'Opéra, Paris, conducted by Georges Prêtre.

Tosca (Puccini)

Recorded in December 1964, issued on AN 149–150 (Mono), SAN 149–50 (Stereo).

Maria Callas as Floria Tosca, with C. Bergonzi, T. Gobbi. L'Orchestre de la Société des Concerts du Conservatoire (Paris) and Chœurs du Théâtre National de l'Opéra, Paris, conducted by Georges Prêtre.

RECITALS

Recordings of Maria Callas on 78 r.p.m. Recorded in February 1949.

Norma (Bellini), issued on R 30041.

Act 1: Casta Diva.
Ah! bello a me ritorno.

I Puritani (Bellini), issued on R 30043.

Act 2: Oh rendetemi la speme . . . Qui la voce.
Vien diletto e in ciel la luna.

Tristano e Isotta (Wagner), issued on CB 20481.

Act 4: Morte d' Isotta.
All with the Turin Radio Orchestra, conducted by Arturo Basile.

PUCCINI ARIAS

Recorded in September 1954, issued on 33CX 1204, with the Philharmonia Orchestra, conducted by Tullio Serafin.

Manon Lescaut

Act 2: In quelle trine morbide.
Act 4: Sola, perduta abbandonata.

La Bohème

Act 1: Mi chiamano Mimi.
Act 3: Donde lieta usci.

Madama Butterfly

Act 2: Un bel di vedremo.
Act 3: Tu, tu, piccolo Iddio.

Suor Angelica
Senza mamma.

Gianni Schicchi
O mio babbino caro.

Turandot
Act 1: Signore, ascolta.
Act 2: In questa reggia.
Act 3: Tu che di gel sei cinta.

MARIA CALLAS SINGS OPERATIC ARIAS

Recorded in September 1954, issued on 33CX 1231, with the Philharmonia Orchestra, conducted by Tullio Serafin.

Adriana Lecouvreur (Cilèa)
Act 1: Ecco: respiro appena . . . Io son l'umile ancella.
Act 4: Poveri fiori.

La Wally (Catalani)
Act 1: Ebben? N'andro lontana.

Andrea Chenier (Giordano)
Act 3: L'altra notte in fondo al mare.

Mefistofele (Boïto)
Act 3: La mamma morta.

Il Barbiere di Siviglia (Rossini)
Act 1: Una voce poco fa.

Dinorah (Meyerbeer)
Act 2: Ombra leggera.

Lakmé (Delibes)
Act 2: Dov' è l'Indiana bruna?

I Vespri Siciliani (Verdi)
Act 5: Mercè, dilette amiche.

CALLAS AT LA SCALA

Recorded in June 1955, issued on 33CX 1540, with the Orchestra of La Scala, Milan, conducted by Tullio Serafin or Antonino Votto.

La Sonnambula (Bellini). (From the complete recording of the opera.)
Act 1: Come per me sereno.

I Puritani (Bellini). (From the complete recording of the opera.)
Act 2: Oh rendetemi la speme . . . Qui la voce.
    Vien deletto e in ciel la luna.

Medea (Cherubini). (From the complete recording of the opera.)
Act 1: Te due figli.

La Vestale (Spontini)
Act 2: Tu che invoco.
Act 3: Caro oggetto.

CALLAS MAD SCENES

Recorded in September 1958, issued on 33CX 1645, with the Philharmonia Orchestra, conducted by Nicola Rescigno.

Hamlet (Thomas)
Act 4: À vos yeux . . . Partagez-vous mes fleurs.
    Et maintenant écoutez ma chanson.

Il Pirata (Bellini)
Act 2: Oh! s'io potessi .´. . Col sorriso d'innocenza.

Anna Bolena (Donizetti)
Act 2: Piangete voi?
    Al dolce guidami castel natio.

CALLAS PORTRAYS VERDI HEROINES

Recorded in September 1958, issued on 33CX 1628, with the Philharmonia Orchestra, conducted by Nicola Rescigno.

Macbeth
Act 1: Nel di della vittorai . . . Vieni! t'affretta!
Act 3: La luce langue.
Act 4: Una macchia e qui tuttora.

Nabucco
Act 2: Ben io t'invenni . . . Anchio dischiuso un giorno.

Ernani

Act 1: Sorta e la notte . . . Ernani! Ernani, involami.

Don Carlo

Act 4: Tu che le vanita.

MARIA CALLAS IN FRENCH OPERAS

Recorded in April 1961, issued on 33CX 1771 (Mono), SAX 2410 (Stereo), with l'Orchestre National de la RTF, conducted by Georges Prêtre.

Orfée et Eurydice (Gluck)
Act 3: J'ai perdu mon Eurydice.

Alceste (Gluck)
Act 1: Divinités du Styx.

Carmen (Bizet)
Act 1: L'Amour est un oiseau rebelle (Habanera).
Près des remparts de Seville (Séguedille).

Samson et Dalila (Saint-Saëns)
Act 1: Printemps qui commence.
Act 2: Amour! viens aider ma faiblesse!

Roméo et Juliette (Gounod)
Act 1: Valse—Je veux vivre.

Mignon (Thomas)
Act 2: Polonaise—Je suis Titania.

Le Cid (Massenet)
Act 2: Pleurez, mes yeux.

Louise (Charpentier)
Act 3: Depuis le jour.

CALLAS A PARIS

Recorded in May 1963, issued on 33CX 1858 (Mono), SAX 2503 (Stereo), with l'Orchestre de la Société des Concerts du Conservatoire, conducted by Georges Prêtre.

Iphigénie en Tauride (Gluck)
Act 2: 'O malheureuse Iphigénie!'

La Damnation de Faust (Berlioz)
Part 4: Romance: D'amour l'ardente flamme.

Les Pecheurs de Perles (Bizet)
Act 2: Me voilà seule dans la nuit . . . Comme autrefois.

Manon (Massenet)
Act 2: Je ne suis que faiblesse . . . Adieu, notre petite table.
Act 3: Suis-je gentille ainsi? . . . Je marche sur tous les chemins.

Werther (Massenet)
Act 3: Werther! Qui m'aurait dit . . . Des cris joyeux.

Faust (Gounod)
Act 3: Il était un Roi de Thulé . . . O dieu! que de bijoux . . . Ah! je ris.

MARIA CALLAS SINGS MOZART, BEETHOVEN, WEBER ARIAS

Recorded in February 1964, issued on 33CX 1900 (Mono), SAX 2540 (Stereo), with l'Orchestre de la Société des Concerts du Conservatoire, conducted by Nicola Rescigno.

Scena: Ah, Perfido! (Beethoven)

Don Giovanni (Mozart)
Act 1: Or sai chi l'onore.

Le Nozze di Figaro (Mozart)
Act 2: Porgi amor.

Oberon (Weber)
Act 2: Ocean! Thou mighty monster.

Don Giovanni (Mozart)
Act 2: Crudele? Non mi dir.
In quali eccessi, o Numi!
Mi tradi quell' alma ingrata.

MARIA CALLAS SINGS VERDI ARIAS

Recorded in February 1964, issued on 33CX 1910 (Mono), SAX 2550 (Stereo), with l'Orchestre de la Société des Concerts du Conservatoire, conducted by Nicola Rescigno.

Otello
Act 4: Mia madre aveva una povera ancella.
Piangea cantando (Willow Song).
Ave Maria piena di grazia.

Aroldo
Act 1: Ciel, ch'io respiri! (Salvami, salvami tu gran Dio!)

Don Carlo
Act 3: O don fatale.

Aroldo
Act 2: O cielo! Dove son io.

Don Carlo
Act 2: Non pianger, mia compagna.

MARIA CALLAS SINGS ARIAS BY ROSSINI AND DONIZETTI

Recorded in July 1964, issued on 33CX 1923 (Mono) SAX 2564 (Stereo), with l'Orchestre de la Société des Concerts du Conservatoire, conducted by Nicola Rescigno.

La Cenerentola (Rossini)
Act 2: Nacqui all'affano.

Guglielmo Tell (Rossini)
Act 2: S'allontanano alfine! . . . Selva opaca.

La Figlia del Reggimento (Donizetti)
Act 1: Romance: Convien partir.

Semiramide (Rossini)
Act 1: Bel raggio lusinghier . . . Dolce pensiero.

Lucrezia Borgia (Donizetti)
Act 1: Tranquillo ei posa! . . . Com' è bello! quale incanto.

L'Elisir d'Amore (Donizetti)
Act 2: Prendi; per me sei libero.

INDEX

INDEX